THE CLASSICAL ROOTS OF ETHNOMETHODOLOGY

THE CLASSICAL ROOTS OF

ETHNOMETHODOLOGY

DURKHEIM, WEBER, AND GARFINKEL

BY RICHARD A. HILBERT

FOREWORD BY RANDALL COLLINS

The University of North Carolina Press

Chapel Hill • London

© 1992 The University of North Carolina Press
All rights reserved
Manufactured in the United States of America

The paper in this book meets the guidelines for permanence and durability of the Committee on Production Guidelines for Book Longevity of the Council on Library Resources.

96   95   94   93   92   5   4   3   2   1

Library of Congress Cataloging-in-Publication Data

Hilbert, Richard A.
   The classical roots of ethnomethodology : Durkheim, Weber, and
Garfinkel / by Richard A. Hilbert ; foreword by Randall Collins.
      p.   cm.
   Includes bibliographical references (p.   ) and index.
   ISBN 0-8078-2039-3 (cloth : alk. paper)
   1. Ethnomethodology—History.   2. Durkheim, Emile, 1858–1917.
3. Weber, Max, 1864–1920.   4. Garfinkel, Harold.   I. Title.
HM24.H536   1992
301'.01—dc20   91-47747
                                                     CIP

Portions of this book appeared earlier, in somewhat different form, in "Anomie and the Moral Regulation of Reality: The Durkheimian Tradition in Modern Relief," *Sociological Theory* 4 (1986): 1–19; "Bureaucracy as Belief, Rationalization as Repair: Max Weber in a Post-Functionalist Age," *Sociological Theory* 5 (1987): 70–86; "Durkheim and Merton on Anomie," *Social Problems* 36 (1989): 242–50; "Ethnomethodology and the Micro-Macro Order," *American Sociological Review* 55 (1990): 794–808; and "Merton's Theory of Role-sets and Status-sets," in *Robert K. Merton: Consensus and Controversy*, ed. Jon Clark, Sohan Modgil, and Celia Modgil, pp. 177–86 (London: Falmer Press, 1990), and are reproduced by permission of the journals and publishers.

Quoted material is reproduced with permission from the following sources: Jeffrey C. Alexander, Bernhard Giesen, Richard Münch, and Neil J. Smelser, eds., *The Micro-Macro Link* (Berkeley: University of California Press, 1987), copyright © 1987, the Regents of the University of California; Egon Bittner, "The Police on Skid-Row: A Study in Peace Keeping," *American Sociological Review* 32 (1967): 699–715; Talcott Parsons, *The Structure of Social Action* (New York: The Free Press, 1968), copyright © 1968, The Free Press, by permission of Macmillan Publishing Company; Melvin Pollner, *Mundane Reason: Reality in Everyday and Sociological Discourse* (New York: Cambridge University Press, 1987), copyright © 1987, Cambridge University Press; and Max Weber, *Economy and Society*, trans. Ephraim Fischoff et al., ed. Guenther Roth and Claus Wittich (Berkeley: University of California Press, 1987), copyright © 1978, the Regents of the University of California.

TO THE MEMORY OF MY FATHER, LOUIS W. HILBERT, JR.

CONTENTS

Foreword by Randall Collins   ix

Preface   xv

1

Ethnomethodology's Peculiar Place

in the History of Sociology   1

2

The Status of Rules in Moral Life   27

3

The Society/Morality Equivalence   46

4

The Society/Reality Equivalence   66

5

Anomie   83

6

Indifference to Order and Ideas   104

7

Empirical Subjectivity and the

Compellingness of Ideas   122

8

Bureaucracy and Rationalization   141

9

Durkheim-Weber Convergence and

Functionalist Rationalization   161

10

Classically Informed Ethnomethodology

in Contemporary Theoretical Context   188

Notes   221

References   233

Index   251

FOREWORD

Some of the great theoretical works in modern sociology have been treatments of previous classics. Talcott Parsons's *Structure of Social Action* in 1937 built up a new synthesis by means of analyzing Durkheim, Weber, and Pareto. Jeffrey Alexander's *Theoretical Logic in Sociology* (1983) adds Marx to Durkheim and Weber among the old classics, and then treats Parsons as the following theoretical generation. Jürgen Habermas's *Theory of Communicative Action* (1981), which is closely contemporary with Alexander's work, does much the same but adds George Herbert Mead to the pantheon. Whoever wants to set forth a major line of theory, it seems, does well to present it as a synthesis of and corrective to the great theoretical efforts of the past.

Richard Hilbert's *Classical Roots of Ethnomethodology* is in this mold. But what constitutes a classic is itself the result of just these sorts of choices as to whom one features. Hilbert's lineup of building blocks and stumbling blocks is a rival construction to those of Alexander and Habermas. For Hilbert, the classics worth building on are Durkheim and Weber—not surprising, perhaps, since these are the constants on everyone's list. But the next step is a contest, in which Parsons plays the part of obfuscating the old classics and turning them into a blind alley; while Harold Garfinkel and his school come to the rescue, rediscovering the key insights of the classics and demonstrating them in empirical detail.

Hilbert's revision will be a gestalt switch for mainstream sociologists and ethnomethodologists alike. When ethnomethodology blew onto the sociological scene in the mid-1960s, it had the aspect first of an underground movement and then of an intellectual revolution. Whether they favored this movement or not, most people on both sides tended to see the situation as a struggle of ethnomethodology *versus* sociology. Now Hilbert tells us that the ethnomethodologists have been the truest sociologists all along.

All such claims, rearranging the symbols of our intellectual identities, are bound to raise emotions. Let us try to detach ourselves for a moment, however, and consider why it is that sociologists are so concerned to get straight the theoretical continuities from the past. Why have major theorists so often found it necessary to work through their predecessors, showing what has been fruitful and where we have gone astray, where the threads should be woven together and where they have been given a false weave? One reason, surely, is that sociologists are polemical and one-sided. We readily divide into schools and denigrate whatever is outside our own. Our famous thinkers often are those who can rise above the partisanship to pick out what the polemicists have been missing and collect it into a fund that should serve for the common good of sociology. Such efforts are only partly successful at best; the syntheses themselves are one-sided, and so there is room for reconsideration and resynthesis, sometimes tearing apart the old syntheses in the process.

Hilbert's *Classical Roots of Ethnomethodology*, like the other major works in this genre, has a historical thread, but it is not primarily a history. Garfinkel was a student of Parsons at Harvard around 1950; and Garfinkel's dissertation was indeed on Weber's theory of action as an alternative to the Parsonian appropriation of Weber. Garfinkel about the same time attended lectures by Alfred Schutz at the New School for Social Research; here too there is a link back to Weber, for Schutz was not only a phenomenologist but a former economist who had begun by attempting to develop the ideal types of action which Weber had barely sketched in his own writings.* Hilbert's work, however, is not primarily in tracing out these details of intellectual biography. Like Parsons before him, and like his illustrious modern contemporaries, Hilbert treats the classics and moderns analytically. He cuts through to a core of central ideas; he shows their resonances and incompatibilities.

We should be aware of the creativity of this kind of work. Many interpretations can be and have been made of this material, and if Hilbert's vision of the underlying pattern is convincing, it is because of his own insight. The work of this book is in Hilbert's demonstration of a synthesis between the research findings of the ethnomethodologists and the major ideas of the classic theorists. Many things come simultaneously into sharper focus: what the ethnomethodologists have been able to do, what is truly

---

*See Christopher Prendergast, "Alfred Schutz and the Austrian School of Economics," *American Journal of Sociology* 92 (1986): 1–26.

central in Durkheim and Weber, and how Parsons shifted the focus to an entirely different frame.

Durkheim's core idea is that there is a nonrational basis for rationality. To put it another way, social solidarity is a moral process which is implicit in interaction, and any utilitarian interests and exchanges can operate only if such solidarity exists. Parsons saw this, and he gives considerable emphasis to the way Durkheim solved the "Hobbesian problem of order," by demonstrating that contracts are possible only if there is precontractual solidarity. If one insists on being rationalistic about this, any rule implies a second agreement to uphold the rule, and that implies a third agreement to uphold the second agreement, and so on ad infinitum. The regress must be broken somewhere, and Durkheim goes on to show that in fact it is cut through immediately when social rituals constitute moral feelings of what is right and wrong.

Parsons and the ethnomethodologists part company on what this means. For Parsons, the lesson of Durkheim is that there is a separate normative order which exists over and above society and which provides the basis for social order. Hilbert makes clever use of Durkheim's theory of crime and the ethnomethodological conception of indexicality to show why this is the wrong lesson. Durkheim's argument on the necessity for precontractual solidarity states that rules are never adequate in themselves; hence whatever the moral dimension of society is, it cannot consist of rules. Crime, in the common-sense conception that Parsons adopts, consists of violation of the agreed-upon rules. But if rules are inherently vague and inadequate to determine social behavior, it is impossible in principle for people always to adhere to them. Why did Durkheim declare that crime is inevitable, that even a society made up of saints would have its sinners? The social process itself creates crime, and it does so in the same process that creates punishment. In Durkheim's famous argument, people frame some behavior as criminal so that they can punish it, and the punishment constitutes a ritual which reminds everyone of the power of society and of the ideal of followings its rules.

Hilbert points out the similarity between Durkheim's argument that rules alone are never adequate—for instance, that people always need some implicit understanding as to when and how to apply the rules—and the ethnomethodological conception of indexicality. Garfinkel expanded the problem from rules to all semantical expressions and pointed out that their meaning varies with the context and depends upon implicit methods for making use of them to sustain social life. No amount of further clarification of what is said can get around the fact that the final set of expressions used for clarification is also indexical. This was demonstrated in the breaching experiments in which subjects asked for further explanations of ordinary talk until finally their partner blew up in exasperation—a Durkheimian ritual in itself, as Hilbert points out, restoring the taken-for-granted normal procedures of social life by punishing the violator.

In Durkheim's conception of crime, punishment rituals arise because the rules are not inherently self-applying. They are vague unless they are specified, concretely and in practice, and the way in which this is done is by punishing someone. What has seemed like an uncharacteristically paradoxical or cynical element in Durkheim follows directly from his central insight about the nonrational foundations of rationality, and this is the same insight as ethnomethodological indexicality.

Durkheim had also pushed very far in his theory of the social construction of reality; the fundamental categories of thinking are sacred objects, symbols of group membership, which arise from the pattern of social interactions. Parsons was unwilling to accept this, since he wished to give culture an autonomous status, separate from social interaction and exerting influence upon it. Here again, Hilbert argues, Parsons took the wrong path. What Garfinkel terms "reflexivity" is the process by which people organize their actions tacitly, and at the same time give the impression that there is a stable social order. As Hilbert puts it at the beginning of chapter 5, "whatever members do to sustain a sense of stable society is also the very activity that sustains the impression of an inherently stable and objective reality." There is no "culture" out there which can push people around, because "culture" is what people are producing, using their implicit techniques for dealing with indexicality whenever they carry out any social action.

Hilbert gives this a characteristically Durkheimian slant. Durkheim was fond of showing what constrains people by focusing on what happens when they violate the normal; the invisible, taken-for-granted barriers become dramatically present when someone bumps into them. If it is the normal process of social life to generate meanings which one believes are objective and universally shared, any time when this does not happen will be experienced as abnormal. Hilbert shows this in the case of chronic pain. The feeling of pain is private; it cannot be shared. This means that there are no social categories for understanding what is happening in oneself, no way of distinguishing what is really there and what its shape is. Pain is anomic, Hilbert shows, and thus there is suffering which goes beyond the pain itself. It is a loss of social contact, a failure of the most common ethnomethods for giving a sense of objectivity; it is a loss of reality. The only way out of this, Hilbert suggests, is shifting one's attention away from the hopeless task of trying to understand one's pain and onto a meta-level where religions or philosophies attempt to account for why there are things that cannot be understood. It is a point worth following up: the transcendence of religions comes from putting a social meaning around the regions of life which most escape from society.

Hilbert similarly traces how Weber's central themes are closer to ethnomethodology than to the normatively structured order which Parsons made of them. Again rules and rationality provide the touchstone. Weber carefully indicates that people act in terms of various kinds of legitimate orders, whether traditional or rational-legal. But these are beliefs people orient toward, not entities that independently exist. Thus when Weber describes the ideal-type characteristics of bureaucracy, he is referring to the common beliefs subscribed to by its members: that actions are to be carried out according to formal regulations, that records are to be kept, that promotion is to go through procedures which are regarded as selecting "merit," that each job has its own sphere of competence and its incumbent sticks within it. Sociological studies of organizations have long ago shown that organizations do not operate like this, that there are informal groups, spur-of-the-moment adjustments, organizational politics. Ethnomethodological research in organizations has strengthened the point; as one might expect, rules do not give their own grounds for when and how to apply themselves, and even when people are being most bureaucratic, they have a tacit understanding of how to go about it.

Here Hilbert adds some punch from his own research. He examines what happens when an organization tries to spell out explicitly everything that a member must do. The result is a growing list of rules, such as the 900-plus rules formulated by administrators trying to specify what a competent classroom teacher should do. Yet every rule remains unspecified in various ways, so each rule can branch out still further into other rules. This leads Hilbert to show why bureaucratization is an endless process. Formal rules can never cover all the contingencies and occasions for their own application. To try to make rules perfectly comprehensive is an impossible task; and the effort to do so makes people proceed endlessly onward, formulating new rules. Hilbert gives a chilling projection of the Weberian iron cage as a historical trend.

It has often been charged that ethnomethodology deals with the small-scale and the trivial and has little to say about the big concerns of sociology—about political and economic power, massive social conflicts, the directions and causes of long-term social change. Hilbert argues, however, that ethnomethodology is not inimical to large-scale questions. It is, rather, indifferent to questions of structure, whether these are characterized on the macro or the micro level. Ethnomethodology has been concerned with the tacit procedures by which persons create a sense of social structure, and it brackets the question of whether such structure really exists. If we wish to consider what happens when people use ethnomethods over a long period of time, for instance patching up rule failure with further rule creation, we come out with the proliferation of rules and enforcement procedures that characterizes the bureaucratization of our world.

Hilbert shows the relevance of ethnomethodology to what had been considered a traditional macro question, because for him ethnomethodology is not merely microsociology. If ethnomethodology continues the core concerns of classic sociology, it should be able to cast light on all the topics which Durkheim and Weber dealt with. And here we see that connecting ethnomethodology back into the classical lineage of sociological problems and insights is also a practical activity. It opens a broad agenda of tasks for the future.

Randall Collins

University of California, Riverside

PREFACE

Any attempt to shed light on Garfinkel requires more than a passing interest in ethnomethodology and in Garfinkel's texts. Any attempt to connect
Garfinkel with Durkheim and Weber requires more of the same plus a
tendentious disposition and a strong teaching presence somewhere in the
background. For me that presence includes D. Lawrence Wieder, who
patiently saw me through my formative training in ethnomethodology,
preventing the missteps and almost automatic mistakes one makes when
reading Garfinkel for the first time. Don Zimmerman and Tom Wilson
later helped solidify my own evolving sense of ethnomethodology as a
sense worth owning and developing, though nobody ever told me in graduate school that I would be writing a book on ethnomethodology's classical
roots—a subject at once subtle and quite daunting.

My interest in classical theory goes back to undergraduate days, with
Nicos Mouratides and Orrin Klapp at San Diego State, where I began to
suspect that classical sociologists were on to a good deal more than the
theory of norms and values. Also at San Diego was Eugene Troxell, who
taught me about Wittgenstein and the importance of thinking clearly.
These teachers are the kinds of heroes that often go unsung in the ac-
knowledgments sections of midlife publications.

Next come my formidable, and sometimes unwitting, helpers during
the book project itself. There's Deirdre Boden, who told me to *write* the
thing and not to put it off to retirement. There are countless people whose
generous responses to earlier exploratory articles and papers encouraged
me along the way—Norbert Wiley, for example, and Jeff Alexander. Mel
Pollner is always an inspiration in any conversation. Joe Schneider probably does not realize how his confidence in my work helped me to follow it
through. And Randall Collins has simply been one of the most gracious
and encouraging personalities I have encountered on this ever-uncertain
trail.

Collins also tops the list of people who read and commented upon drafts of the book as it moved along. He wrote page after page of detailed commentary on the entire manuscript in one of its early stages. Doug Maynard (how fortunate I am to know him) also wrote very penetrating ideas and suggestions on several chapters, as did Tom Wilson (ever rigorous, ever informed) and Deirdre Boden—although Dede ended up telling me most of her ideas over the phone. Gary Fine responded to chapter 1, reminding me of the need to further distinguish my project from simply reading one text in terms of another. Each of these people helped in ways that I might have to say are indexical, and to each of them goes my very special, indexical gratitude.

Next we come to officials in the publication process itself. The anonymous reviews were wonderful and helped provide an architecture for the book that it surely would have lacked without them. And Paul Betz did more to nurture the book along than one would automatically expect from an editor.

Finally, I am grateful to Gustavus Adolphus College for several research grants and the time released from teaching so helpful in finishing up a project like this, and to my students for their patience in allowing me to develop some of the ideas of this book in spoken form.

A book such as this should be therapeutic for an author as well as informative for an audience. I have tried to clarify much of what I have been thinking about for the past seven or eight years concerning ethnomethodology and classical sociology, things I have been longing to say all at once, together in the same place, and in some kind of order that brings it all together. I hope that readers will find some insights that are new and helpful.

THE CLASSICAL ROOTS OF ETHNOMETHODOLOGY

1

ETHNOMETHODOLOGY'S PECULIAR PLACE

IN THE HISTORY OF SOCIOLOGY

My main purpose in writing this book is to demonstrate specific historical continuities between classical sociology and ethnomethodology. That these continuities are historical, rather than simply the result of reading the classics or ethnomethodology in terms of each other, is a central focus of my demonstration. Ethnomethodology's origins in Talcott Parsons's functionalist sociology, together with the origins of functionalism in Emile Durkheim and Max Weber, account for these continuities.

This historical connection presents a more dramatic tale than one of simple linear cumulation. My thesis involves three generations of ideas, with the first finding confirmation in the third by way of its transition and latency in the second. Specifically, Parsons derived a theory from Durkheim and Weber while silencing some of their key theoretical contributions. Parsons often expressed his exceptions to Durkheim and Weber by way of correction and dismissal; at other times he ignored classical themes altogether. The result was a functionalist sociology based on negation and suppression that provided precisely the theoretical spaces in which Harold Garfinkel launched his empirical studies. Garfinkel's studies in turn served as a correction of Parsons. My primary thesis is that in correcting Parsons, Garfinkel's empirical studies also resurrected the very classical ideas that Parsons had suppressed. Thus the connection between classical sociology and ethnomethodology is indirect, involving Parsons as the carrier of classical ideas in their inverted form to Garfinkel, who serendipitously reversed this "negative image" back to its original positive form found in classical sociology.

An important auxiliary thesis in this book expands upon early ethnomethodological criticism of "traditional sociology" as an example of the social phenomena it supposedly set out to study (see Zimmerman and Pollner 1970; Zimmerman and Wieder 1970). This early commentary was widely received as a criticism of sociology generally, contributing to the impression that ethnomethodologists were attempting to rebuild sociology anew from the ground up. However, ethnomethodological criticism was expressly directed at Parsonian functionalism, not classical sociology, though established associations between Parsons and the classics may have fed the false impression, even among ethnomethodologists, that this criticism automatically extended to Durkheim and Weber. Once the principles of my primary thesis are established, we shall be in the position to see Parsonian functionalism not only as an example of the society it set out to study but also as an example of the phenomena Durkheim and Weber wrote of and prognosticated about. My auxiliary thesis, then, is that functionalist theory is a fascinating microcosm of Western society, the rational social order Weber speaks of together with its Durkheimian methods of self-preservation.

BRIEF HISTORICAL BACKGROUND

The 1937 publication of Parsons's monumental *Structure of Social Action* was a watershed for American sociology in at least two ways. First, it introduced the works of Durkheim and Weber to the English-speaking world and established orthodoxies relative to these works that stood for several decades (see Ritzer 1988, p. 180). Second, through detailed textual analysis Parsons derived the outline of his own "voluntaristic" theory, which later served as the foundations for functionalist sociology.[1] In many ways functionalism became almost synonymous with "sociology" in the United States, a hegemony it enjoyed at least through the late 1950s (Davis 1959; Ritzer 1988, pp. 201–2; cf. Alexander 1987b). In its raw form, functionalism asserts the existence of a factual behavioral order that is caused by another order, a normative order consisting of norms, values, roles, and statuses; socialization into normative order and its internalization by societal members produces or "causes" the behavioral order sociologists can observe (Parsons 1968b, p. 91; see Zimmerman and Wieder 1970, p. 286; cf. Alexander 1984, p. 22).

The original appeal of functionalist theory lay not only in its tacit reasonableness but also in its apparent derivation from Durkheim and Weber.[2] Parsons made much of the fact that while the two classical theorists came from different intellectual and cultural backgrounds and were relatively unaware of each other's work, they nevertheless implied the same conclusion, which later served as the foundation of Parsons's functionalism (see e.g. Parsons 1968b, pp. 697–726). Each, said Parsons, nearly reached that conclusion, but each missed it because of some idiosyncratic mistakes and blind spots. Thus there was an inevitable intertwining between the scholarly respectability of American functionalism and the orthodoxies Parsons established concerning the theories of Durkheim and Weber.[3]

Parsons's derivations were of an analytic sort, even though Parsons called the mere possibility of his derivations, particularly the fact that they converged on his own theory, itself empirical verification of the theory (see Alexander 1984, pp. 152–69). The bulk of later functionalist theorizing, as exemplified in such work as Parsons 1951, Parsons, Bales, and Shils 1953, and Merton 1968, consisted of *figuring out* what kinds of norms, processes, and other principles are necessary for socialization to produce social order. The functionalist agenda was not, in other words, based upon the empirical discovery of a concrete system of norms and values but rather upon logical necessity.

The functionalist agenda is to be contrasted with that of one of Parsons's more innovative students, Harold Garfinkel. What set Garfinkel apart from Parsons's other students and colleagues was his extreme commitment to *empirical studies*. Rather than ask, for example, what kinds of normative networks are necessary to sustain family structures, Garfinkel would more likely ask: "What normative networks *are* there?" or "Are there any normative networks?" or "How can we see normative networks?" or even "Where is the family structure in the first place?" Garfinkel's *look-and-see* attitude toward social phenomena led him to a distinctively empirical sociology, though always rooted in Parsons's theory and engaging key Parsonian themes—social structure, normative prescription, and shared understandings, to name a few (see Heritage 1984, p. 9). His investigations led him to a domain of previously unexamined social phenomena which he called "members' methods" or "artful practices" (see Garfinkel 1967, pp. vii–ix, 31–34), and he coined the term "ethnomethodology" to name his investigations as the study of those artful practices (see Garfinkel 1974).

In 1967 Garfinkel published the bulk of his investigations under the title *Studies in Ethnomethodology*, which soon became the foundational text for subsequent work by later generations of ethnomethodologists. As a whole, ethnomethodological studies undercut the premises and theoretical orientations of functionalism, and they did so in ways that enable one to see the "real and actual society" in "the concreteness of things" (Garfinkel 1988, p. 106) rather than simply as the achieved result of a priori theorizing and formally administered research methodologies. In fact, part of Garfinkel's recent assessment of functionalism is that Parsons assumed that "the real and actual society . . . is *not* to be found in the concreteness of things" but only as the product of formal theory and methodology, a general stance Garfinkel calls "formal, constructive analysis" (p. 106). A consequence of such analysis is that it provides concepts and categories predetermined by logical necessity, common-sense reasoning, intellectual heritage, and so on; in this way the presumption of nonempirical entities can legislate to sociologists what surely must be, somehow, empirically the case. Thus the theoretically constructed society replaces the "concreteness of things" as the "real and actual society" (p. 106). It is this "concreteness of things" that Garfinkel turned to and that ethnomethodologists have been studying ever since. In that way, ethnomethodology is radically empirical in the tradition of natural science (see Hilbert 1990a). To whatever extent sociology is supposed to be empirical, ethnomethodology is radically sociological as well (see Garfinkel 1988).

CLARIFICATION OF THE PRIMARY THESIS

Ethnomethodology's place in this historical scheme is not well known. Many sociologists are hardly aware that ethnomethodology sprang from functionalism or that Garfinkel was Parsons's student, despite periodic reminders (e.g. Heritage 1984). An early tendency was to view ethnomethodology as a complete break with practically everything sociological, an impression fed by the difficulty of the primary texts and by a reluctance among ethnomethodologists to theorize their own works systematically.

Ethnomethodologists themselves originally expressed little positive interest in sociology that preceded their studies, but this was partly due to

American functionalism's claim on the classics. Inherent in the functionalism with which early ethnomethodologists did battle is Parsons's readings
of Durkheim and Weber, which claim that these theorists implied and
converged upon Parsons's own theory. If in fact Parsons derived his theory
from Durkheim and Weber, then any break from Parsons would be equally
a break with Durkheim and Weber. Yet the positive association between
Parsons and the classics is no longer an uncontested fact (see Alexander
1984, 1987b; Pope 1973; Pope, Cohen, and Hazelrigg 1975; Cohen,
Hazelrigg, and Pope 1975; Warner 1978). Today, therefore, we are better
prepared to see how ethnomethodological empiricism, while engaging
Parsons, would quite naturally return us to the classical themes that Parsons negated or suppressed. I should emphasize that Garfinkel himself
made no deliberate effort to recover these lost themes, making their recovery by ethnomethodology all the more remarkable.

Against this historical backdrop, I can now state my primary thesis
more succinctly: I am arguing that similarities in methodological policy,
working assumptions, and empirical findings of Durkheim and Weber on
the one hand and those of ethnomethodology on the other are more than
fortuitous. I contend that Durkheim's and Weber's genius, together with
ethnomethodology's uncompromising empiricism, accounts for these similarities and moreover that the connection is historical: Parsons's roots in
the Durkheim-Weber genius passed through his work like recessive genes
to his student Garfinkel, who became deeply empirical about the profound
issues Parsons had handed to him, later overthrowing most of the solutions
Parsons himself crafted in response to those issues. Yet while Parsons was
preparing the path for Garfinkel, he was also reconstructing Durkheim
and Weber, claiming they both implied and converged upon Parsons's own
theory, the same theory that Garfinkel supersedes. Thus when the phe-
notypical Durkheim and Weber reemerge and blossom in ethnomethodology, they are unrecognized. Instead, what ethnomethodologists have been
almost obliged to do is present their case as radical, unprecedented, and
discontinuous with respect to what they call "traditional sociology," focusing on the theoretical groundedness that derives from contemporary philosophy, such as phenomenology or ordinary-language analysis (see e.g.
Mehan and Wood 1975, pp. 192–204). Although these movements in philosophy played an important role in the development of ethnomethodology,
focusing on them obscures ethnomethodology's preeminent grounding
in sociology. This produces a vision of accumulating ethnomethodologi-

cal wisdom as preempting sociology, when it really only preempts Parsons and American functionalism. I will demonstrate how ethnomethodology can claim its classical roots and present itself as sociology to the very core of the discipline.

My demonstration of ethnomethodology's classical roots will be by way of ethnomethodological case studies. Each of the empirical studies discussed in later chapters addresses a key principle (or several principles) in Parsonian sociology. In each case, I will show how Parsons derived his principle from Durkheim or Weber, especially in terms of what he had to negate or suppress in order to establish the principle. And in each case I will show how the empirical study reverses the damage, not only negating Parsons, but also negating his negation—recovering the classical principles he suppressed. I shall show, in other words, that each classical idea has its analogue in ethnomethodological studies mediated by its negation in American functionalism. The result is an almost one-to-one correspondence between classical sociology as theoretically conceived and ethnomethodology as empirically practiced. The continuity between ethnomethodology and the classics is therefore quite real, but it is indirect by way of "negative images" transmitted to Garfinkel through Parsons by the problems in Parsons's work caused by his suppression of certain classical matters. Once again, this continuity is all the more fascinating since Garfinkel was not himself making an effort to reconnect with the classics or even to spell out his theory systematically.[4]

The auxiliary thesis mentioned above is more difficult to restate succinctly at this point, since it depends upon establishing the primary thesis in detail. I do not therefore argue the auxiliary thesis fully until chapter 9, though it begins to come forth in bits and pieces earlier, particularly in the chapters on Max Weber. As I have already indicated, I will argue that American functionalist reasoning, rather than being a viable theory of society, is a feature of the very society it seeks to explain and in that capacity is a rarefied *example* of the very social phenomena that Durkheim and Weber wrote about and that ethnomethodologists reveal through empirical studies. Taken this way, classical sociologists might have predicted the rise of American functionalism as part of advanced Western civilization. This is an extension of early ethnomethodological characterizations of "traditional sociology" as an example of the social phenomena it set out to illuminate, a "folk science" that assimilates to these phenomena, losing them as topical concerns in the process. Combined with my primary thesis, we shall be prepared to see Parsonian functionalism as an active case of Durkheimian ritual repair and as an active case of a Weberian rational-legal, bureaucratic orientation. Indeed, we shall see the Parsons derivation itself, the conversion of Durkheim's collective conscience to norms and values, as an instance of Weberian rationalization, that is, the rationalization of morality and society.

ETHNOMETHODOLOGY AS AN UNDERTHEORIZED ENTERPRISE

One favorable by-product of finding ethnomethodology's roots is that we can put ethnomethodology to use, in a more systematic way than is usual, in the development of sociological theory. The one-to-one correspondence I just mentioned provides a classical way of understanding ethnomethodological findings, while these same findings also tell us more about the phenomena Durkheim and Weber were writing about. There is progress to be made, therefore, in general theory. I will address this question directly in chapter 9, where I take up the question of "classically informed ethnomethodological theory."

Yet because of ethnomethodology's deep commitment to empiricism, even the term "ethnomethodological theory" may seem anomalous to some readers. Ethnomethodology has to a significant degree resisted theorization, certainly systematic theorization, resting instead on an accumulation of a variety of fascinating empirical findings which, to the inquisitive nonethnomethodologist, may seem only vaguely or peripherally related to each other (cf. Heritage 1984, p. 1; Wilson and Zimmerman 1979/80, p. 52). Among ethnomethodologists themselves, there have been implicit understandings concerning the underlying theoretical directions running through their work, but there has been a reluctance to assert these directions boldly in the style of theoretical claims. In a way, this has been an enlightened reluctance, and expressed as such, since central to ethnomethodological findings is a sense in which preordered theoretical orientations can legislate what will be found in advance of an investigation. Thus premature theorizing among ethnomethodologists could be counterproductive to the long-term gathering of substantive findings, deflecting ethnomethodology from its course at the very point where its empirical findings are most enlightening. In arguing for this stance, for example,

Mehan and Wood (1975, p. 152) state, "No unifying resolution of these disparate 'theories' and 'methods' [within ethnomethodology] need be attempted."

Ethnomethodology is not without theory, however, and it is not without theorists (see Maynard and Clayman 1991). Early efforts to communicate ethnomethodology to a wide academic audience expressed, often rather directly, theoretical orientations to the social world (see e.g. Zimmerman and Wieder 1970; Zimmerman and Pollner 1970). Yet it is difficult to distinguish these theoretical assertions from programmatic statements about what ethnomethodological studies should consist of. Early substantive studies also contained useful theoretical commentary relevant to general sociology (see Pollner 1974b; Bittner 1965, 1967; Sudnow 1967; Wieder 1970), and Garfinkel's (1967) seminal classic was laden with theoretical vision. However, once again, many of these discussions were tailored to the specific studies they were about, with little ambition to connect these studies with each other by way of overarching theory. They also were often couched as methodological policy statements regarding ethnomethodological research.

Most important, as I mentioned, many formulations of ethnomethodology seemed to deny continuity with previous sociological concerns, characterizing ethnomethodology by way of direct contrast with "traditional sociology." While much in these characterizations was largely pedagogical, nevertheless they foster an image of ethnomethodology as discontinuous with respect to nearly everything sociological, a denied continuity I am affirming in this book. This inability or unwillingness to claim sociological turf has also been an inhibition against bold sociological theorizing. Occasionally ethnomethodologists have used such ideas as Durkheim's "social facts" or "exteriority" and Weber's organizational theory as counterexamples to their recommended line of research (e.g. Wieder 1974a; Bittner 1965). Sometimes they even seem to be speaking of "ethnomethodology" on the one hand as opposed to "sociology" on the other (e.g. Mehan and Wood 1975; Wilson and Zimmerman 1979/80).

Wilson and Zimmerman (1979/80) specifically take up the question of sociological theory in relation to ethnomethodology. They take special pains to distinguish between ethnomethodological theory as it relates to sociology in general—that is, the sociological theory that justifies ethnomethodological research in the first place—and the kind of theory within ethnomethodology itself, which is to say, the theoretical principles ethnomethodology generates with regard to its own subject matter (p. 53). With regard to general sociological theory, the authors identify ethnomethodology largely by contrast with "conventional" concerns, though they draw some common ground across the contrast saying that ethnomethodology has affinities with sociological traditions broadly conceived (pp. 53–55). They also adapt ethnomethodological focus on context-dependency to argue that sociological theory is itself context-specific—indeed, historically situated—and cannot be removed from its historical circumstance to describe "society" as a more general theoretical object (pp. 63–67). Interestingly, the authors cite Max Weber and Karl Marx as friendly forebears of this view, though they cite Durkheim as a counterexample (pp. 55, 56).

When it comes to theoretical matters within ethnomethodology itself, Wilson and Zimmerman (1979/80, pp. 67–75) discuss the turn-taking model of conversation developed by Sacks, Schegloff, and Jefferson (1974) and used extensively in conversation analysis. They treat this as an example of theory internal to ethnomethodology, not subject to critical tests for confirmation or rejection of hypotheses, but useful mainly for purposes of framing empirical investigations and suggesting new theoretical puzzles for investigators (1979/80, p. 72). Given the general location of ethnomethodology within general sociology, these "internal" ethnomethodological theories are more like the foundational assumptions of a discipline, just as for example biology has foundational assumptions that provide for its subject matter. Moreover, since these theories are not about structure but about the methods whereby people assemble and theorize about structure, these internal theories may even designate context-free or transhistorical phenomena. Wilson and Zimmerman leave open the possibility that these foundational ethnomethodological assumptions might themselves eventually turn out to be historically specific, but they argue that to date there is no evidence to indicate this (p. 74).

By contrast, my arguments do not distinguish between ethnomethodology as it relates to general sociology and as it relates to its own internal subject matter. I am suggesting a lineage between classical sociology and the substantive findings of ethnomethodology. This means that theoretical justification for ethnomethodological research within sociology generally and theoretical development within ethnomethodology proper need not be distinguished. If ethnomethodologists turn up empirical findings continuous with respect to the phenomena Durkheim and Weber wrote about, this in itself recommends these studies to sociology. At the same time, whatever is "news" about these phenomena within ethnomethodological circles is deeply connected to what motivated sociological studies at the outset.

GARFINKEL'S ROOTS IN PARSONIAN SOCIOLOGY

One of the most ambitious attempts to theorize ethnomethodology is John Heritage's (1984) *Garfinkel and Ethnomethodology*. The most noteworthy aspect of this work is the way the author systematically brings otherwise disparate ethnomethodological studies together in line with a set of thematic issues that underlie them. Furthermore, Heritage demonstrates how Garfinkel became interested in these issues and where he derived his principal insights. Heritage's third chapter, for example, reviews the contribution of phenomenology to Garfinkel's thought as well as the intellectual puzzles being addressed by phenomenologists at the time Garfinkel brushed shoulders with them in his early days as a graduate student, most notably Alfred Schutz and Aron Gurwitsch (Heritage 1984, pp. 37–38).

Most significant is Garfinkel's graduate school career at Harvard University, specifically his direct intellectual ties to Talcott Parsons (Heritage 1984, pp. 7–10). In his dissertation (Garfinkel 1952), supervised by Parsons, "he sought to dig still deeper into the basic problems in the theory of action which had been raised, but incompletely dealt with, in [Parsons's] *The Structure of Social Action*" (Heritage 1984, p. 9; cf. Garfinkel 1988, p. 104). Quoting the dissertation, Heritage reminds us that Garfinkel originally set out to explore an implication in Max Weber's work, an alternative implication to the one Parsons worked on, this alternative having to do with "experience structures" as opposed to systemic social structures. Indeed, writes Heritage, Garfinkel's interest in phenomenology's concern with cognition and experience derives from the fact that phenomenologists Schutz and Gurwitsch "entered [this concern] at exactly the most troubled point of Parsons's treatment [of cognition]" (Heritage 1984, p. 38). Phenomenologists had troubles of their own, writes Heritage, particularly in that the Hobbesian problem of social order, which motivated Parsons's entire intellectual career, remained unsolved and indeed unaddressed (p. 76). In fact, Schutz even generated a new kind of order problem, one having to do with cognition as opposed to structured behavior. These troubles remained for Garfinkel to solve, even as he drew upon phenomenological insights to overcome weaknesses in Parsons's theory. The point here is that Garfinkel was from the outset addressing the puzzles and paradoxes in Parsons's work, this as opposed to his ever having set out to integrate phenomenology with sociology as an end in its own right. As Heritage (p. 9) puts it,

> While the theoretical vocabulary to be used in [Garfinkel's] task was to be drawn from the phenomenological writings of Schutz and Gurwitsch, it would be used to analyze classical problems in the theory of action and to propose entirely novel avenues toward their solution.

To lay emphasis on ethnomethodology's roots in sociological matters, consider Garfinkel's (1988, p. 104) recent comments about Parsons's *Structure of Social Action.*

> Ethnomethodology has its origins in this wonderful book. Its earliest initiatives were taken from these texts. Ethnomethodologists have continued to consult its text to understand the practices and the achievements of formal analysis in the work of professional social science.
>
> Inspired by *The Structure of Social Action* ethnomethodology undertook the task of respecifying the production and accountability of immortal, ordinary society.

It still seems odd to think of Garfinkel's studies as rooted in Parsonian sociology. But to miss this fundamental point is to miss the heart of Garfinkel's insights. That these insights have been largely missed by so many readers in just that manner is at least partly due to so many challenges to functionalism arising at precisely the time that early ethnomethodological findings were first being published (see Heritage 1984, pp. 2–3). Superficial similarities between ethnomethodology and these new challenges, with their varying emphases on the social construction of reality, interpretation, and humanism, set the stage for misunderstanding, or worse: acceptance on a misguided basis. As Heritage (p. 3) puts it:

> The net result was an assimilation of a range of perspectives . . . into a single category: the "sociology of everyday life." In the process, Garfinkel's fundamental and enduring analytical achievements

were lost from sight at the very moment at which "ethnomethodology" became a household word in sociology.

Thus we see, for example, Lyman and Scott's (1970, p. 1) conflation of ethnomethodology, labeling theory, and "neo-symbolic interactionism" and Denzin's (1969, 1970) arguments that ethnomethodology and symbolic interactionism converge on the same substantive concerns (but see Zimmerman and Wieder's [1970] reply). These misunderstandings have proven most intractable and have become well entrenched over the past quarter century (see Maynard and Clayman 1991), frequently appearing as factual background material in sociological textbooks. Recently, Stephan and Stephan (1990, pp. 29–31) placed ethnomethodology and Goffman's "dramaturgical school" as the two subheadings under the general heading "Offshoots of Symbolic Interactionism." This could not more fully miscast the ethnomethodological enterprise as well as its historical origins.

In short, Garfinkel derived his thematic issues from Parsons. As Heritage (1984, p. 3) shows, these were not newly minted issues but rather issues that "have been central areas of investigation throughout the history of [sociology] and, in their various aspects, have persistently concerned its distinguished practitioners." These issues and concerns include "the theory of action, the nature of intersubjectivity and the social constitution of knowledge" (p. 3). My way of expressing this is to say that Garfinkel conducted highly observational investigations relative to theoretical matters within and contained by Parsonian sociology. Consequently, as the Parsonian edifice began to crumble in the wake of Garfinkel's studies, some of the very themes Parsons suppressed from Durkheim and Weber in the derivation of this edifice began to resurface.

In order to see how this happened, it helps first to review Parsons's sociology. I begin with the basic requirements Parsons says are necessary for a theory of social action, that is, the bedrock of his sociology that he does not claim to derive from anywhere other than logical necessity. I begin here in order to show that even Parsons claims to derive only the upper edifices of his voluntaristic theory from Durkheim and Weber; the bedrock of his theory was not at all derived from them but rather from Parsons's own sense of logical necessity. Next I review Parsons's negative evaluation of utilitarianism in terms of this theoretical bedrock and also of its only conceivable alternative, also derived in terms of this bedrock: radical positivism. This review will help us understand how Parsons conceived the problematic for sociology as embedded in utilitarian thought, how he conceptualized the inability of positivism to solve the problem, and how he saw his own advanced theory as responsive to that analytic puzzle. This in turn enables an appreciation of exactly where Garfinkel entered the Parsonian discourse, a development worked out by Heritage (1984) and more recently discussed by Garfinkel himself (1988). At the same time, a review of the Parsonian bedrock helps in understanding what Parsons had to read into and out of Durkheim and Weber in order to find their alleged flaws and to derive his own theory from those classical texts.

THE BEDROCK OF PARSONS'S THEORY ANTECEDENT TO ITS DERIVATION FROM THE CLASSICS

Parsons's long-range goal was a "theory of action" that could describe human behavior in ways that would solve the "problem of social order." The problem of order has it origins in presociological utilitarian thinkers, particularly Thomas Hobbes, who is so noted for first stating the problem that it is also known as the "Hobbesian problem": Why is human behavior coordinated; why does it display patterns; why is it orderly and structured as opposed to random and chaotic; how, indeed, is society possible? Parsons's initial objective was to show how this question would be puzzling to presociological commentators on human behavior, how sociology overcame deficiencies in these commentators' vision, how classical theorists Marshall, Pareto, Durkheim, and Weber all worked within postutilitarian frameworks (i.e. emerging sociological ones) to solve the problem of order, and how their work fell just short of the solution. From there, Parsons finishes the task, providing the solution nearly reached by the classical thinkers.

Classical sociology most certainly arose in part as a response to questions concerning social order, more generally to answer questions regarding why people behave collectively the way that they do. But the solutions Parsons ultimately provides are couched in terms of some logical assumptions offered in chapter 2 of *The Structure of Social Action*, well before his analysis of classical sociology, indeed even before the detailed examination of utilitarian thought. In other words, Parsons does not claim to derive his rock-bottom assumptions from Durkheim or Weber. Rather, these assumptions are expressly modeled after axiomatic principles within the natural sciences which, Parsons says, define their subject matter by reference to its "units," which exist only in terms of their "basic properties" (Parsons 1968b, p. 43). As an example, Parsons offers physicists' interest in particles, which "can be defined only in terms of their properties, mass, velocity, location in space, direction of motion [sic], etc."[5]

In the science of human action, Parsons identifies the fundamental unit as the "unit act," which can be said to exist only as a consequence of its formal properties. These properties are (1) an *actor*, or agency of action; (2) an *end* of action, a "future state of affairs" that the action brings about; (3) a *situation* the actor is in which differs from the future state and which in turn consists of present objective *conditions* (which the actor cannot control) and the *means* of altering the situation in conformity with the end; and (4) a "normative orientation," which is to say that the action proper (means) is neither chosen at random nor determined for the actor by the conditions (Parsons 1968b, pp. 43–45; see Warner 1978, pp. 1321–22). This last property indicates that the actor has an element of subjective choice relative to the means. Since ends are analytically distinct from conditions, there is a necessary element of choice relative to ends too, but once ends are decided, choice regarding means are subject to limitations concerning the actor's ability to make correct choices—that is, choices that in fact accomplish the ends (Parsons 1968b, pp. 45–46).

Parsons views social order as systems of these unit acts, analytically conceived. Therefore any theory of society will have to take account of unit acts and their formal properties. Without each of these formal properties, unit acts and systems of action are inconceivable (cf. Bershady 1973, pp. 66–68). Once again it is important to realize that this analysis of action, which marks the opening of Parsons's sociology, is not derived from classical sociology. This analysis, rather, is Parsons's presociological offering and the bedrock of his theory. He proposes unit acts and their formal properties as logically necessary. They become axiomatic to his theory. He goes on to discuss the utilitarian problem of order in just such terms. Utilitarianism fails to solve the problem however, so Parsons begins the derivation from Durkheim and Weber in order to solve the problem as already set forth by these logically prearranged axioms. He spends most of *The Structure of Social Action* deriving the outline of the solution through addressing Durkheim's and Weber's relative abilities to overcome the limitations of utilitarianism while handling action in terms of these essential, logical properties. They do well, he says, but not quite well enough. Had either theorist sufficiently followed the implications of his work in terms of action and its properties, he would have arrived at Parsons's voluntaristic theory; had they both done so, they would have converged upon this theory.

UTILITARIANISM AND RADICAL POSITIVISM

Utilitarians could not, however, have reached Parsons's conclusions, he says, for they had inherited a "common sense" of their era so entrenched in individualism that they could not begin to conceptualize any sort of integration between ends in complex systems of action. Consequently their version of organized life, which Parsons (1968b, p. 51) says "was built essentially out of the kind of units described but put together in a peculiar way," displayed an "atomistic" tendency to see complex systems of action as simply sum totals of internally unrelated unit acts. More important, utilitarianism displayed a naive version of the normative orientation as consisting only of rationality, modeled after scientific rationality. That is, actors' deviations from rationality were conceived only negatively as irrational or nonrational, as error (p. 56). Consequently, actors' voluntaristic element could make sense only relative to choosing means once the ends were already known. Choices were correct to the extent that they were rational and achieved ends; all other choices were simply based on error.

But actors had no basis, rational or otherwise, for choosing ends themselves. Thus utilitarian conceptions of large-scale systems of action necessarily displayed this additional critical feature: *randomness of ends*. Randomness of ends could not help but make the facticity of society puzzling to analysts working within a utilitarian framework (see Parsons 1968b, pp. 51–60; cf. Bershady 1973, pp. 41–43).

Parsons identifies utilitarianism as one form of positivism in its inability to conceptualize normative frameworks other than scientific rationality (1968b, pp. 60–61). From here, he considers two analytically conceivable departures from pure utilitarianism that overcome randomness of ends while complying with the strictures of more general positivism (pp. 60–69). In order to develop his own action theory, Parsons would have to abandon positivism entirely (p. 63), but within the positivist framework, there are only two alternatives to utilitarianism. In one, the actor's choice of *ends* is based on rational knowledge of the *situation*. This solution assimilates ends to conditions, losing the integrity of the analytic properties of action and making action solely a consequence of conditions. In such a vision human action is predetermined by the objective conditions of heredity and environment, a vision which eliminates the actor or the active agency of action. Thus the integrity of the analytic properties is lost, and social action as such becomes inconceivable. Parsons calls this "radical rationalistic positivism" (pp. 63–65). In the second alternative, the actor chooses ends irrationally, based on ignorance and error (pp. 65–69). Irrationality, in a positivistic frame, is conceivable only as a departure from a scientifically rational mode; hence irrationalities, if they are not to be random, are a consequence of actors' flawed knowledge of relevant factors which themselves are analytically capable of being known (pp. 66–67). Irrationality, within a positivistic mode, is explainable solely with reference to the scientifically knowable aspects of the actor's overall life situation that would produce such ignorance and error, that is, the actor's objective conditions. Parsons calls this position "radical anti-intellectualistic positivism" (cf. Alexander 1984, p. 24; Bershady 1973, pp. 44–45).

These two positivistic alternatives to utilitarian randomness of ends therefore lead, says Parsons, "to the same analytic result: explanation of action in terms of the ultimately nonsubjective conditions, conveniently designated as heredity and environment" (1968b, p. 67). In other words, the agency of the actor, subjectivity, is denied in either alternative. Ultimately, Parsons seeks to remedy this by moving beyond positivism itself, simultaneously saving all of the necessary elements of action.

On a less abstract plane, Parsons next characterizes two major utilitarian thinkers, Thomas Hobbes and John Locke, in terms of the analytic properties of action he has outlined. Hobbes, who was the first to point out the problem of order with clarity, conceived of people as rational. But reason for Hobbes was subordinate to passions, the ultimate driving force of human behavior (Parsons 1968b, pp. 89–94). That is, people rationally pursue their passions; yet inherent in this state, if left alone, is the routine possibility that different people's rational pursuits would conflict with each other. People would be obstacles to each other's goals, and the rationally efficient mode of action would be for people to overcome each other through force or fraud. Thus the predicted state of nature is the famous Hobbesian "war of all against all." Empirically, this natural state does not prevail, leading Hobbes to say that people, fearing this natural state, were motivated by that fear to give up natural liberties in exchange for security. Security would be guaranteed by a sovereign authority—government— which enforces social order. This agreement to exchange natural liberties for security is the "social contract," and it is the basis of order for Hobbes.

In Parsonian terms, passions are "discrete, randomly variant ends of action" (Parsons 1968b, p. 90). The nightmare world envisioned by Hobbes is the deducible world predicted by utilitarianism, and Parsons congratulates Hobbes for having so adroitly recognized the problem.[6] But as for solving it, the "social contract" is an almost facile response, one requiring more of the actor than the utilitarian model will allow. Actors must somehow transcend their individualized circumstances to gather a "big picture" enabling them to transcend the natural state. How could this happen? Hobbes does not say. Parsons (p. 93) says the Hobbesian solution stretches "at a critical point, the conception of rationality beyond its scope in the rest of the theory." Notice, too, that once a contract was operational, there would be nothing in Hobbes's theory, or within Parsons's action theory as he has outlined it so far, that could account for why actors do not routinely abandon the contract whenever that would be the rationally expedient method of obtaining passionately desired ends.

The other utilitarian philosopher Parsons discusses is Locke (Parsons 1968b, pp. 95–102). Locke's thinking moves within the same analytic space as Hobbes's, as Locke "envisions no clear conception of any positive mode of relations between [ends]" (p. 95). However, Locke saves social order with what Parsons calls a "metaphysical prop" (p. 102): the natural identity of interests. These "ultimate ends" are just naturally given to all reasonable people—they are life, health, liberty, and possessions. Given these ultimate ends in nature, people still use reason to attain ends, but reason here is not the servant of mere passions but is "the dominant principle of nature itself" (p. 96). The natural identity of interests leads reasonable people to some related discoveries about natural order: all people are created equal, they have reciprocal obligations to each other, they should subordinate immediate personal interests to the long-term gain of all, and so on. These fundamentals have been assimilated almost non-reflectingly by various kinds of political theorists; Parsons says the doctrine of the natural identity of interests is "the device by which it has been possible for utilitarian thought, with few exceptions, for two hundred years to evade the Hobbesian problem" (p. 97). Parsons concludes his discussion of utilitarianism with a restatement of the problem for sociology in light of these considerations.

> How is it possible, *still making use of the general action schema*, to solve the Hobbesian problem of order and yet not make use of such an objectionable metaphysical prop as the doctrine of the natural identity of interests? (p. 102, emphasis added)

Parsons (1968b, pp. 102–25) also discusses concrete positivistic alternatives to utilitarianism, showing how they exemplify the inevitable turn toward radical positivism already outlined in abstract form. Several are analyzed, notably Malthusian doctrine (pp. 102–7), Darwinism (pp. 110–14), behaviorism, and hedonism (pp. 115–22). The details are not necessary to spell out here other than to say that all of these positivistic theories turn out to be variations of environmental or behavioral determinism; they necessarily turn out to be "radical positivism" of either the rationalistic or the anti-intellectualistic kind. Parsons's point in these pages is that "so long as one remains genuinely positivistic, the transition to radical positivism [from utilitarianism] is inescapable" (p. 122).

Parsons, then, set as his task the transition out of positivism completely toward a "voluntaristic theory of action" that would save the integrity of the action model and solve the problem of order (cf. Heritage 1984, pp. 13–14). Four major authors nearly made this transition, according to Parsons. Of these four, Durkheim and Weber are most convincing to Parsons's line of reasoning. This is because both Durkheim and Weber were expressly developing new lines of empirical analysis specifically *sociological*. They were doing so at about the same time in history, within different national and cultural settings, and with relatively little awareness of each other's work. Most important, they began their work in roughly opposite intellectual traditions. According to Parsons, Durkheim came from the positivistic side, was correctly motivated by his research to abandon positivism, but then, unable to see the implication, moved over to idealism, a position as objectionable as positivism. Weber, in contrast, began with idealism and was motivated by his research to move toward the positivistic camp. It is the novelty of Parsons's analysis, and perhaps his genius, that he was able to analyze these authors' works according to their abilities to capture social action with the elements Parsons posits as logically necessary—agency, conditions, means, and ends—and to show how these respective works both implied the same thing: Parsons's voluntaristic theory of action. The bulk of *The Structure of Social Action* is devoted to deriving action theory from the classics.

PARSONS'S VOLUNTARISTIC THEORY
OF SOCIAL ACTION

Few approaching Parsonian functionalism for the first time will not at once be struck by its massive complexity. Attempts by commentators to simplify matters for explication do not help much; the impression is of an enormously complicated phenomenon—society—that requires an enormously complicated theory to explain it. Thus we see myriad conceptual tools and variables, specified and clarified with summarizing figures and drawings that locate concepts and processes in relation to each other with an expanding set of ever-familiar arrows (for a summary, see Lackey 1987; for a fascinating discussion of pictures, drawings, and vectors in social theory, see Lynch 1991).

In the main, functionalism's complexity was developed by Parsons and his followers in work subsequent to *The Structure of Social Action* (see Heritage 1984, pp. 16–18), such famous work as *The Social System* (Parsons 1951), *Toward a General Theory of Action* (Parsons et al. 1951), and *Working Papers in the Theory of Action* (Parsons, Bales, and Shils 1953), not to mention the work of Parsons's colleagues writing more or less independently, such as Merton 1968. I will discuss the resultant complexity of functionalism as a separate topic in chapter 9. Here it is necessary to remember only that it originated in the outline of the theory developed by Parsons in *The Structure of Social Action* (see Parsons 1968b, pp. xv–xx). Parsons claims to have derived this outline from the unfinished implications of Durkheim and Weber, and at that level the model is simplicity itself.

Parsons formalizes the problem of order as the problematic relationship between *factual order* and *normative order* (Parsons 1968b, pp. 91–92; see Zimmerman and Wieder 1970, p. 286; cf. Alexander 1984, p. 22). Factual order is the order that presents the intellectual puzzle in the first place, the order identified in "the problem of order." It is the preliminary phenomenon of sociology; it is empirically present for sociologists to inspect, just as the orderly motion of stars and planets is available for astronomers. Factual order is the objectively present phenomenon of regularity in human affairs; it is a behavioral order. It can be seen in the ways that bodies line up at banks and supermarket checkout stands; it is witnessable as the orderly way in which people sit and space themselves in bus stations. On a larger scale, it is present in rates of crime, divorce, and so on. Factual order is also structural in being observable independently of the individual people who happen to be manifesting it at the moment and independently of their subjectivity or ideas about their behavior. Factual order is, in a word, the society. It can be compared with its opposite: social chaos or random behavior (Parsons 1968b, p. 91). Factual order is empirically undeniable; Hobbes could not deny it, even though his intellectual model of behavior could not account for it and indeed predicted chaos. In the simple recognition of factual order, then, lies the *problem* of order: what is it doing there, how could there be such a thing, how can we account for it? Summarized, the question becomes, How is society possible?

Normative order, in contrast with factual order, refers to actors' points of view and the element of active agency that radical positivism denies. Utilitarians sustained agency, but at the expense of factual order, which was nevertheless unaccountably present (Parsons 1968b, pp. 51–125). In Parsons's theory, normative order is a system of norms, values, roles, and statuses which actors actively subscribe to. Normative order is *moral* in that actors voluntarily surrender to it their deepest subjective respect (Parsons 1968b, passim). And normative order is *prescriptive*, such that when actors subscribe to it, they can follow it and do what it tells them to do, the result being their objective behavior. On a large scale, the result is factual social order: society (p. 92).

Normative order, then, contains rules—norms and values—that stabilize behavior (Parsons 1968b, passim). It differs from the "natural environment," or biological conditions of radical positivism, in that it is distinctively social, relative to the society in question, and impressed on actors through the mechanisms of socialization and internalization. It allows for agency in action, even as that agency is regulated by the very order it voluntarily surrenders to. Normative order also has the following features: it is institutionalized in that it is externally enforced upon individuals at various levels of formality, the most extreme being incarceration or punishment. But it also is internal to individuals; that is, actors internalize it to such an extent that it becomes the content of their consciousness. It motivates them to act from within. In that its objective content is now subjectively present, actors have a common subjective base. Normative order, in other words, is the source of shared understanding, or *inter*subjectivity. It also is learned through the process of socialization and thereby is passed along from one generation to the next.

Here the outline of the theory is complete. The visible factual order is caused by another order more difficult to access: the normative order. It is the job of sociologists to ferret out the subjectivity of actors by ferreting out the normative order actors subscribe to, explaining the factual order that can be observed independently of questions about subjectivity (see Zimmerman and Wieder 1970, pp. 286–87).

Parsons's voluntaristic theory explains the facticity of society by means of a normative network while retaining the necessary properties of the unit act that lie at the foundation of Parsons's sociology. As I indicated, the agency of the actor is maintained, and "conditions" have not been a problem in the presociological theories Parsons reviews except where they are required to "determine" action in radical positivism. Means toward ends are also retained in normative order; actors' choices regarding means are governed by *norms*. Finally, actors' choices of ends themselves are governed by *values* (cf. Heritage 1984, p. 14). Parsons's theory requires neither norms nor values to be rational, and indeed values, governing the ultimate ends of action, cannot be rational. Instead norms and values are social "givens" internalized by actors through processes of socialization. In later functionalist writings, Parsons would specify an ontology of *systems*, including cultural systems that provide values and social systems that provide norms, these tied in a general action theory to personality and biological systems at the individual level.

FROM PARSONS TO ETHNOMETHODOLOGY: HERITAGE'S REVIEW OF THE TRANSITION

Heritage (1984, pp. 7–18) reviews Parsons's voluntaristic theory of action with a developing emphasis on what it contained that first caught the eye of one of Parsons's students, Harold Garfinkel. Specifically, Heritage focuses on Parsons's "science of subjectivity," which was supposed to overcome positivistic determinism and save the active, subjective agency of the actor. Ironically, says Heritage (pp. 20–22), it did just the opposite. When normative order becomes the content of subjectivity, this order, rather than actors' subjective agency, becomes the formal cause of behavior. Heritage reviews how Parsons allowed actors' subjectivity to remain an analytic element in action theory *for the theorist*, expressly disconnected from the concrete subjectivity of concrete actors. The facts of the actor's personality are by this account equivalent to the facts of normative order through the mechanisms of socialization and internalization. Thus while actors are no longer buffeted about by environmental and biological conditions, they are still buffeted about by normative order, albeit working "from within" actors. Indeed, as Parsons develops the theory in *The Social System*, actors need have no knowledge whatever about the normative order operating on them from within; as Heritage (p. 30) puts it, "Parsons conceptualized patterns of cultural values as operating to motivate the actors 'behind their backs.' Accordingly, the actors will tend to lack 'insight' into the normative underpinnings of their own action."

This development is ironic in that Parsons was trying to transcend utilitarianism while saving the subjective element negated by radical positivism. It is ironic, too, because Parsons was attempting to move beyond positivist visions of rationality as the only conceivable subjective orientation besides ignorance and error. This he did, but he retained rationality for his own science, says Heritage, with the consequence that while actors may internalize all manner of nonrational norms and values, the fact that those norms and values would produce the behavior they do among actors is itself rationally understandable and predictable from the point of view of the scientist (cf. chapter 9). This is why actors, having internalized this nonrational normative order, will be ignorant of why they do what they do (Heritage 1984, pp. 19–22, 24–27). For functionalism, then, there was a "rapid and straightforward suspension of interest in what the actor concretely believes and acts upon" (p. 21).

Within these analytic spaces Garfinkel began his work and found help from phenomenologists' disciplined interest in subjectivity, says Heritage, reminding us that Parsons corresponded with Schutz for some time (Grathoff 1978) about just such matters (Heritage 1984, p. 21). Garfinkel was trying to further insight initiated by Parsons relative to the phenomenon of institutionalized action, and he wanted to do so in ways that would incorporate such troubling "residue" phenomena in Parsons's theory as these: (1) actors account for their own actions (pp. 22–23), that is, have their own versions of what they are doing and why; (2) actors coordinate activity in line with presumptions of shared understanding (p. 23), that is, subjective content distinct from what actors share as normative order according to functionalists; and (3) actors often invoke theories of norm-governed behavior for strategic purposes having nothing to do with accurate description or conformity to norms—Heritage offers the example of "finding an excuse" not to go to a party (p. 23).

Another trouble spot in Parsons's theory that Garfinkel was quick to spot was its reliance on a "correspondence theory of truth" version of reality that allows biological and environmental reality, not to mention a factual behavioral order, to exist independently of the ways people go about knowing it. This is precisely what would allow functionalist versions of social action to stand as corrective to actors' flawed versions (Heritage 1984, pp. 24–27). Still another trouble spot concerns the "logic" with which institutionalized norms and values, internalized by actors as shared subjectivity, guide action. Since actors orient to norms and values through nonrational subjective modes, the only way norms and values could pre-scribe actors' behavior for functionalists (who would presumably be look-ing on with full knowledge of actors' "institutionalized error") would be for them to designate standardized meaning in advance of actors' conformity with them. Parsons had no interest in explicating this matter (pp. 27–30).

These issues are where Garfinkel stepped into Parsonian sociology. His studies were detailed and empirical, and eventually these issues proved to be more than Parsonian sociology could contain. As Heritage (1984, p. 33) puts it, "In reacting to the theories of his famous teacher, Garfinkel formed fundamental disagreements with almost every major aspect of Parsonian sociology."

THE THESIS RESTATED AND THE PLAN OF THE BOOK

That ethnomethodology derives from anomalies within functionalist theo-ry is not in question. Also not in question are functionalism's roots in Parsons's derivation from the classics. What remains unexplored is the consequences both of these connections have for the relationship between ethnomethodology and the classics. That is my concern in this book.

In general, Parsons claims that the system of norms and values—his normative order—is what Durkheim implied by *collective conscience* and that Weber nearly reached the same conclusion coming from the other theoretical direction. This derivation is predicated on the correctness of Parsons's bedrock assumptions concerning the nature of social action; thus his interpretations of the two authors are informed by his own analytic directions rather than the other way around (cf. Pope 1973; Pope, Cohen, and Hazelrigg 1975; Cohen, Hazelrigg, and Pope 1975). More important, in order to read Durkheim and Weber the way he did, Parsons had to argue with these writers, overriding key points otherwise incompatible with his own theory. The resultant theory of action contained the analytic weak points within which Garfinkel launched his empirical studies. My primary thesis is that these studies, through no deliberate effort of Garfinkel or of ethnomethodologists generally, resurrected the very key classical themes that Parsons overrode.

In chapters 2–5 I demonstrate my primary thesis in detail relative to the works of Emile Durkheim. Chapter 2 begins with Durkheim's rendering of morality and Parsons's rerendering of it as rules. Chapter 3 extends the discussion of morality to Durkheim's idea that society and morality are equivalent. In chapter 4 I take up the further Durkheimian equivalence between society and reality. Parsons worked diligently to suppress both of these equivalences; Garfinkel's empirical studies recovered both of them even without an express interest in reconnecting with Durkheim. Moreover, if anomie is a breakdown in society, then it is a breakdown in all that Durkheim says society is equivalent to: morality, reality, experience, and ideas—a subject I take up in chapter 5.

Chapters 6–8 pick up Max Weber in relation to my primary thesis. Chapter 6 begins with Weber's assertions that sociologists cannot invoke the existence of social organization without reification, a position that Parsons ignored but that ethnomethodologists recovered in their critique of Parsonian "factual order." Chapter 7 discusses how ideas are compelling to actors who subscribe to them. Parsons's solution to this question required massive tampering in an ecology of Weberian principles, particularly ideal types. Ethnomethodology finds ideas compelling in concrete, empirical social practices, recovering what Weber called the universal "psychological roots" of ideas. Chapter 8 examines Weberian bureaucracy in light of these principles, particularly Weber's antireification stance relative to social organization. Ethnomethodological studies are instructive in this area and reveal how rationalization, which Parsons saw as a weakness in Weber's work, is empirical for sociology.

Chapter 9 includes a comprehensive and integrated summary of classically informed ethnomethodological theory. The "negative image" of classical sociology that passed through Parsons's voluntarism extends to his theory of convergence. In other words, Durkheim and Weber do converge, but not in the manner Parsons imagines. Chapter 9 also develops an ironic observation that plays a relatively minor role in earlier chapters: while Parsons argues against the possibility of "pure rationality," his own theory is an example of it. Indeed, Parsonian sociology is a distinctively *bureaucratic* model of society. In that light I will make explicit the auxiliary thesis mentioned above and show how American functionalism is a twentieth-century maturation of trends and tendencies in Western civilization analyzed in their nineteenth-century homunculus form by Durkheim and Weber. Put differently, functionalism is a feature of modern society rather than a viable theory about it and accordingly was predicted in its essentials by classical sociologists.

Finally, chapter 10 situates theory developed in this book within a wider field of contemporary sociological theory which addresses such issues as relationships between micro and macro social phenomena. I will argue that ethnomethodology is neither a micro nor a macro form of sociology but remains significantly indifferent to questions of structure—indeed, its very existence, let alone its "size." Here I will address issues raised by the most recent expression of ethnomethodology: conversation analysis. I will also speculate, somewhat freely, on what might come of these developments, including continuities between ethnomethodology and Karl Marx. Marx plays no role in the main body of my arguments precisely because he played no significant role in Parsons's thought.

Since this book concerns theory development, I have not attempted to cover all of the ethnomethodological studies or even all of the most important ones. I discuss studies that illustrate the theoretical points I wish to make; I could well have chosen other studies. Moreover, since I am establishing links between classical theory and ethnomethodology at its origins in Parsonian issues, I deal mainly with what might be termed "early" ethnomethodology. This is not always so, but I tend to focus on Garfinkel's (1967) *Studies in Ethnomethodology* and the kind of work that came out of that period. I do not, for example, discuss conversation analysis except in the final chapter.

Finally, a word about vocabulary is in order. I retain Parsons's terms "normative order" and "factual order" (1968b, p. 91) throughout my arguments, even though Parsons did not himself systematically retain these specific terms. There is no distortion in this, only a convenient shorthand for designating key Parsonian ideas (cf. Zimmerman and Wieder 1970, p. 286) with the terms Parsons himself uses to introduce these ideas. Another taxonomic matter is my use of the term "functionalism," here interchangeable with "American functionalism" or "Parsonian functionalism." The outline of this theory is Parsons's voluntaristic action theory, which I have reviewed in this chapter. Despite some authors' impressions that a transition from voluntarism to structural-functionalism was "muddled" (Alexander 1978; Menzies 1977), Parsons saw functionalist development as a refinement of, not a departure from, voluntaristic theory in that aggregate concrete action was understood to be caused by normative systems that stabilize behavior into corresponding systems of action (see Parsons 1968b, pp. xv–xx). Thus according to Parsons, functionalist reasoning is predicated on the logic of voluntarist action theory. I will not therefore pursue any terminological distinctions between different "phases" of functionalism as it logically progressed.

But I do want to distinguish American functionalism from what some might call "Durkheim's functionalism." In fact, I see the popular idea that Durkheim was a functionalist as itself a product of American functionalism's claim on the classics. If Durkheim was a functionalist, he was a functionalist of a different kind. When addressing Durkheim's sociology as representing a more generic type, I prefer the nineteenth-century term "organicism."

2

THE STATUS OF RULES

IN MORAL LIFE

In opposition to the functionalism from which it sprang, ethnomethodology attacked the norm-governed model of society on at least two fronts. First, the model could not work, even in the abstract; the very feasibility of such a society is in doubt. Second, detailed empirical studies into organized social life did not always yield rules. Either of these is significantly devastating for functionalism.

Either would be devastating for Durkheim too if in fact his "collective conscience" consisted of norms and values, as Parsons supposed in deriving his own theory from Durkheim's sociology. Here I consider this derivation as well as the analytic and empirical status of the derived theory in light of ethnomethodology. I will argue that a formal rule-governed society is not implied in Durkheim's work and that his commitment to empirical science militates against that understanding. Moreover, ethnomethodological arguments and findings do not damage Durkheim's theory but set the stage for rediscovering Durkheimian moral order.

DURKHEIM'S ORGANICISM AND
SUI GENERIS MORAL ORDER

Though we may weary of analogies between society and bio-organisms, it helps to be reminded that the purpose of this nineteenth-century imagery was not so much to characterize society as an animal as it was to identify society at its own unique level, to recommend a topic of study. The analogy was to point out that biologists do not examine their phenomena as mere collections of atoms and molecules but as entities with their own defining workings and features. Likewise society could be examined at its own level of integrity without resorting to the biology or psychology of its members.

Following this line, Durkheim promoted and encouraged such an examination, and by example: throughout and at every turn he argued and demonstrated that there is a sui generis order of social phenomena that transcends individual psychology or behavior (Durkheim 1938; Pope, Cohen, and Hazelrigg 1975). To illustrate the intuitive reality of this transpersonal order, Durkheim reminded us that society precedes the life of each of its members and survives each member's death. During the course of a biography, a member confronts and experiences the society as an external reality that regulates both behavior and subjective experience. Its status as an "out there" reality is beyond question and is experienced directly by anyone who tries to flout it (Durkheim 1938, pp. 2–3). Indeed it controls and assimilates to individual consciousness to such an extent that flouting it is for the most part unthinkable; consequently it may, from a common-sense vantage point of those living within it, go unnoticed (pp. 2–6; 1953, p. 55).

It was these transpersonal sui generis phenomena that Durkheim was describing with his famous concepts "exteriority" and "constraint." Their status outside of and independent of individuals rendered them unamenable to investigation as collections of psychologistic traits (Durkheim 1938, pp. 14–46; Lukes 1972, p. 9). But it was precisely their character as external to any individual that rendered them factually present for empirical sociology apart from anyone's common-sense awareness of them or ideas about them (Coser 1971, pp. 129–30; Parsons 1968a). Hence Durkheim recommended that we view society as social facts, and these in turn as *things* (Durkheim 1938, p. 14). In that way, exteriority and constraint were concepts crucial not only as theoretical claims about society but also as cornerstones of methodological policy (Coser 1971; Giddens 1971). If social facts are "there" and experienceable for societal members, they are likewise "there" and examinable for scientists (Parsons 1968a, pp. 314–15). Durkheim's main accomplishment, therefore, was to establish the existence of this independent sphere, to supplement what might otherwise be mere organicist rhetoric with empirical discovery. Thus did he carry Comte's newly coined discipline, "sociology," to fruition.

Beyond the existence of social facts, Durkheim's main claim about them was that they are *moral*. Indeed Durkheim began his work as a science of moral life (see Giddens 1971, pp. 66–79) and took such pains to illuminate the moral dimension of social control that society and moral control became largely synonymous (Durkheim 1933, p. 228). This flew in the face of conventional wisdom, as represented by Tönnies (1963), which argued that morality was receding in modern society, no longer the glue that binds people together, giving way to advancing individualism and requiring the surrogate glue of rational, legalistic contracts (see Lukes 1972, pp. 140–47). The community-based morality that Tönnies nostalgically recollects is, for Durkheim, but one kind of morality, a morality of "sameness" and social uniformity that Durkheim calls *mechanical solidarity* (Durkheim 1933, pp. 111–99). In large part because of an advancing division of labor which shattered uniformity, mechanical solidarity was giving way to increased human diversification and rational contract specification, as Tönnies observed. But for Durkheim, this is not a retreat from morality but a shift in moral content from mechanical solidarity to *organic solidarity*, a morality of differentiation throughout society. In other words, modern society, far from being removed from the jurisdiction of collective morality, was experiencing a new collective morality which included principles such as moral individualism and other principles that sustain rational contracts, principles that are not asserted in contracts themselves but that cause people to abide by what these contracts do assert (Durkheim 1933, pp. 200–229, 396–402; Giddens 1971, pp. 69–72; Lukes 1972, pp. 147–57). As the division of labor advanced, so also did the gradual replacement of mechanical solidarity with organic solidarity (Durkheim 1933). Individualism, then, was a morality collectively arrived at, collectively shared, and collectively enforced (pp. 172–228).

That modern society displays the famous twin features of exteriority and constraint no less so than elementary societies is no happenstance of history. Moral constraint is indeed the essence of collective life for Durkheim. When individuals confront moral reality, they are confronting society; society and morality are one and the same (Durkheim 1933, p. 228). Thus a society lacking these twin features is inconceivable, as is a legal contract without a moral commitment to contract-following (pp. 200–206).

Morality is not simply an extrasocietal phenomenon attached to society that makes it run smoothly, without which it would run less than smoothly. Absence of morality *is* absence of society; any tendency toward that state is a tendency toward anomie.

NORMS AND VALUES: THE STATUS OF THE DERIVATION

One of the early moves Parsons makes in his derivation of functionalist theory is to reject as "error" (1968b, p. 392) Durkheim's equivalence between society and morality. In Parsons's theory, society becomes an observable factual order *caused* by morality, the latter being an analytically distinct kind of order—normative order—consisting of norms and values that people respect. Parsons acknowledges that Durkheim "scarcely takes notice" of a normative order distinguishable from factual order (p. 377n) but argues nevertheless that Durkheim's hypothetical society of "perfect integration" implies another perfectly integrated system (p. 377), which Parsons most often refers to as "a body of rules," sometimes a "system" (p. 314), "a body of normative rules" (p. 320), or "a vast body of customary rules" (p. 312).[1] This prescriptive moral order was a frequent target of early ethnomethodological commentary. The dispute was essentially with Parsonian functionalism; however, it appeared to be a dispute with sociology generally, in part because of the impression that Parsons's theory was derived from the classics. Yet Durkheim, at least in his early work, had relatively little to say about the concrete character of moral regulation,[2] spending most of his energy on establishing its ontological and omnipresent status. For example, the mere fact that something external to psychological processes could affect the types and distribution of acts as private as suicide was an innovative and counterintuitive finding for Durkheim's audience (cf. Lukes 1972, p. 194)—this whatever the concrete character of that "something" turns out to be.

To view Durkheimian moral regulation mainly as norms is nevertheless quite understandable. For one thing, within contemporary common-sense terms moral regulation often *means* following rules. And for another, Durkheim made many references to moral rules that suggest that this may indeed have been what he had in mind (e.g. Durkheim 1938, pp. 2–3). Note, for example, that where Durkheim speaks of the moral foundations of organic solidarity as something underlying the legalistic rules of rational contract, he sometimes summarizes these moral principles as "other rules." The question is whether these characterizations invite a formal analysis of moral regulation in terms of rules or whether they just provide a vocabulary for discussing it.

Durkheim definitely did not formalize and develop the concept of "rule," nor was that a particularly common characterization of moral control in his work. Indeed Durkheim employed a wide vocabulary with reference to moral regulation. He used "rules" occasionally, but not systematically or most of the time. Durkheim's other concepts and characterizations are neither synonymous nor even quite compatible with "rules." We see in his work a large family of terms that together denote social facts but that do not reduce, even by implication, to norms or rules. Other terms that weave in and out of Durkheim's work include "a collective force of a definite amount of energy" (1951, p. 299), "moral conscience" (1933, p. 42), "social currents" (1938, p. 4), "a unified system of beliefs and practices" (1947, p. 47), "ways of thinking and feeling" (1933, p. 172), "very strong collective sentiments" (1938, p. 67), a "state of conscience [which] is a source of life" (1938, p. 96), and "the very society itself" (1933, p. xlviii). The most famous and comprehensive term he used is *collective conscience*.[3]

These are highly charged imageries for someone who was supposed to have meant, after all, mere rules. They do not translate easily into rules, much less a formal Parsonian normative system. Furthermore, while Durkheim does not address this specifically, there are reasons in his work for suspecting that something beyond rules, or other than rules, is required for morality to regulate. A tantalizing clue is provided in the way Durkheim does analyze rules whenever they are empirically available for analysis. He notes, for example, that legal codes and contracts cannot enforce themselves without an underlying moral commitment to abiding by them that is itself not spelled out (Durkheim 1933, pp. 200–229). But of what does this commitment consist, and how does it work? One might argue, as does Parsons (1968b, pp. 308–24), that this underlying commitment consists of yet further rules that do not need to be spelled out because they are already known and respected by everyone.[4] This makes the underlying commitment of organic solidarity formally equivalent to morality in general in mechanical solidarity, where little if anything is ever spelled out, but which nevertheless, in analogous fashion, would have to be analyzable in terms of known and respected rules.

So in the case of organic solidarity: *could* this underlying commitment be written into the contract? What would then cause anybody to abide by *its* terms? Or in the case of mechanical solidarity: *could* mechanical morality be specified in contractual style? And how would its members then abide by it? In either case, can an entire morality be expressed, can either a mechanical or organic collective conscience be expressed, as rules that could of their analytic nature prescribe behavior? A negative answer would suggest that rules are no more sufficient for moral regulation than legal contracts; one might suspect that rule-governed regulation presupposes a Durkheimian "moral something" (cf. Collins 1985; Giddens 1971, pp. 88–89; Takla and Pope 1985; see Durkheim 1933, p. 227).

It would appear that Durkheim's argument against the adequacy of formal rules applies no less to any set of rules, no matter how deeply they are presumed to underlie the formal rules or how respected they are. There is no theoretical reason for thinking that a sociologist could bring to light a set of underlying rules that would tell people how to behave without in turn requiring still deeper underlying rules to prescribe their application. The solution Durkheim offers, though in his early work he is largely silent on its concrete character, is morality as such, something that for him is *equivalent to society* as a sui generis phenomenon. Morality and social facts are identical things for Durkheim, phenomena subject to scientific investigation in their own right and at their own existential level.

THE ANALYTIC CASE AGAINST RULES

Parsons did not provide a justification or an analytic defense of his model, saying simply that it was implied by both Durkheim and Weber and therefore probably correct. This permitted Parsons to avoid probing either the theoretical underpinnings or the presuppositions of the model and instead to develop and elaborate upon the model in subsequent work. One of the first tasks of early ethnomethodology was to characterize these underpinnings.

A striking example is Wilson's (1970) characterization of the functionalist model as a "normative paradigm." The unstated unifying theme of the paradigm is a literal correspondence between situations and behaviors linked by stabilizing rules which designate specific action as appropriate for each specific situation. This requires an unambiguous prescriptive meaning for the rule in each case of its being applied, understood, or followed. The paradigm takes this for granted as necessary, for in no other way could a factual order be a necessary outcome of adhering to normative order. If norms are supposed to stabilize behavior, then the norms themselves have to be stable.

By current standards, the above reading of functionalism seems over-stated and rigid (see e.g. Warner 1978, p. 1334). Yet this rigidity is abso-lutely mandated by the perspective, even where its advocates disavow such rigidity. Once we assume that the source of behavioral stability lies in stabilizing rules, we are inevitably committing ourselves to the possibility of literal and unequivocal prescription. Attempts to back away from that commitment by including "interpretation" as a feature of rule use not only fail to solve the Parsonian problem of order but reproduce the problem: interpretation according to what? Some kind of standards are necessary for deciding the adequacy of rule interpretation; without standards, interpre-tation of a rule can lead to anything, and the problem of order remains unsolved. Yet standards are nothing more than further rules, and they in turn have to be literal in order to stabilize rule interpretation and ulti-mately behavior. If standards themselves are imprecise and have to be interpreted, there need to be yet further rules for deciding the adequacy of that, and so on. Eventually the premise that rules produce stability requires the analytic possibility of some general set of rules whose uses are not matters of mere interpretation; otherwise there would be no factual social order. This is so even with respect to ambiguous rules whose innovative uses supposedly fall within general parameters; the parameters themselves would need literal boundaries in order to prevent random decisions as to where the boundaries are, decisions that would produce correspondingly random behavior.

We find the necessary prerequisite of literal prescription embedded even in certain forms of symbolic interactionism, where the attempt to transcend functionalist rigidity is most deliberate. Consider, for example, Ralph Turner's (1962) role theory. In "role making" we find a stated rejec-tion of static models of role conformity in favor of a dynamic one wherein actors actively interpret their roles as they move through social interaction. Yet Turner retains the analytic *feasibility* of literal conformity in at least two ways. First, he discovers role innovation by comparing actual role behavior with what would take place if rules were literally followed. In that vein he says that bureaucratic organizations reduce innovation by "substituting role prescriptions," a strategy he says is "only partially successful" (p. 27). Here we see that the implicit possibility of literal conformity is part of Turner's theory, even if only used as the analyst's reference point. Put differently, "only partially successful" presumes a criterion of success: lit-eral conformity is a possibility, albeit seldom if ever witnessed. A second and more important way Turner retains the feasibility of literal prescription is by way of his criterion of "the folk judgment of consistency," which "requires that some more general principle than those arising from the unique contingencies of the interaction be invoked" (p. 25). This is the general norm that binds various interpretations of other norms together. Without it, interpretation of norms would be as random and fancy-free as the expected world of the utilitarians. Interpreting rules according to this norm would stabilize behavior, but the consistency norm would itself have to be stable and not subject to interpretation without requiring yet further norms to stabilize that process. Thus even interactionist role theory depends upon the analytic possibility of literal prescription and literal conformity to explain the factual behavioral order spread out before us (see Hilbert 1981).

Another criticism of functionalism which sustains its very premises is Wrong's (1961) claim that the model produces a vision of "oversocialized" societal members. Wrong does not argue that the model could not work in the abstract but only that life does not proceed as the model suggests. In fact, Wrong's criticism depends on the feasibility of the model, since actors working within a "free-will space" are nevertheless constrained by structural rules if and when they bump against them. Thus even for Wrong, rules retain their analytic capability of constraining behavior and are theoretically required to prevent chaos. What distinguishes Wrong's theory from straight functionalism is that for Wrong the rules simply do not, as a factual matter, control behavior at every turn. People are free to innovate and tailor their individual behaviors within the uncontrolled spaces between, among, and within rules (cf. DiTomaso 1982). Yet notice that without the analytic possibility of literal constraint, people could behave randomly and interpret whatever they do as within the uncontrolled free-will spaces of rule specification and therefore within the parameters of rule conformity. Parsons's problem remains unsolved.

The idea that rules stabilize behavior or that behavioral stability requires rules is a common-sense assumption of our time and therefore a particularly difficult one to question or abandon. This is perhaps why it underlies so many different kinds of otherwise disparate sociologies. Ethnomethodology nevertheless questions the very foundation of the prescriptive model, the possibility that it could work even in a fantasized social universe, and it does so in a way similar to Durkheim's critique of his contemporaries' understanding of modern social regulation strictly in terms of rational rules: rules alone could not regulate without morality. Durkheim agreed with contemporaries such as Tönnies that morality was not the same thing as modern rules but disagreed that it was being driven out and replaced by such rules through modernization. Morality was, probably, "something else."

It is difficult to assess how far Durkheim would have been willing to go in diagnosing the inadequacies of rules. However, we can extend his insights from the insufficiency of rational contracts to that of rules in general by briefly considering some insights of linguistic philosopher Ludwig Wittgenstein, one of several wellsprings of theoretical inspiration for ethnomethodologists (e.g. Coulter 1979, 1989). Though not a sociologist, Wittgenstein exhaustively examined the model of rule-governed activity as perhaps no other, and he extended these insights to a wide range of rules, from the daily and routine to the paragons of formality and precision, including deductive logic and mathematics (1953, 1956, 1958). His work provides a most succinct access to ethnomethodological ways of thinking. I also cite him here because his polemic against the adequacy of rules parallels Durkheim's argument against the possibility that rational contracts by themselves could be moral (cf. Bloor 1983, pp. 57, 93).

Throughout Wittgenstein's discussions, he maintains that even highly formal cases of rule-governed procedure do not by their very nature require rules for their correct performance. Yet neither are they, by their very nature, self-evident. Whether they are dependent on rules or self-evident is part and parcel of the requirements of the people engaged in them. People, for example, often explain procedure to others unfamiliar with it or clarify a misunderstanding by referencing "underlying rules." These are practical requirements in applied settings, rather like defining words or providing instructions. But Wittgenstein notes this about rules as they come up in such settings (here I paraphrase): their *own* meanings are neither self-evident nor in need of clarification; whether they are one or the other is again part and parcel of somebody's practical requirements. Moreover, there is no point in the clarification process where this would be otherwise, no point where some clarified intent would display either a self-evident status or require further clarification independent of someone's practical requirements. In terms of sociological prediction, there is no place beyond which people cannot require further clarification, nor is there any analytic reason for suspecting that at any given point they will call for any clarification whatsoever (cf. Garfinkel 1967).

Another Wittgensteinian point concerns the relationship between rules and the activity they prescribe. The observation is that rules and procedure are not synonymous, equivalent, or deductively related in precise ways. Rules are used to clear up trouble; when the trouble is cleared up—which means that the procedure can be performed—then the rules fall away as superfluous. In that regard, rules are more like rough paraphrases of the activity they prescribe. This can be seen in teaching someone proper use of a word like "perhaps." While we might provide definitional prescriptions, successful use of the word does not consist in following these prescriptions, nor do fluent users of language attend to any such policies. Fluent users engage the word "point blank," as it were, finding and creating any required stability as they go (cf. Heritage 1984, pp. 120–22).

Wittgenstein also demonstrated the impossibility of ever reducing procedure to a set of unequivocal basics that could be literally prescribed. One example Wittgenstein uses is color recognition, long treated as a paragon of simplicity by philosophers. The traditional argument is that reality might eventually be reduced to these "simples" (Locke 1959). Yet even color recognition will not yield the sought-after precision. Wittgenstein asks rhetorically, "Could you tell me what is in common between a light red and a dark red?" (1958, p. 130). To anyone suggesting a mental image of a color, he asks:

> Which shade is the "sample in my mind" of the color green—the sample of what is common to all shades of green? . . . What *shape* must the sample of the color green be? Should it be rectangular? Or would it then be the sample of a green rectangle? So should it be "irregular" in shape? And what is to prevent us then from regarding it—that is from using it—only as a sample of irregularity of shape? (1953, p. 35)

This excerpt clearly shows the essential impossibility of literal prescription. No matter how clearly we spell out the norms of Parsons's normative order, they could not do the analytic work Parsons requires of them. Rules cannot be intrinsically clear (or for that matter intrinsically ambiguous), independent of actors' practical requirements. Moreover, whether rules even "stand behind" behavior in the first place depends on whether or not actors require such explanations (cf. Mills 1940). But left to their own analytic integrity, rules can no more stabilize behavior than behavior can be already in itself inherently stable.

To summarize, proper procedure, or the facticity of stable human behavior, does not require rules, although people sometimes make such requirements. It should be no surprise, however, that actors never require the analytically impossible literal prescription before they proceed—they never require the theoretically satisfying closure on the rule-governed model —as their interests are generally practical and not theoretical. Moreover, they could not act if they were to wait for that kind of theoretical clarity. Therefore, whether actors require rules or not, how they require them, what such requirements consist of in terms of clarity sought—all of this remains, for sociology, an empirical question. But this much is certain: norms cannot be required as ongoing prescriptive entities as Parsonian functionalism supposes. As we shall see, actors probably require rules a bare minimum of the time.

These considerations are intriguingly similar to Durkheim's commentary about the insufficiency of contractual relations. Durkheim knew that rational rules of modern life would be insufficient for social solidarity, no matter how carefully and exhaustively they were spelled out (Durkheim 1933, pp. 200–209). Organic solidarity indicated something beyond mere rules, a "moral something" that underlay rules and provided for their stabilizing influence. Parsons saw this morality as more rules,[5] but it would seem that Durkheim's observations about rational rules can be extended to rules in general. Durkheim did not make this extension, perhaps because "rules" was a peculiarly modern idea that contrasted with late nineteenth-century notions of morality. Tönnies, for example, did not view morality as formal rules and in fact saw the proliferation of rules as evidence that morality was declining. Thus as Durkheim sought to designate the omnipresence of morality, he had to establish the Gemeinschaft (unruled) dimensions of modern rational (rule-governed) life. That Durkheim analyzed mechanical solidarity itself in terms of ritual practices (Durkheim 1947), and thereby did not have to raise questions about the sufficiency of rules in elementary moral life, is instructive in itself. This is to say that at that point no one had yet hypothesized that morality in general consisted of rules. In any case, Durkheim's critique of morality-less contract would be moot if it were possible to specify underlying morality itself in terms of rules—if morality were rules, then it could simply be written into the contract, thereby rendering contracts themselves sufficient.

THE EMPIRICAL CASE AGAINST RULES

The normative order Parsons postulates as distinct from observed factual order is not something that has been observed and described by empirical science. It is, rather, a working explanatory hypothesis. Parsons's subsequent theoretical development depends on the adequacy of this formulation, but he never establishes that adequacy empirically. Indeed most of Parsons's later work is argument on behalf of what is theoretically required for this normative regulation to work. He argues from a position of logical necessity, describing what normative order surely must include for it to work, given that such a thing exists in the first place (see Garfinkel 1988; cf. Bershady 1973). But that existential assumption does not itself have empirical reference.[6] To be sure, the arguments are convincing, just as the premise seems intuitively correct to Western ears—to say that behavior conforms to rules accords with common-sense ways of talking about and explaining behavior. Still it remains notable that no one has yet "seen" a normative order or found empirical evidence that norms govern human action at every turn, or even at most turns. People do talk that way on occasion, especially where ongoing behavior is disrupted, and they can be induced to talk as "informants" about rules in response to questionnaires and in interviews, but they can also be induced to talk about demons; to date a normative order has yet to be scientifically observed.[7]

Yet the premise of Durkheim's early sociology was that morality is empirical, that moral regulation is part of the natural world and thereby factual for sociology (see Alexander 1982b, p. 90). He backed away from this occasionally, such as in his suggestion that moral solidarity was not directly measurable. But the indices of solidarity were themselves empirical, which is why Durkheim studied legal codes as a "visible symbol" of moral solidarity (Durkheim 1933, p. 64). He did not suggest that sociologists should simply be able to figure out, on the basis of analytic incisiveness alone, the character and workings of moral regulation. Sociologists supposedly could *see* morality, could witness it for science. Note the empirical status of rules, for example, when Durkheim studied them: legal codes are observably there, on paper; they can be analyzed as things, as social facts. In that regard they differ markedly from the abstract normative order of American functionalism (see Lackey 1987). Again, the norms of

American functionalism are a working theoretical premise rather than the empirical indices of solidarity that Durkheim recommends.

By contrast, ethnomethodology was uncompromisingly empirical at the outset. As Garfinkel (1988, p. 106) has expressed it, ethnomethodology returns sociology to "the concreteness of things," steering away from what he calls "formal, constructive analysis." This does not make ethnomethodology atheorctical or remove analysts as interpreters of data, but it does seek to eliminate the practice of allowing formally theorized and unseen social phenomena, documented with formally administered research methodologies, to replace the empirical "concreteness of things" as the "real and actual society" (p. 106).

Concrete ethnomethodological studies show us that morality cannot possibly be the same thing as rules. Put differently, when we look for rules in the context of stable and morally regulated behavior, we do not always find them. An intriguing example comes from Bittner's (1967) investigation into the peacekeeping practices of police on skid row. Here is professional activity that practitioners attend to and regulate in great detail, yet there appear to be few if any governing rules.

Peacekeeping involves police activities that do not derive from law enforcement per se; its general character and specific instances are not implied in legal prescriptive guides. They include such matters as regulating traffic, monitoring activities within local establishments (e.g. bars, hotels, shops), using sanctions alternative to arrest in cases of minor offenses or invoking the power to arrest even when no violation has occurred, intervening in nonlegal affairs (e.g. aiding people in trouble, arbitrating quarrels), controlling crowd behavior (with force if necessary), and exercising special duties toward people considered marginally competent (for example underaged or mentally ill people) (Bittner 1967, pp. 702–4). Bittner studied this activity among the police on skid row, where it looms large in routine police work.

Bittner's choice of setting provides a look at a theoretically provocative phenomenon, the non-rule-governed activity of police. Skid row is viewed as a setting apart from the rest of society, a setting which exhibits few of the regularities known to most societal members. Consequently peacekeeping is a nebulous occupation in which "patrolmen make decisions based on reasons that the law probably does not recognize as valid" (Bittner 1967, p. 709) and in which, even where the use of the law can be seen as valid, "the law is the outward appearance of an intervention that is actually based on altogether different considerations" (p. 710). The considerations which take precedence over all others include "a richly particularized knowledge of people and places in the area" (p. 707) and momentary expediency, with little regard for long-range effects (pp. 706–7).

In order to illustrate the intricate and tenuous character of police work, it helps to quote one of Bittner's examples in its entirety.

A man in a relatively mild state of intoxication (by skid-row standards) approached a patrolman to tell him that he had a room in a hotel, to which the officer responded by urging him to go to bed instead of getting drunk. As the man walked off, the officer related the following thoughts: Here is a completely lost soul. Though he probably is no more than thirty-five years old, he looks to be in his fifties. He never works and he hardly ever has a place to stay. He has been on the street for several years and is known as "Dakota." During the past few days, "Dakota" has been seen in the company of "Big Jim." The latter is an invalid living on some sort of pension with which he pays for a room in the hotel to which "Dakota" referred and for four weekly meal tickets in one of the restaurants on the street. Whatever is left he spends on wine and beer. Occasionally, "Big Jim" goes on drinking sprees in the company of someone like "Dakota." Leaving aside the consideration that there is probably a homosexual background to the association, and that it is not right that "Big Jim" should have to support the drinking habit of someone else, there is the more important risk that if "Dakota" moves in with "Big Jim" he will very likely walk off with whatever the latter keeps in his room. "Big Jim" would never dream of reporting the theft; he would just beat the hell out of "Dakota" after he sobered up. When asked what could be done to prevent the theft and the subsequent recriminations, the patrolman proposed that in this particular case he would throw "Big Jim" into jail if he found him tonight and then tell the hotel clerk to throw "Dakota" out of the room. When asked why he did not arrest "Dakota," who was, after all, drunk enough to warrant an arrest, the officer explained that this would not solve anything. While "Dakota" was in jail "Big Jim" would continue drinking and would either strike up another liaison or embrace his old buddy after he had been released. The only thing to do was to get "Big Jim" to sober up, and the only sure way of doing this was to arrest him. (Bittner 1967, pp. 709–10)

This example illustrates a pervading practical problem for the peace-keeper on skid row: the rationale for action, here arresting "Big Jim" in order to sober him up, cannot be abstracted from the concrete circumstance in which the action is carried out. There are no general formulas for policemen to follow in deciding whether to sober someone up or whether to arrest someone. Indeed whatever professional criteria are available, such as legal definitions of public drunkenness, are sometimes skillfully disregarded by the successful peacekeeper. In the example, "Dakota" was drunk enough to be arrested, yet this officer ignored that fact in favor of a better solution to potential trouble: arrest "Big Jim," even though he was not immediately available for scrutiny by this officer and even though the precise terms and circumstances of the prospective arrest were necessarily unknown by anyone. Moreover, the rationale for this prospective solution is so tied to this particular officer's knowledge concerning the habits of these two men—and men like them—and to the particular details of their immediately recent activities passed along through informal channels that it defies standardization for future use. The rationale is neither a previously known prescription for peacekeeping nor a prescription for future peacekeeping. Instead it is irremediably tied to the specific action proposed and is in that sense part of the action itself. It defies a literal "fit" either with past action or with future action.

In other words, policemen must attend to here-and-now considerations that take priority over any formulas for behavior arising from outside context-specific circumstances. So dependent are policemen on their abilities to synthesize fresh solutions to unanticipated problems that they are unable to derive lists of rules, regulations, and recipes concerning what competent policemen do. Instead, as Bittner puts it, they make decisions "without the intervention of explicitly reasoned chains of inferences," admitting that they "do not seek to defend the adequacy of their method against some abstract criteria of merit" (Bittner 1967, p. 712). In short, they "play it by ear."

"Playing by ear," however, does not mean that policemen can act arbitrarily or that their competence does not depend upon practice and practical knowledge or that just anyone could do it. Despite their inability to describe their activities in terms of behavioral recipes, policemen maintain a distinction between competent and incompetent police behavior; indeed they "generally maintain that their own procedures not only measure up to the working of [the formal complex of social welfare/legal/medical institutions] but exceed them in the attitude of carefulness" (Bittner 1967, p. 712). To use Garfinkel's expression, the police engage in "ad hoc" practices (Garfinkel 1967, pp. 21–23), but they must do so with exquisite skill. Novices failing to realize the skillful nature of the enterprise often experience frustration; that is, the attempt to perform the role without preparation and practice is "ready-made for failure and malpractice" (Bittner 1967, p. 715). Notably, policemen skillful in peacekeeping are also skillful in diagnosing the relative degrees of skill in others.

We see in Bittner's study what must be an anathema for Parsonian functionalism: social order without rules. Yet this ordered life proceeds, and it does so in a manner that remains, ultimately, beyond the control of individual policemen. It is not the case that individuals can do just anything, yet whatever they must do cannot be prescribed in advance. The constraint exercised on individuals does not derive, then, from behavioral recipes but from the availability of such concepts as "professional competence" and "incompetence" and, more important, the uses to which these concepts are put by concrete others in concrete circumstances. Bittner's analysis thus retains the Durkheimian principles of exteriority and constraint locating social constraint exterior to all individuals, yet finds such constraint in the practical real-life actions of people—that is, the empirical constraint people exercise on each other.

Still, a committed functionalist might argue, there surely *must* be rules, whether or not actors talk about them or know about them. Notice that such a claim reveals a requirement for rules that belongs to the theorist. Police do not require rules; their mere behavior does not require rules for its facticity, so if rules are required, this is because *functionalists themselves require rules*. Notice too that this is a requirement born of a commitment to Parsonian theorizing as opposed to anything empirical about police work, a classic case of a theoretical perspective leading the investigation and dictating to the investigator what surely must be, somehow, observable (cf. Garfinkel 1988).

The tacit reasonableness of the functionalist approach is reflected in artificial-intelligence research, where computer scientists are attempting to find programs that enable a computer to simulate intelligent cultural competence. In fact their needs are considerably less than those of functionalists; all computer scientists require is a program that produces results whether or not this is a program that people themselves actually follow. Yet their codification efforts fail, these failures are unyielding, and there are many reasons for suspecting they are inevitable (see Dreyfus 1979; Suchman 1987; cf. Wolfe 1991). Imagine how much more difficult these efforts would be with the added requirement that the program be equivalent to the body of prescriptive norms and values that societal members themselves orient to, respect, and follow.

Yet the tacit reasonableness of the functionalist line is supported by the mere fact that, despite the anomalous case of the skid-row police, members of our society generally tend to *think* of their behavior as in conformity with rules. Indeed, social sciences as taught in elementary-school contexts are often summoned to impress children with the need to respect rules and follow them as a guard against chaos. But it has not been the historic role of scientific inquiry to reinforce, elaborate, verify, or otherwise reproduce the common sense of an era, even where no alternative form of theorizing is immediately available. The empirical persistence of the Galileos of history has repeatedly placed them at odds with the conventional wisdom.

Some of Garfinkel's studies indicate occasions where there are no rules, even where actors think there are. In one such study Garfinkel (1967, pp. 68–70) asked 135 students to violate a presumed rule, the "institutionalized one price rule" (which Garfinkel got from an unpublished paper by Parsons [1959]), by bargaining for merchandise in department stores and offering less than the sticker price. Many students who completed six tries were surprised to discover that such bargaining was not only possible but likely to produce favorable results; they expressed plans to continue the practice in the future. More significantly, of the 68 students who were asked to complete only one try, 20 percent either refused or terminated the assignment, compared with only 3 percent of the other 67 students, who were asked to perform six trials. In the latter group, anxiety decreased with successive trials, with most students enjoying the assignment by the third trial.

The experiment points to an artful dimension of human life as opposed to a rule-governing dimension. It suggests that the reason people routinely pay sticker prices is not because there is an institutional rule causing such action but because there is an artful way of presuming such a rule that people are comfortable with. When asked, in other words, to live an alternative art form, people are anxious because of inexperience, just as novices might be in Bittner's (1967) study. However, as they practice the new art form, they become more skilled at living it. Indeed their anxiety, which is always highest on the first attempt, seems to be considerably less so for those who know there are going to be other attempts—and that they will have further opportunities to practice and cultivate competence, thereby gaining mastery over preliminary fears—than it is for those who know their first attempt will be their only attempt.

Garfinkel sees these results as suggesting how functionalists make societal members out to be "cultural dopes" by describing a member as "one who operates by the rules when one is actually talking about anticipatory anxiety that prevents him from permitting a situation to develop" (Garfinkel 1967, p. 70). As for societal members' belief that they are following standardized rules, Garfinkel calls this "the standardization that could consist of an *attributed* standardization that is supported by the fact that persons avoid the very situations in which they might learn about [standardized expectancies]" (p. 70). In other words, it is through the routine avoidance of terra incognita that people continue to convince themselves and each other that institutionalized proscriptions exist. These tactics of avoidance are, apparently, equally convincing to Parsonian functionalists, who formalize the impression to the status of scientific knowledge. Furthermore, as Garfinkel (p. 70) puts it, "the more important the rule, the greater is the likelihood that knowledge [of the nature of rule-governed actions] is based on avoided tests."

These empirical studies begin to undermine the Parsonian assumption of a rule-governed society. In any case, we see that whatever else is going on with stable behavior, there need not be rules to explain it. But this does not undermine the Durkheimian principle of exteriority and constraint. Neither Bittner's police nor Garfinkel's students, even in the latter's methodic violations of presumed rules, were "free" to engage in any action whatever or to justify any behavior whatever on the grounds that there are no rules. These studies make Durkheimian exteriority and constraint available for observational study by locating it either in the concrete action that others take toward an actor or in the actor's anticipatory anxiety concerning what kinds of actions might be taken. This is a distinct advantage over finding constraint within the logical integrity of unobservable functionalist norms.

These considerations thus provide an imagery of standardized behavior, that of *artful* as opposed to *programmed*. Within the "programmed" discourse, it is difficult to imagine an alternative to prescribed behavior (or behavior-in-accordance-with-something) and random, arbitrary behavior. But a third alternative is something practitioners of the fine arts know well. A piece of great art is neither in conformity with what has gone before (which in the extreme would be plagiarism), nor does it disregard conventions (which in the extreme would be chaos). A new symphony is celebrated neither when it literally reproduces a well-known Mozart composition, even though the Mozart piece already has the stamp of greatness, nor when it consists of random, disorganized notes, even though that exact combination of notes is wholly original with the composer. Instead, there is a sense of the new symphony that seems to provide continuity and innovation at the same time. Similarly, jazz musicians know that expertise consists in the artist's ability to "play along" with others similarly playing along in ways that conform to improvisational competence but that were not set out in advance by agreement or any other kind of notational prescription (see Sudnow 1978). This art imagery more convincingly captures the Durkheimian constraint in social order than does the functionalist model, and it is likely that this is roughly what Garfinkel (1967, p. vii) had in mind with his designation of the methods whereby people accomplish social order (ethnomethods) as "artful."

Thus ethnomethods are essentially social and thereby never under anyone's full creative control. Although they do not transcend (and are no different than) empirical human activity, that very activity stands outside each individual and is morally constraining upon each individual's participation in that very activity. In that way ethnomethods retain their status as social facts and their Durkheimian characteristics of exteriority and constraint.

3

THE SOCIETY/MORALITY

EQUIVALENCE

Ethnomethodologists abandoned the rule-governed model of society in favor of a new topical domain known as ethnomethods. These consist of empirical social practices whereby people produce order, activities that retain their Durkheimian features of exteriority and constraint. But the fact that they are artful and not prescribed requires new understanding of how deviance within social order is possible and indeed how there could be such a thing as conformity.

Garfinkel's use of the term "indexical" helps in developing such new understanding. Interestingly, it also captures a sense of conformity and deviance contained in Durkheim's work that was lost in Parsons's rendition. Moreover, subtleties of indexicality are inextricably linked to Garfinkel's other seminal concept, *reflexivity*; this in turn recovers a Durkheimian sense of social order as sui generis, a self-contained order sufficient unto itself, one that is both moral and factual. Thus ethnomethodology, through no deliberate intent, resurrects a Durkheimian principle that Parsons expressly rejected: the equivalence of society and morality.

INDEXICALITY AND CONFORMITY

As we have seen, Parsons assumes that rules are analytically capable of prescribing behavior. They will not automatically do so, however. What is necessary for Parsons, beyond the mere existence of rules, is that societal members respect them and voluntarily conform to them (Parsons 1968b, pp. 383–90). Subjective respect is normally generated through the mechanisms of socialization and internalization. But once the subjective respect is supplied, the connection between prescriptive order and behavior is not problematic for Parsons.

This model of behavioral conformity inhabits Parsons's rendering of Durkheim on the inevitability of crime. Parsons (1968b, p. 379) suggests that Durkheim's reasons for saying there will always be law violators is simply that a legal rule logically implies its violation. He states, "So long as this mode of relation persists [that 'a body of normative rules implies the possibility of their violation'], some men will violate such rules some of the time; there will be crime" (p. 375). This characterization makes crime a product of either imperfect socialization or the diversity of people in relation to moral rules perhaps accountable in terms of personal idiosyncrasies, which is to say that not all people respect norms and values sufficiently. Behavior which logically falls outside of moral compliance will inevitably be produced by somebody. This is presumably a generalization of an empirical sort, since nothing theoretically would prevent the unlikely occurrence of total and simultaneous conformity throughout a society.

However, Durkheim's comments on the inevitability of crime are far more profound, and they have nothing to do with insufficient subjective respect for rules. At the risk of overstating his case, it would be more proper to state that *no one* conforms with morality (Durkheim 1938, pp. 69–70), at least not in a logical or deductive way (cf. Coser 1971, p. 142). This feature of the collective conscience is part of what makes it transcendent to all individuals, something no concrete person can ever embody, manifest, or become. Any concrete behavior can be found to be more or less in violation of it. As Durkheim (1938, p. 70) expresses this point, "There cannot be a society in which the individuals do not differ more or less from the collective type." Left to continue, this state of affairs would reduce the collective conscience in the minds of people to a point of phenomenal nonexistence, simultaneously weakening the fabric of society, which is the same thing. This is the condition Durkheim calls *anomie*.

One of the ways, then, that societal members are recalled to collective morality is through the ritual identification of whoever the most "extreme" violators are and judging the status of their behavior (through arrest and trial or other forms of deviance recognition) in terms of the collective conscience as an otherwise unavailable ideal (Durkheim 1938, pp. 67–70). This is a ceremony essential to the maintenance of society, or morality, as such. It is, in other words, a ritual prevention of anomie. Hence the twofold reason for why crime is normal and why it cannot be eliminated: (1) whatever specific behavior is eliminated, something would still be the most extreme behavior vis-à-vis the collective conscience and would be crime (pp. 67–69), and (2) this recruitment from the fringe for trial and punishment is crucial for the maintenance of social order and the avoidance of anomie (Durkheim 1933, pp. 85–103; 1938, p. 70). Note, then, that in Durkheim's theory literal conformity is not only not required but not possible. If it were possible, there would be nothing inherently destabilizing in the elimination of crime, nor would crime be necessary and theoretically inevitable.

Thus Parsons's theory requires the possibility of literal conformity to morality where Durkheim's theory does not. Crime, in Parsons's reading of Durkheim, is conceived not as the impossibility of deductive conformity but only in the logical possibility of a violation. Certain behavior really is conformity; anything else is a violation. These categories are clear for Parsons, and there will always be behavior in the society to fit either category. This imagery articulates with the "rules" idiom, for if we are to view the collective conscience as something one could conceivably conform to deductively, naturally its most promising characterization would be a "body of rules." As we shall see, even this characterization does not help much. In any case Durkheim's theory does not require that imagery, nor does his moral regulation require conformity as most people commonly think of conformity.

Ethnomethodologists, in placing their empirical findings against the background of Parsonian functionalism, have recovered a theory of conformity remarkably similar to Durkheim's. This theory emerges in Garfinkel's (1967, pp. 4–11) introduction of the term "indexical." While the principle of indexicality extends far beyond mere rules, considering it in this light here will be helpful shortly in a discussion of members' rule use as an empirical matter.

Most simply put, "indexical" is the term Garfinkel uses to describe a property of semantic expressions indicating that their specific sense or meaning varies with the context and is, at the general level, equivocal and imprecise. Garfinkel (1967, pp. 4–7) introduces the concept by citing others who have noticed a free play in everyday talk, going on to discuss how modern sociologists tend to view such ambiguity in their science as an unsatisfactory technique for capturing the objective social world as it happens. Thus social scientists seek to standardize their descriptive vocabulary by creating new concepts, fine-tuning ordinary ones, and operationalizing expressions and categories for purposes of mathematical and statistical modeling—a general strategy Garfinkel (p. 4) calls substituting "objective for indexical expressions." The goal, in the long-term development of a science, is to develop objective vocabulary capable of rendering literal description of acts and events in the social world in ways that are scientifically precise as opposed to common-sensically loose.

But the goal has not been realized; indeed the goal, says Garfinkel, is unrealizable because *all* expressions are indexical, including those used to clarify and remedy the indexicality of other expressions. Sociologists for the most part recognize each instance of their inability to defeat indexicality and, in the need to get on with the practical goal of research or meeting a publication deadline, postpone the long-term goal, finding reasons to relax the anti-indexicality campaign for the moment. As Garfinkel (1967, p. 6) puts it, "In every actual case without exception, conditions will be cited that a competent investigator will be required to recognize, such that in *that* particular case the terms of the demonstration [that objective concepts are in use and not sloppy ones] can be relaxed and nevertheless the demonstration be counted as an adequate one." Meanwhile, the long-term project recedes to methodological appendices, where this same practice takes place, and to focused methodological discussions in their own right, where this same practice takes place—in short, to "endless occasions [for researchers] to deal rigorously with indexical expressions" (p. 6).

Indexicality can be apprehended with a brief consideration of any linguistic concept, for example the term "have" with regard to someone's "having" something. Criteria for correct use or intended meaning of "I have . . ." vary indefinitely whether the object of the sentence is "a pen," which designates copresence of a physical object with the interactants and the speaker's ability (even willingness) to make a loan; "a dog," which indicates an object without copresence and without implying a potential loan; "the time," which almost implies a physical object (a watch) but which nevertheless indicates information freely sharable; "a secret," which indicates information not freely sharable; "a cold," which designates neither information nor a physical object; "rhythm," which designates something like an internal ability or appreciation; "an idea," which also indicates something internal yet altogether different from any of these, and so on. The list could go on indefinitely, with subtle differences and radical differences criss-crossing each other in unspecifiable ways. The point is that for users of the language, all of these are instances of the "same" relational state of "having," even though there are no commonalities, other than the use of that term, that bind the instances together; what it takes in order to "have" something varies from occasion to occasion.[1] Moreover, it is not an unusual complexity or abstraction level of "have" that allows for this; Wittgenstein performed a similar illustration with "game" (1958, pp. 31–32) and, as we have seen above, with the color green. Phenomenologists know this illustrative practice as the method of "free variation" and have shown how it can be performed on any perceptual act, no matter how apparently simple (see Gurwitsch 1964).

Determined slayers of indexicality might counter with attempts to standardize meaning by listing the contexts or the types of possible use and substituting professional terms for each of these. Such attempts would presume that the number of contexts is finite and that each context is itself unambiguous in character. This does no good when one considers that contexts themselves are specified with indexical expressions, or as Garfinkel (1967, p. 10) puts it: "Not only does no concept of context-in-general exist, but every use of 'context' without exception is itself indexical." Thus a long-term standardization project would be truly endless in the sense that each occasion of clarification would itself stand in need of clarification.

This mode of analysis can be extended to any element of linguistic expression, whether one is talking about a single term like "have," a phrase, a sentence, a paragraph, an "assumption," a folk theory, or, as some postmodernists have shown, an entire text. Ethnomethodologically conceived, all of these are *cultural resources* for making sense. Their use is not determinate, yet neither is it arbitrary. It is *constrained*, in Durkheim's terms, but this constraint manifests itself in the actions of people rather than in the inherent logical integrity of cultural resources themselves. People do not allow each other to get away with just any arbitrary usage. For example, where the cultural resource is role behavior, such as the "competent police work" Bittner (1967) studied, people do not allow each other to count just any behavior as competent, even though they do not have, and cannot themselves provide, access to the specifics of competency in advance of its recognition.

Yet as it happens, actors do not always or necessarily experience constraint as "merely" a constraint people impose on each other in their artful productions, or when they do, such constraint is seen as imposed or enforced "for a reason." In either case, actors sense that their linguistic use or behavior either conforms or fails to conform with some known, albeit unspecified, "underlying pattern" of the sum total of all possible uses of the resource in question. For example, each use of "have," for users, documents a stable underlying pattern of "people having things," even though that pattern, however familiar, may be presumed by users to be complex and impractical to spell out. The same goes for each instance of competent police work. More generally, each concrete use of a cultural resource is presumed to document an underlying pattern such that the pattern could have predicted this specific use; in that sense, then, for actors, each documented instance of the underlying pattern points out more about the pattern that actors "knew about all along" but never had need of explicating. This "documentary method of interpretation" (Garfinkel 1967, pp. 77–79) is therefore, in a prospective/retrospective fashion, a constituent method of societal members' accomplishment of conformity or nonconformity to patterns.

For ethnomethodologists concerned with empirical events, such "underlying patterns" are myths, in that they cannot be found. Indeed indexicality prevents their ever being found. Yet they are matters of profound common-sense knowledge among societal members. For that reason they can be understood as folklore, or *conceptual idealizations*. But for ethnomethodologists, only the concrete use of cultural resources displays their empirical status. That is, such expressions do not refer to any semantic entities or logically cohesive patterns of use that provide either for their sense or for their proper use. In that regard, then, they have no core meaning whatever but only an open and expanding set of applied meanings.

Yet notice this about applied meanings as they come up: it is precisely the constraint imposed on the use of cultural resources that sustains the impression that there are literal, core meanings. If there are right versus wrong ways to use an expression, so the impression goes, then there must be "something" to which specific uses more or less conform. Thus we see in members' artful management of indexical expressions a collective method of sustaining the folklore of relatively fixed underlying patterns. Notice that without constraint, this impression would wither and disappear. If *anything* were allowed to pass as correct use, or if nothing were recognizably incorrect use, then the very idea of use-in-conformity would vanish, and with it, in fact, notions of correct use. In other words, it is the very possibility of error and correction that provides the impression that certain usages and not others are in conformity with underlying patterns.

These considerations resonate strongly with Durkheim's observations about the collective conscience. Conceptual resources seem to transcend their concrete occasioned uses, even though they are incapable of prescribing these uses. The concept "have," for example, cannot be prespecified in terms of its proper use, nor can a "core meaning" be identified or expressed. Yet constraint imposed on its occasioned use continually reproduces the necessary impression that it has a core meaning. Likewise for Durkheim, the collective conscience cannot be manifested or expressed by anyone's behavior, yet its status as transcendent morality, its sacred character, is sustained by the recruitment of behavior designated crime by a rigorous comparison with it. In both cases, social constraint is concrete and empirical, and in either case a reduction or absence of social constraint yields meaninglessness, in the case of a concept, or general anomie, in the case of the collective conscience.

An obvious question concerns whether or not Durkheim intended the collective conscience to be mythological in quite the same way "core meaning" or "literal use" has been designated here. My answer to that is that the mythological status is analogous to Durkheim's qualification of the collective conscience as incapable of thinking or acting on its own, independent of the people who make up a society. Better, its mythological status is equal to its status as sacred, as transcending the concrete daily affairs of people. Note, for example, that while the collective conscience is said to contain religious symbols, Durkheim's empirical studies focus not on the symbols themselves as empirically determinate entities but on their *use*—for example in concrete aboriginal life (Durkheim 1947).

Furthermore, the status of the collective conscience as objectively present for science, exterior to individuals, is analogous to the empirical availability of concepts like "have," "competent police work," and so on in the language. Indeed it is analogous to the empirical availability of language per se as part of culture. The very existence of language can be established independently of studies of actual language use. Notice that the availability of concepts and of language precedes and survives all societal members and is exterior to them in precisely the manner of Durkheim's collective conscience. Thus it is not an unreasonable theoretical move to envision the collective conscience as the repertoire of available cultural resources (including language) as discussed here. This move simply adds explanation to Durkheim's assertions regarding the sacred and transcendent character of the collective conscience: it is experienced that way because it cannot be expressed or conformed to; it cannot be conformed to because it is sterile in its capacity to prescribe; but it can be used. Indeed people *must* use it in order to sustain the impression of morality as sacred and transcendent, as stable and prescriptive. Its use, moreover, is collectively monitored and constrained. Without such concrete, occasioned, and constrained usage, the sterility of the collective conscience would become apparent, the very essence of anomie.

I should emphasize that the availability of cultural resources does not imply an "already empirical" status of whatever else can be made from them, anymore than a block of wood implies a figure that is carved from it. If laws and rules, complex concepts and higher categories, assumptions and other kinds of organizing ideational principles are all constructed with language, their empirical status does not derive from their potential construction but only from their actual empirical status-as-constructed and, moreover, their concrete use, by actors. Thus, for example, if someone invokes a rule in the course of accounting for behavior, that invocation, itself an empirical event, does not in and of itself provide evidence that the rule was ever present prior to the invocation. It may have been, but insisting that it must have been is analogous to positing the previous existence of any created art form.

This is an additional troublesome aspect of Parsons's version of the collective conscience in that its content, limited by Parsons's analysis to norms and values, is required to include whatever rules are necessary for prescribing whatever factual behavior is observed prior both to the behavior and to the invocation of the rules. This is not to say that such rules cannot be empirically present prior to their invocation; formal laws and other written codes are, for example. But even in these latter cases, where rules are themselves cultural resources, the actual use of rules on specific occasions need not be prescribed or contained within a normative order as prescriptions prior to the construction of their newly created "underlying intents." So in a sense Parsons posits more in the collective conscience than it could possibly contain, including rules that have yet to be constructed, while simultaneously limiting its repertoire of available resources specifically to rules. Yet he needed rules, and he needed them to be prescriptive, for reasons having to do with his very recognition of factual order. It is to that matter that we now turn.

REFLEXIVITY AND THE SUI GENERIS ORDER

That Parsonian normative order is unobservable should in itself cast doubt on the notion that Durkheim implied such a mechanism, for morality was empirical for Durkheim. A related source of doubt is the mere fact that normative order is analytically distinct from the factual order that Parsons says both Hobbes and Durkheim were trying to explain. Factual order, again, is the observed behavioral order, organized behavior as distinct from random utilitarian behavior—in a word, the society. Normative order is another system entirely, one which, if it is sufficiently respected by the membership, causes factual order. Yet for Durkheim, society itself is moral (Durkheim 1933, p. 228); social facts and moral facts are identical. It is the moral nature of society that provides for its own possibility. Society is, in that sense, truly sui generis.

The term "sui generis" (literally, "of its own kind") suggests that the society observed has a life of its own, even in its moral capacity, not that there is something else separate from it that causes it. Moral constraint need not regulate everyone simultaneously by arising from a source external to the whole, to the society (see Durkheim 1951, p. 320). In fact, the very organicist analogy postulates an organism whose parts are interdependent in such a way as to produce a whole that can be understood only with regard to those interdependencies—that is, a whole that cannot be understood as simply the sum of those parts, their features itemized separately, compiled, and added together. "The whole is more than the sum of the parts" does *not* mean that the organism requires some external animating principle, something in addition to the empirically available organism itself that makes it happen or causes its parts to work the way that they do. Why, then, would we expect to find something beyond the observed factual order to produce observed behavior? Why must that which transcends the sum of society's parts be other than the whole of which the parts are parts—that is, the factual order, the society?

It seems more faithful, then, to Durkheim's sui generis principle to seek the phenomenon of moral regulation directly in the empirical workings of society itself, there in the "interrelations" of parts (see Giddens 1971, p. 87). Thus while factual order cannot be explained by examining psychologies of its members, the question at hand becomes: how does it nevertheless produce itself, by itself, with no help from the outside? Answers, following Durkheim's organicist analogy, would have to have something to do with how society's members stand in relation to each other. The challenge comes in finding these relations empirically within the very order we are seeking to explain, which is the sui generis order. Success would eliminate the need for a mythological normative order. For Durkheim, the whole thing is factual, and the whole thing is moral. It cannot be split into separate factual and moral spheres.

Parsons, however, was most deliberate in his separation of the factual and moral spheres, arguing that Durkheim's society/morality equivalence was an "error" (Parsons 1968b, p. 392).[2] Instead, Parsons saw factual order as by its very nature patterned, repetitive, and standardized independently of morality and the active role of the investigator; it is this incorrigible order, featured by its contrast with the Hobbesian war of all against all, that he set out to explain. He found analogous structure in the minds of actors, this second structure shared as culture internalized by individual actors. As opposed to the primary factual order, this second structure that Parsons derives is moral, and it is prescriptive and analytically capable of producing the factual order.

But if Durkheim is correct about the equivalence of society and morality (see chapter 2), we would expect to find moral order already constituted in the behavioral order that Parsons begins with as factual. We would expect, in other words, Parsons's prescriptive order to be implied already in his very recognition of the structured society as factual. It would be impossible to distinguish between behavioral and moral order, more specifically between Parsons's factual and normative orders. Notably, these Durkheimian predictions are born out in early ethnomethodological studies— even though ethnomethodologists did not specifically address Durkheim but directed their argument against the functionalist theory Parsons said he derived from Durkheim.

Notice that had Garfinkel begun with Parsons's premise of an independently observable factual order, then his observations about indexicality and the essentially nondeterminateness of culture would run into the following problems: How could inherently indexical cultural resources, incapable of prescribing their own use, nevertheless produce the factual social order we see before us? How could any amount of subjective respect for a collective conscience produce order if the collective conscience cannot tell anyone what to do? These are questions, however, that Garfinkel does not have to answer, since he speaks not only of indexical expressions but of indexical actions (Garfinkel 1967, pp. 5, 10–11). This is to say that just as cultural resources, including linguistic expressions, mean nothing in particular independent of their use, likewise no human behavior is any behavior in particular independently of its being cast in categories by users of culture. That is, behavior is not inherently behavior-of-a-sort such that it can be seen to be repeating itself or fitting together with other types of behavior to form patterns. In short, Garfinkel is denying the factual social order as Parsons conceives it. Instead, Garfinkel invites us to see how societal members use indexical expressions to organize indexical actions in such a way as to produce, *for them*, an impression of stable social order.

This is the phenomenon Garfinkel (1967, pp. 7–11) terms "reflexivity." While it does not remove behavior from the jurisdiction of empirical study, and while in that sense behavior retains its "factual" status for science, that behavior includes actors' verbal displays, including (among other things) actors' talk and theorizing about their own behavior. Through the use of cultural categories actors organize their behavior as the behavior-that-it-is, as behavior of a certain sort, as structured, recognizable, repetitive, patterned behavior. It is also this behavior as organized that provides the context for the indexical expressions used to organize it, thus reducing or managing the ambiguity of these cultural resources for actors' immediate practical purposes. Thus for Garfinkel the problem of social order cannot be addressed without examining how people actually produce the order they talk about and take for granted as factual. These methods of order production, or ethnomethods, are observable in what members of a setting do and say; thus these methods are part of the very setting they organize as factual. As Garfinkel put it, "Members' accounts, of every sort, in all their logical modes, with all of their uses, and for every method for their assembly are constituent features of the settings they make observable" (p. 8).

For Garfinkel, then, description of social order is part of the very social order it describes. When sociologists step back from this process and observe it from the outside, they will witness a reduction of ambiguity, though by no means its elimination, through the juxtaposition of behavior and the terms used to describe that behavior in local settings. They will witness a stability sufficient for the purposes of those assembling the stability— which is to say, a stability for all practical purposes. They will witness the societal membership assembling, disassembling, and reassembling order as they require, and they will witness the membership living within and taking for granted the objective reality of the products of their artful work (cf. Zimmerman and Pollner 1970). But sociologists will *not* witness, if they step outside this process, an inherently structured behavioral world. They will not witness behavioral events that recur or line up into patterns. They will not see Parsons's factual order. If they do, this is sound indication that they have not stepped out of the process. Instead they are unwitting participants in the process. In this regard, Parsons can accurately be said to have "gone native" in the very recognition of his preliminary phenomenon: factual order.

It can be understood from this that where Parsons sees two orders, both structured and one causing the other, Garfinkel sees neither one, or more strictly he sees one self-organizing, "incarnate" (Garfinkel 1967, p. 1) order. As he puts it in his introduction to ethnomethodological studies:

> I mean, too, that [accounting] practices consist of an endless, ongoing, contingent accomplishment; that they are carried on under the auspices of, and are made to happen as events in, the same ordinary affairs that in organizing they describe; that the practices are done by parties to those settings whose skill with, knowledge of, and entitlement to the detailed work of that accomplishment—whose competence—they obstinately depend upon, recognize, use, and take for granted. (p. 1)

This would appear to come intriguingly close to Durkheim's expressive "sui generis" with regard to the categorical uniqueness of society. As I have indicated, there is no recommendation in Durkheim to split society into two parts, particularly when one of them is invisible. Garfinkel's approach has the advantage of retaining the singularity of the Durkheimian phenomenon as sui generis—as in-and-of-itself—as well as retaining its status as empirical and as morally regulated.

To repeat for clarity: First, the two orders that Parsons postulates now merge as one. The body of rules, for the most part unobservable in Parsons's scheme, become nevertheless, to whatever extent they are empirical, part of the order that can be observed. That is, their empirical presence in the form of written codes or oft-repeated maxims, their presence as newly coined innovations, and their routine use in concrete instances can be witnessed for science. Moreover their use is essential to the order of which they are a part for its status as factual.

Second, and conversely, the order as factual is also essential for the sanctionable use of cultural resources. This unified phenomenon is thereby moral in that its organization as an outcome of the use of such resources cannot be accomplished at random or according to the will of disembodied individuals without the predictable degeneration into anomie. That is to say, members, like artists, work on and within their practical projects with a definite need to innovate but with certain knowledge that not just any account will do. However, where for Parsons the origin of constraint is in the logical integrity of an invisible yet hypothesized normative order, here the constraint is found in concrete human activity—members do not allow each other to get away with any descriptive accounts whatsoever. They regulate each other's work, with the result that for anyone the work cannot proceed without constant attention to that exterior regulating activity. Thus for anyone this constraint is factual, unifying the factual and the normative aspects of the Durkheimian sui generis order that are artificially severed in Parsons's theory.

Finally, rules per se constitute far less of the collective conscience than Parsons imagines, and far fewer rules than he imagines are part of this repertoire. Indeed, his theory would require an infinity of rules in this normative body. And beyond the rules in the repertoire is the broader class of cultural resources: proverbs, maxims, categories, concepts, assumptions, organizational idealizations, folk theories, and so forth, all subsets of and constructed with a more general resource: language itself.

EMPIRICAL STUDIES IN INDEXICALITY AND REFLEXIVITY: MEMBERS' USE OF RULES

The principles of indexicality and reflexivity can be illustrated with societal members' use of any type of cultural resource. This does not necessarily mean rules, and in fact I have already discussed occasions of stable behavior where no rules whatever are used. In many studies, however, rule use has been a preferred topic of ethnomethodological investigation. This is true for several reasons. One has to do with the simple fact that American sociology before Garfinkel was routinely organized around the Parsonian assumption of rule-governed behavior. Thus early ethnomethodologists displayed a continuity of concern with functionalism—that is, with functionalism's interest in rules—although it came to ethnomethodologists to provide the corrective in this vision, distinguishing their own interest in rules as radically different than the interest of what they termed "traditional sociology" (see Zimmerman and Wieder 1970).

Another reason for the focus on rules has to do with the frequency with which societal members themselves use rules in organizing their world, this in turn resting on a folk belief that behavior is rule-governed. Along with this goes an observation that cultural resources in general can be grammatically transformed into a rule format. For example, someone could turn competent use of the word "have" into a prescriptive definition or express "competent police work" as the rule "Do competent police work," or turn an assumption into a prescriptive "Think this way." This is in fact a predominant way members of society help each other with unfamiliar procedures, clear up trouble as it comes up, instruct each other in the ways of the world, and so on. As we have seen, trouble with rules themselves is often cleared up by invoking or generating other rules. This common-sense practice in our society, as well as the common-sense assumption that behavior is rule-governed, also accounts for ethnomethodologists' interest in rules, for when they look into the Durkheimian order, this practice is often what they see.

It should hardly need repeating that the rules invoked, created, or interpreted by societal members cannot do the prescriptive work required by Parsonian functionalism. These are cultural resources that *members* use in the construction of order, but they do not in themselves prescribe order. Nor, as we have seen, are they theoretically required by order or for order. But when they are required, they are required by members as practical matters; if they are not required that way, they are not required at all. It is an interesting corollary to Parsons's having "gone native" in the recognition of factual order that he *required rules himself* at almost every turn to account for that very presupposed order. Indeed, in presupposing order, Parsons presupposed rules. From this presupposition sprang his entire general theory. This explains his focus on the collective conscience as rules, for while cultural resources in general are in themselves prescriptively sterile, and while this is no less true with rules, nevertheless resources expressed as rules are formulated in a grammar of prescription, a presumptive case thereby made that rules are what patterned behavior requires.

And so ethnomethodologists, insofar as they remained interested in rules at all, turned to members' use of rules as a constituent part of the order to be investigated. This is distinct from using such resources themselves to account for order or creating new rules to explain behavior. Functionalists who did the latter, ethnomethodologists claimed, were continuing members' activity, that is, they were acting as members of the order, doing the same work characteristic of that order, thereby becoming examples of what they had ostensibly set out to study (Zimmerman and Pollner 1970; Zimmerman and Wieder 1970). Ethnomethodologists designated as their topic members' use of cultural resources, including (but not limited to) rules, to produce order. Moreover this was an occasioned order organized around the practical purposes of members, an order for members, not an objectively apparent structured entity for ethnomethodologists. Sociologists who instead used such resources to explain order were simultaneously producing the order themselves, thereby missing their chance to witness the phenomenon they were after. Using these resources in the production of an alleged topic, rather than topicalizing their use as a distinct and unifying phenomenon, is what was called "confusing topic with resource" (Zimmerman and Pollner 1970).

Empirical investigations into members' use of rules as part of social order rather than explanations of it have revealed that the practical purposes to which rules are put go far beyond the functionalist concern with behavioral prescription. As one might have predicted from Durkheim's society/morality equivalence, rules are implicated in the *very identity of behavior as factual*, even as these same rules are presumed by members to be prescriptive and explanatory. This is the phenomenon discussed above as reflexivity.

Superb examples of reflexivity permeate Wieder's (1974a, 1974b) seminal ethnography of a halfway house. Here Wieder found a set of rules for governing residential life, a "convict code," which included the following: Do not snitch, do not cop out, do not take advantage of other residents, share what you have, help other residents, do not mess with other residents' interests, do not trust staff, and show loyalty to other residents (Wieder 1974a, pp. 115–18). If Wieder had limited his investigation to Parsonian concerns, this code would have become the rules that explain the factually observable behavior of convicts in and around the halfway house. But instead he extended the analysis to include the telling of the code as a very part of that behavior. Notably the code was analytically incapable of prescribing specific behaviors; indeed its expression as eight governing rules was Wieder's own rendition, a far more organized and prescriptive format than what he actually observed in the halfway house. In practice, residents, though oriented to the code as a set of rules, could not recite the rules in ethnographers' style (p. 115).

The embeddedness of the convict code in residential life makes Wieder's study a revealing glimpse at reflexivity and the sui generis order. For the very factual behavior engaged in by residents depended on the code in more ways than Parsons will allow. Not only was the code invoked by residents, by staff, and by Wieder himself as explanations of observed behavior, and not only was it invoked as guides for future behavior, but it was invoked as an index of what the behavior on display actually was, how it was patterned, objective, and factual: "Hearing the code and employing it as a 'guide to perception' gave behaviors of residents a specific and stable sense" (Wieder 1974a, p. 131). Thus the factual status of what was explained by the code depended on the code for its very identity. If the notion of a device used both to generate and explain a phenomenon seems uncomfortably circular, nevertheless this is what empirical observation reveals as a fundamental property of social order. As Wieder (p. 146) captures this double use, "Somehow through the vehicle of ordinary conversation, residents made it happen that their behavior would be seen as regular, independent of their particular doing, and done as a matter of normative requirement."

Reflexivity within the halfway house is further illustrated by the fact that the code was often "heard" in the nonverbal behavior at hand rather than the reverse. It is not that novices first learned the code and then followed it; often they learned the code in the process of seeing or participating in behavior, indeed even "conforming" to the code. Eventually Wieder turned these ethnographic observations on himself as ethnographer within the setting, revealing how he came to learn the code, often through such behavior, ironically, as residents' refusal to discuss it with him.

Thus behavior and resources for organizing the behavior are mutually elaborating features of each other. Their juxtaposition reduces ambiguity to a point sufficient for members' purposes at hand, but, it should be repeated, these purposes never approach the rigorous, unsatisfiable requirements of functionalist sociology. "Purposes at hand" are practical purposes, not purposes for a disinterested or analytically satisfying theory of the halfway house, but purposes such as explanation, justification, persuasion, and interpersonal control.

It should be noted, again, that while no member of the halfway house setting was "free" in the sense of being able to generate general rules in any way whatsoever or being able to engage in behavior without constant attention to the constraining aspect of the social environment, these constraints were those exercised or exercisable by members on one another rather than anything emanating from the grammatical integrity of deductive norms. Sanctions for violations of the code could be severe, but the specifics of compliance were matters of persuasion and control with the ever-present possibility of failure, more like successful social "passing" (Garfinkel 1967, pp. 116–85; Hilbert 1980) or "impression management" (Goffman 1959, pp. 208–37), this as opposed to conformity with a body of rules. Thus constraint is an art form within the social order it constrains.

Still, prescription is one of the many practical uses to which rules are put. Given the analytic impossibility of prescription, then, one might wonder how members could use rules for that purpose. The prototype example in our society is bureaucracy (see Bittner 1965); because this is a central concern in Weber's work, I shall return to it in chapter 8. But it is instructive to note, in terms of a sui generis order, that even where rules are used to prescribe the order that is sought and expected, they depend for that use upon routine knowledge of that very order; they cannot stand outside that order and prescribe it. Moreover, what that order consists of, as well as the specific intent of a prescriptive rule, is unique to every occasion of its being artfully constructed or "reproduced" and cannot thereby be specified in advance of this construction (Hilbert 1981, 1982; Wieder 1970, 1974a, 1974b). Thus each instance of a rule's having prescribed behavior involves an active determination, on the parts of members working artfully together, of other "underlying rules" or some underlying meanings of present rules that were never specified but are now, in the course of their construction, oriented to as "known all along." Simultaneously each of these determinations is an occasion to construct more case-specific knowledge about the routine workings of competent behavior as it factually exists. Thus reflexivity is no less a phenomenon for the prescriptive use of rules than it is for a descriptive use. Indeed the analytic distinction between normative prescription and factual description drops out of the sociologist's lexicon altogether.

The reflexive properties of prescriptive rules were found by Garfinkel (1967, pp. 18–24) in his famous investigation of coding practices. Here coding rules were prescriptive and rationally designed as clear for coders' purposes of explicating criteria used by the staff of a clinic to process patients through various treatment stages. The premise was that while these criteria as written and routinely spoken were loose, their underlying stability could be captured by (1) keeping rigorous and very detailed records on patients' clinic careers and (2) coding this information in a methodologically precise way to discover standard selection criteria for patients moving through these treatment phases. Coding instructions had to be precise in order to render what was otherwise loose as stable, quantifiable, and subject to a reliability test. Garfinkel's central finding was that coders had to use more knowledge than was contained either in the coding instructions or in the patient folders in order to code folder contents into code categories—that is, to follow the coding instructions. Coders had to use "loose" knowledge about routine clinic events and operations—knowledge which was itself not coded, standardized, or even thematized prior to its use, that is, its construction for use in particular coding cases. In other words, coders had to use the "loose" knowledge that they were seeking to standardize in order to assess the adequacy of the standardization. In this sense the loose knowledge took priority over clinic events, folder contents, and coding instructions.

Garfinkel called this coders' work "ad hoc" considerations, noting that while conventional research could see them as unwelcome and obtrusive flaws in objective coding practices, they were nevertheless essential to the very discovery of folder events as correctly coded. That is, they were part and parcel of the recognition of what instructions were instructing coders to do in each instance of a folder event's being coded. Indeed, asking coders to repress these ad hoc considerations produced bewilderment (Garfinkel 1967, p. 21). Thus once again prescriptive rules occur within a setting and are about that setting, not standing outside that setting as its cause. It is not, therefore, that coders' activities could be understood from the outside by consulting the instructions they followed, no matter how precisely they were formulated. Rather, the intent of the instructions was, as was their use, ongoing and accomplished features of the setting itself. So was the reasonableness and very identity of specific instances of coders' activities having been done well.

That a setting "self-organizes" this way is deeply suggestive of a Durkheimian sui generis order, for sufficiency in following the instructions, as well as the prescriptive adequacy of the instructions, is accomplished in the very art of following them, that is, in the course of observable behavior: "How ever coders did it, it was sufficient to produce whatever they got" (Garfinkel 1967, p. 20). Similar findings are reported in Zimmerman's

(1970) study of the intake procedures at a welfare establishment, where exceptions to prescriptive rules were determined by members to have been implied by the rules "all along" but never before thematized. While intake workers were expected to adhere to the rules, they were expected to "know more" about the rules' intent as the orderly processing of applicants such that they could abandon the rules whenever necessary for this orderly processing in ways that could be seen as "nevertheless" in compliance with the rules. In the event of poor processing, it would do no good to appeal to a rule's literal meaning as a way either to exonerate the intake worker of bad judgment or to implicate policymakers in poor rule construction. Indeed, as we have seen, there is no "literal rule"; such an appeal would be simply *one more use* of the rule, here a poorly crafted one. Thus intake workers are expected not simply to "follow" rules, though this may be part of the setting vocabulary; they are expected to *use* rules, and to do so with some degree of skill. These same practices were also found in the use of rules for correct legal and medical procedures by Sudnow (1965, 1967).

Thus normative and factual orders are the self-same sui generis order. It is the order that Durkheim called society, and it is empirical in both its normative and factual aspects. Modern research reveals it to be like an ongoing work of art, more like a jazz musicians' jam session than a computer program—even an ambiguous program that allows individual "free space" as suggested by those attempting to draw compromises between sociological determinism and psychological reductionism (DiTomaso 1982). In any case, its normative dimension cannot be separated from its factual status. It can be observed in both these aspects, as can the consequences of these aspects for members of it, but it cannot be observed in either aspect independently of the other. It is enforced, moreover, on the membership, but it is, in the final analysis and as a matter of empirical observation, members who are enforcing it and using it.

Finally, members of society can organize and see the regularities of their behavior. When done with the organizing assumption that behavior is rule-governed, each case of recognized behavioral stability is simultaneously a case of recognized prescription. That is, order constructed with this folk theory will inevitably yield whatever rules are required to produce whatever is allowed to count as order. Order construction need not make use of this organizing assumption, nor need it require rules. But when it does, results are guaranteed. Therefore it is no profundity, though it is an intriguing finding, that functionalists, in buying into this organizing premise, are able to find any degree of complexity in normative order that is necessary to prescribe factual order in its corresponding degree of complexity (see Hilbert 1990b). For ethnomethodology, and for Durkheim, they are the same order.

4

THE SOCIETY/REALITY

EQUIVALENCE

In chapter 3 we saw the Durkheimian order as the society generating itself from within, in both its moral and factual aspects, through the artful practices of its membership. But Durkheim had more to say about society than that it is moral. Society is also, in Durkheim's most radical commentary, equivalent to objective reality as known and recognized by societal members. This means that whatever it takes to sustain membership—which is to say, whatever it takes to sustain society—is precisely what it takes to sustain stable experience of a known and knowable objective reality.

Parsons rejected Durkheim's society/reality equivalence as a misguided degeneration from empirical science into idealist philosophy. Ethnomethodology, however, recovers this equivalence through empirical research. In essence, the exterior and constraining ethnomethods that produce social order simultaneously produce an objective world, including what members take to be nonsocial reality. Thus objective reality and the sui generis order are indistinguishable phenomena accomplished by and for the membership.

DURKHEIM AND THE SOCIETY/REALITY EQUIVALENCE

Parsons assumed that normative order is, by virtue of its logical and grammatical integrity, analytically capable of prescribing behavior. This does not in and of itself guarantee that such an order will be obeyed, however; even for Parsons a system of rules can only regulate to the extent that it is *moral*. Moreover, he is clear that the morality of rules does not mean simply that they are enforced through social institutions or other external sanctions, for this would have the effect of assimilating social control to other natural environmental constraints to which people adapt (Parsons 1968b, pp. 378–83), a position Parsons rejected earlier as radical positivism. For Durkheim, notes Parsons, moral behavior is not simply a matter of adaptation, of avoiding negative consequences of violation, but rather includes a sense of duty, of subjective commitment on the part of individual actors. For Parsons, having already posited the "body of rules" as analytically capable of prescribing, this commitment becomes subjective respect for the body of rules and voluntary conformity to them (pp. 383–90). People conform to rules as a matter of duty and subjective moral obligation; this makes social order.[1] As he puts it, "The solidarity of individuals is the unity of allegiance to a common body of moral rules, of values" (p. 389).

Thus for Parsons, Durkheimian morality is tied to the subjective dimension of social action. He calls this by various names, including "the 'subjective' sense of moral obligation" (Parsons 1968b, p. 385), "the attitude of respect" (p. 390), and "the creative or voluntaristic side [of the relation of people to norms]" (p. 396). Morality, then, consists of a body of rules concomitant with subjective orientation to these rules.

Here we come to a revealing difference between Durkheim and Parsons on the role of subjectivity. In Parsons we have a two-termed causal scheme with objective behavior on the receiving end of the arrow and shared subjectivity on the causing end, the latter including norms and values that societal members internalize and subjectively respect. But for Durkheim, especially in his late work, subjectivity cannot stand outside the phenomenon being regulated as a feature of a regulating mechanism, for *subjectivity is itself regulated* (Pope 1973, p. 409; Pope, Cohen, and Hazelrigg 1975, p. 419). Indeed Durkheim indicates that subjective respect for collective representations is a result of objective social pressure exerted upon individuals by exterior and constraining social phenomena, roughly the opposite of subjectivity giving rise to those phenomena.[2]

Durkheim's general stance on subjectivity suggests that what gets regulated by society includes human experience of objective reality (Collins 1985, p. 150), encompassing what is "out there" as warrantably experienceable. This is to say that objectivity, as warrantably "out there" and subject to experience, is itself regulated. The categories of thought that provide for a recognizable existence in an orderly world, including notions of space and time, derive from society and arise from the manner in which society regulates human experience (Durkheim 1947, pp. 10–14, 440–43; see Lukes 1972, pp. 435–49). The objective orderly world, then, is the sui generis society.

Mechanical solidarity indicates the clearest circumstance in which *society and reality are one*: "For the Australian, things themselves, everything which is in the universe, are part of the tribe; they are constituent elements of it and, so to speak, regular members of it; just like men, they have a determined place in the general scheme of organization of the society" (Durkheim 1947, p. 141). What might be termed the ultimate reality of a society, the god in the society, that which embraces all knowable reality and sees beyond what any individual knows, is equivalent to that very society (p. 206). The sacred energy shared by sacred objects, which among North American Indians and Melanesians is called *mana* (p. 194), is symbolized in Australia by the totem, which simultaneously symbolizes the identity of the clan group (Giddens 1971, p. 109; Coser 1971, p. 138). The unity expressed in elementary ontological systems "merely reproduces the unity" of mechanically based solidarity (Durkheim 1947, p. 145).

As the division of labor advances and as mechanical solidarity gives way to organic solidarity, this unity of world vision breaks down (cf. Berger, Berger, and Kellner 1973, pp. 63–82). More precisely, it recedes into the background as supporting axioms for more complicated systems of thought and experiences congruent with the advancing complexity of society (Durkheim 1947, pp. 431–47; Giddens 1971, pp. 112–15). In short, knowledge (which is to say, knowledge of reality) becomes diversified, such diversification finding its resting point on an "ultimate" unifying principle of moral rationalism, or rational individualism, the same working principle that sustains laws and contracts (cf. Alexander 1982b, pp. 263–67, 276–79).

Thus in the modern world, no less than in earlier cultures, society remains the wellspring of the possible when it comes to experiencing the world, no matter how complex the world is found to be (Coser 1971, pp. 139–40). Cosmologies, ontologies, and all of their derivatives—which is to say, entire systems of thought, *including those of the natural sciences*—are socially derived (Durkheim 1947, pp. 13–20). In terms of social evolution, scientific thinking owes its origins to the religious experiences of mechanical solidarity (Bloor 1976, pp. 40–44; Lukes 1972, pp. 444–49). Such insight dovetails nicely with what was later to be called the sociology of knowledge and with Mannheim's (1936, p. 3) insistence that individuals do not think by themselves but participate in thinking.

Thus does society provide for its membership the possibility of experiencing reality. Notably, reality is invariably and inevitably experienced, by anyone experiencing it, in a mode identical to the empirical features of Durkheimian society: exteriority and constraint. That is, reality displays, in experience, an organization all its own that transcends individual consciousness and that cannot be apprehended in any way the individual happens to choose. The individual is *obliged* to experience the world in certain ways and not others, even though such obligations seem to the individual to arise from the objectively arranged nature of reality as such. The independence of reality from the subjective knower appears to be essential for anyone to experience an objective reality. In Durkheim's terms, however, this independence is the independence of society from each person, and obligation to experience reality in certain ways is nothing more or less than socially derived moral constraint. Without that social constraint, no such reality experience would be possible. More radically, without the exterior and constraining society, there would be no reality given to experience.[3]

Note the varied phenomena which are experienced by societal members as transcendent to their here-and-now practical lives: the religious reality of mechanical solidarity, including its god or other supernatural entities; ideal morality as the absolute standard for judging mundane activity; real reality in all of its assorted expressions in organic solidarity, including scientific, objective reality; and the "underlying reality-qua-reality" of organic solidarity to which all expressions of it are subordinate. All of these are equivalent in Durkheim's theory to the exterior and constraining society itself, to the collective conscience.

These equivalences make vast worlds of phenomena available as social facts for sociology, including what the natural sciences regard as their "empirical world" and whatever they regard as the nonempirical, nonscientific, or metaphysical worlds. All of this becomes empirical for sociology in light of the society/reality equivalence. Indeed, reality per se is available to sociology, whatever its content; reality and society are one. Individuals experiencing reality, whatever the content, are not experiencing illusions but the empirical society (Durkheim 1947, p. 225; Lukes 1972, pp. 459–61; Jones 1986, p. 136). The implication for Durkheimian research is to examine the "facts of the world" for their congruent empirical (exterior and constraining) status as sui generis social facts (cf. Giddens 1971, pp. 109–10).

Yet whatever its content, reality retains its transcendent status over individuals in precisely the way society is transcendent. As people first awaken to the power of society in early elementary mechanical solidarity, reality takes on a global religious expression; this accounts for Durkheim's use of the term "sacred" to society. But it should not be thought that sacredness applies only to religious societies. The moral principles of organic solidarity that underlie reality diversification, natural science, individuation, and rational contracts display a godlike transcendence over every societal member, are therefore accorded godlike respect, and consequently warrant the label "sacred" as Durkheim uses it relative to religious symbols in mechanical solidarity (Bloor 1976, pp. 40–43). Indeed in either case it is the society that transcends individuals and the society that is sacred (see Alexander 1982b, pp. 242–43). Consequently Durkheim amusingly designates individualism, known by him as a counterreligious moral tendency, with a collective religious vernacular: "cult of the individual."

It is a problem for Parsons's derivation, therefore, that subjectivity is tied up with a regulating mechanism rather than itself subject to regulation. Granted, when subjective respect wanes, which it will do for Parsons because of a tendency of individuals to behave egoistically, society moves in with its institutional controls (Parsons 1968b, pp. 399–408), hoping to correct this lapse and to reestablish moral respect for norms and values. But even here such regulation is a "substitute" (p. 404) moral regulation of behavior, and to whatever extent it corrects the subjective factor, it is restoring it to its place in the natural causal sequence in human behavior, as a causal factor. For Parsons, then, subjectivity is the mechanism in the individual that makes morality work. But for Durkheim, subjective experience is regulated by society and is experience of society; it is morally regulated and is experience of morality; it is constrained by reality and is experience of reality.

So reality and society are one. Experience of reality is experience of a known and knowable society. Society, the collective conscience, provides the terms of experience making experience and knowledge possible. Reality, of either a mechanical or organic sort, is naturally not knowable to anyone in its entirety. Societal members experience that ultimate un-availability as an incorrigibly transcendent property of reality as such; though it is knowable in particulars, it never becomes available in totality. This is true for reasons identical to the reasons that deductive conformity to the collective conscience is impossible. No one "knows" it, just as no one "becomes" it. It would recede from consciousness, therefore, wither away into anomie, if it were not for rituals of reaffirmation and recognition.

I have already discussed one form of these celebrations as the recruit-ment of deviance from the "fringe" of society for direct comparison with the collective conscience, thereby restating, rearticulating, and reconstitut-ing its terms. Another form of anomie-prevention practices is the religious ritual of mechanical solidarity, described in detail by Durkheim (1947) throughout *The Elementary Forms of the Religious Life*. Here people are temporarily removed from mundane daily considerations, elevated to a context in which the ideal predominates—the ultimate (metaphysical) re-ality for the religious practitioner, which is the force of empirical society for sociology. Here people are reminded of the ideals that have been neces-sarily languishing in everyday practices and that would die out altogether, except for these transcendent rituals. People leave these settings feeling stronger, and they *are* stronger, says Durkheim, for having so directly encountered the power of the collective conscience (Durkheim 1947, p. 346; Giddens 1971, pp. 110–12). It is notable that such rituals involve symbols and material objects held sacred and kept physically separate from the mundane, the "profane" world, whose segregation from the sa-cred world is routinely enforced through these very rituals (Durkheim 1947, pp. 36–42). Sacred things symbolize transcendent reality and so-ciety, one and the same.

In order to sustain the causal role of subjectivity in his own derivation from Durkheim, Parsons worked expressly and diligently to defeat Durk-heim's society/reality equivalence (1968b, pp. 428–29). The equivalence, says Parsons, leads to "a complete ethical and religious relativism" (p. 429). He also reassigns ritual from its critical role in the maintenance of society as such to its more common and restricted association with re-ligious practices (p. 433), where it reinforces the social system by reassert-ing elements in Parsons's own theory: subjective respect for rules. More-over, the reason ritual is necessary, says Parsons, is for reasons analogous to the functions of institutional control: to prevent egoistic drifters from going too far afield, to reinstate voluntary conformity to norms and values. Finally, Parsons (p. 445) makes the now-familiar claim that Durkheim eventually ended up abandoning science and moving "clean over" to idealism. Thus Parsons can claim a derivation of his theory from Durkheim while rejecting the defining features of the late phase of Durkheim's work.[4]

EMPIRICAL STUDIES OF THE SOCIETY/REALITY EQUIVALENCE

Whatever the merits of Parsons's arguments, ethnomethodological studies have empirically resurrected the very Durkheimian themes he tried to suppress. In general, the principle can be stated this way: whatever activity it takes to sustain competent membership, whatever it takes to "conform" in social order, that activity is equivalent to the very practices that it takes to experience the world correctly (i.e. correctly within that social order). The empirical sui generis order for Durkheim and the reflexively self-organizing membership activity for ethnomethodology are identical to and exhaustive of reality-as-known-and-experienced. In other words, what members of an order bump up against and know as "reality" is available to sociology as the empirical activity that provides for the possibility of perceived social order. Thus experiencing social order, from within that order, is simultaneously to experience reality from within that same regulated reality.

In many ways the social construction of reality is no stranger to social science apart from ethnomethodology. Anthropologists well know that differing cultural memberships produce differing versions of the world and, consequently, the kinds of experiences that are possible in a society. W. I. Thomas's famous "definition of the situation" theorem designates an equivalence between defining something as real and its being "real in its consequences," thus eliminating the possibility of standing outside of culture to view a "really real" nonsocial reality. Even allegedly private or individualistic realities are subject to culture—for example, the very sense of one's self as an integrated, experiencing person, that is, the body/brain as the locus of consciousness and subjectivity. The very notion of the self as that which thinks, feels, and perceives is subject to culture for its possibility (Cooley 1902; Mead 1934; Vygotsky 1978). In social-psychological terms, the individual cannot see itself by turning inward and viewing itself directly but only by turning outward, "taking the role of the other" (Charon

1979, pp. 97–110), and experiencing itself as a cultural object whose nature is subject to social sanction and public display no less than any other thing-in-reality (Bem 1972). For example, Zborowski (1969) found that even the experience of the "internal" phenomenon of pain varies by ethnic affiliation among hospital patients (cf. Kotarba 1983a; Kopel and Arkowitz 1974). Similar conclusions derive from experimental and ethnographic studies of how other kinds of physiological arousal are experienced (Becker 1953; Schachter and Singer 1962).

At a more general level, the social construction of reality has been taken up by such diverse perspectives as symbolic interactionism (Blumer 1969; Hewitt 1976; Manis and Meltzer 1967; Rose 1962; Shibutani 1961), labeling theory (Becker 1963), existential and phenomenological sociology (Douglas and Johnson 1977; Psathas 1973), dramaturgical sociology (Goffman 1959, 1961, 1967, 1974; Brisset and Edgley 1975;), plus a variety of specialized expressions, including Berger and Luckmann's (1967) sociology of knowledge and Lyman and Scott's (1970) sociology of the absurd. The special offering ethnomethodology brings to all this is to demonstrate how reality and experience are *actively regulated* (Mehan and Wood 1975). In short, the activities that members know as standard society are the same empirical activities they know as objective reality, even as members are both constrained by and participating in those very activities.

Garfinkel's work is most illuminating in this area. An excellent example is his study of how members of the Los Angeles Suicide Prevention Center (SPC) investigated cases of death to determine "what really happened"—that is, how deaths actually took place, deaths whose candidate causes included suicide, murder, accident, and natural causes (Garfinkel 1967, pp. 11–18). Here the practices used to generate facts about cases, relevant evidence, and so forth, and eventually conclusions about "what really happened" as a historical event in reality were identical with the very practices that displayed competent SPC membership, that is, "conformity" with good investigative work. As Garfinkel (pp. 13–14) expresses the equivalence:

Members were required in their occupational capacities to formulate accounts of how a death *really*-for-all-practical-purposes-happened. "Really" made unavoidable reference to daily, ordinary, occupational workings.

The occupational capacities Garfinkel alludes to in this passage included access to "what everybody knows" about the world (e.g. how people die, what kinds of events lead to what kinds of appearances), inseparable from "what everybody knows" about the SPC and competent SPC membership. Knowledge of the latter included matters that a naturalistic philosopher might say have nothing to do with reality or actual mode of death: how a decision might be handled by relevant others, what an investigator's investigating procedures might be later decided to have consisted of, how a decision might need to include nonforeclosure on the possibility of later revision in light of new evidence, how all of this ties in with careers and professional advancement, the politics of the coroner's office, and so on. But in point of fact, these two "knowledges" collapse into each other; moreover, they collapse into the *methods* of producing a socially adequate account. While there is far more to Garfinkel's study than this, the point here is that there is no "what really happened" that stands outside of whatever SPC members arrive at as "what really happened" in the exercise of their professional duties. Mutual constraint exercised on each other contributes to the impression that "what really happened" stands outside of anyone's doing, just as it contributes to the impression of a corpus of investigative procedures that investigators merely "conform" to, but the construction of the event is an accomplishment of this very regulating activity. Nothing counts as the reality that was never arrived at except insofar as it too is an entity hypothesized in these investigative procedures as a display of competent membership, for example to cover oneself in advance of possible revision, reinterpretation, or new evidence.

According to Durkheim, reality itself, not just pieces of it, are embodiments of society. This is most evident in mechanical solidarity, where society and reality are one, but while the unity of world vision appears to break down in advancing organic solidarity, this unity is actually receding to the background, where it takes expression as axioms, assumptions, and idealizations that provide for the possibility of diversified knowledge and individualized experience (see Hilbert 1986). These are the foundational assumptions of moral individualism and rationality that Durkheim astutely identifies as the unifying bonds that underlie an increasingly complex and differentiated organic society, functionally identical to the unity of mechanical solidarity.

In a fascinating and ground-breaking book, Pollner (1987) articulates these foundational assumptions, the most general of which is the positing of "reality" as an entity in the first place. Reality, in a manner consistent with a Durkheimian transcendence displayed by the collective conscience, is presumed by believers to be massive and huge, objectively determinate, inconceivably complex, presently unknown in its entirety, discoverable through methods of rational inquiry, ideally knowable in its entirety in some hypothesized and hypothetical future, having as its features exactly the features that it has independent of anybody's say so or ideas about it, coherent and internally consistent, containing no contradictions or even any apparent contradictions that could not ultimately be reconciled through further inquiry, and above all factual (pp. 26–47). These are the assumptions hardly anyone ever mentions, so it sounds peculiar to speak of them as "assumptions." Nevertheless Pollner found their use as a continual, ongoing, visible and indispensable feature of people in a wide variety of settings, with special attention to a traffic court.

Consistent with my discussions of "conformity" (see chapter 3), these idealizations do not prescribe their use or dictate to anyone what must be found as facts about reality. As with idealized notions of competent police work, idealized notions of reality as Great Object do not dictate to traffic court judges what specifically has to be the "what really happened" of a case. Nevertheless judges are able to arrive at "what really happened," they are able to document events, in ways that are made out to accord with these same idealizations. Moreover, anything that would contradict these idealizations is rejected out of hand, or not even considered—for example the possibility, in light of conflicting testimony or evidence, that a defendant was driving at two speeds at the same time.

In the above sense, then, this Reality Thesis is like an untested dogma that is used and reproduced in artful, strictly unpredictable ways. The methods of its use are indistinguishable from those used to sustain what from the outside looks like superstitious belief, for example the truth-finding practices of the Azande relative to their oracle (Pollner 1987, pp. 53–58; see chapter 7). The methods are artful in the sense that they cannot be deductively derived from the thesis, nor can they be used at random or arbitrarily. Once again, we find *constraint* upon reality construction, not a prescriptive or deductive constraint, but rather a constraint found in the very activity of reality construction itself. It is a constraint that setting members exercise on each other, know about, and count on. Judges can be reversed or disbarred for constructing outrageous events, for example; yet they will not find the outcome of their decision making prepared for them in the syntax or logical structure of the Reality Thesis or in their legal training. They will not "find" their event at the end of a cultural railroad track that they are adept at staying on.

Here, then, the factual status of events in reality, as they truly and actually happened, as investigated, discovered, and known, as well as the evolving revelation of reality as Great Object, is congruent with whatever it is that judges do that makes them competent judges. That is, the methods of reality investigation are the methods of competent judging. "Conformity" in this sense is simultaneously reality recognition and discovery. The "out there" status of this accomplishment, expressed either as objective reality or as conformity with competent recognition and discovery, is sustained by the constraint anyone knows prevents one from doing any of this at random. As with SPC investigation, this may include a "more might be known" clause that would allow the possibility of a future reopening of the case and reinvestigation in light of new evidence—*if* the judge can demonstrate that such a reopening would not find fault with the conclusion drawn in the case as evolved up to the present time. In that sense, reality is always and irremediably a reality for all practical purposes. But when all that members do to construct reality—which is simultaneously what they do to sustain membership and stable social order—is taken under the sociologist's umbrella, nothing counts as the reality "beyond" that activity or the "what really happened" that stands outside it.

As I stated, Durkheim's equivalence of society and reality extends to the reality of the natural sciences (Durkheim 1947, pp. 13–29). In an interesting article, Garfinkel, Lynch, and Livingston (1981) demonstrate precisely this principle. Their research material included transcripts of taped conversation between astronomers discovering a pulsar at Steward Observatory, January 16, 1969. From the astronomers' point of view, as expressed in their own astronomical article, the pulsar had properties consistent with the Reality Thesis discussed above: it existed prior to its discovery, its features are the cause of whatever is correctly seen or said about it, and its existence, features, and discovery are "anonymous" to the actual discoverers in that (1) discoverers' idiosyncratic work is demonstrably irrelevant to their discovery, and (2) the discovery resulted from adhering to "disembodied proper procedures" (cf. formal norms), such that anyone following these procedures under these exact circumstances would necessarily make exactly the same discovery (Garfinkel, Lynch, and Livingston 1981, pp. 138–39).

Yet analysis of the transcripts reveals quite a different phenomenon. They reveal the ad hoc quality of the work, the artful dimension not reported in the astronomical article, and simultaneously the pulsar as an artfully constructed cultural object. Garfinkel, drawing upon an analogy with the potter's wheel and the potter's object, "construed the [Independent Galilean Pulsar] as a 'cultural object' and in that status incorporated it into [the astronomers'] night's work as a feature of their work's 'natural accountability,' " resulting in an empirical "*intertwining* of worldly objects and embodied practices" (Garfinkel, Lynch, and Livingston 1981, p. 137). That is, the *real time* quality of these practices, and the sociologists' concern with "the pulsar for the way it is *in hand* at all times in the inquiry" (p. 137), revealed the sui generis quality of astronomers' work as it progressed: what they did determined what they had done, in a prospective/retrospective fashion, concluding with the pulsar as well as the work of discovery as having conformed to formal scientific recipes—the pulsar as an independent object fitting into and consistent with an independent scientifically objective universe. The method, in short, was invariably situated, as was the pulsar, any evidence of it, or anything that would later be construed to have been evidence of it. Here again is the congruence of reality and "conformity" or competence. As Garfinkel, Lynch, and Livingston put it:

> It is astonishingly clear in that tape that the possibility of [the astronomers'] discovery and achievements inhabits their work from its outset. But it does so as a situationally conditioned presence and *not* as the pulsar "out there." The possibility of their discovery and achievement is *observable to them* and is a discussable for them in this: *their night's work poses for them their tasks of its own astronomical accountability. It does so as the lived presence of "first time through" in the unfolding vicissitudes of their Runs.* In its own historicity the night's work poses for [the astronomers] their tasks of their work's astronomical observability-and-discourseability. The optical pulsar as a technical phenomenon of astronomy is not different than those tasks. (p. 140)

Or again:

> It is the locally produced and locally recognized orderliness of [the astronomers'] embodied practices as of which the exhibitable objectivity and the observable analyzability and intelligibility of the phe-

nomenon's technical, identifying details consists—definitely, exactly, only and entirely. (p. 141)

One could not ask ethnomethodology for a stronger statement about
the equivalence of social practices and objective reality. Moreover, their
equivalence in idealized expression—society as stable behavior "out there"
and reality as Great Object "out there"—dovetails with Durkheim's so-
ciety/reality equivalence. The impression of either and both of these is
sustained by the constraint people exercise on each other and that everyone knows about, experiences, and counts on. This point is all the more
forceful when we recall the reflexivity inherent in this work. Thus the sui
generis order, which is available as empirical social practices for sociology,
is experienced from within that order both as structured social order and as
objective reality. This also contributes to a deeper understanding of Durkheim's claim that all systems of scientific thought, including scientific
cosmologies and ontologies, are socially derived. Indeed, the pulsar study
cited above is part of an evolving sociology of science literature that treats
the objective facts of the universe in just this way, including mathematical
facts (see Gilbert and Mulkay 1984; Livingston 1986; Lynch 1982, 1985;
cf. Mehan and Wood 1975).

When Parsons (1968b, p. 445) criticized Durkheim for going "clean
over" to idealism, he was complaining especially about the fact that Durkheim eventually draws an equivalence between society and *ideas*. In light
of what has just been discussed, it is not at all hard to understand why
Durkheim would draw this final equivalence. For ideas are, inevitably,
ideas about something, which, given the overarching meaning of reality,
means that ideas are about reality or pieces of it. But precisely in the
manner in which society regulates reality, it provides the categories and
terms for experiencing reality. It is these categories and their organized use
that is empirical about the social regulation of reality for sociology, simultaneously providing, representing, or *being* reality for societal members.
Moreover, there is no reality experienceable independent of these social
terms. There are no criteria for correct or incorrect experience, no *constraint* exercised on experience, independent of the regulation of these
terms and categories. They are the *medium* of ideas, and their regulation
(constraint) is the source of ideas about an independent, incorrigible objective reality. This seems reasonable and consistent with Durkheim's initial
methodological policy: to study social things and account for their working

on their own level, in terms of other social things, rather than resort to psychological, biological, or physical levels as sources of explanation (cf. Giddens 1971, pp. 105–7).

IMPLICATIONS

Parsons could not have viewed Durkheim's society/reality equivalence as having relativist implications without "going native" in the society under investigation, as discussed above. For example, despite Durkheim's claim that natural sciences are social and part of the cultural ethos of advanced organic solidarity, Parsons (1968b, p. 429) asks, "Why should religious ideas take symbolic form in a way in which scientific ideas do not?"[5] The question is clearly framed from *within* the scientific ethos that Durkheim says is social. Similarly, Parsons (p. 429) says that if society and reality were equivalent, then sociology should be able to document the empirical accuracy of religious ideas directly. Again, this assertion is framed as though sociologists and societal members are oriented to the same subjectively accepted universe of facts and ideas.

Durkheim did not directly address relativistic implications in his sociology, but it is apparent that when he wrote of society and its god as one (Durkheim 1947, p. 206), he was not making a theological statement, much less an aboriginal religious claim whose content could be evaluated or interpreted in aboriginal terms. Likewise, where the natural sciences became socially derived (pp. 13–20), Durkheim was not writing a corrective that physicists or chemists should be able to accept or reject on their own disciplinary terms. Durkheim was not, then, writing either as a religious practitioner or as a natural scientist. He was writing from the unique perspective of sociology, which offers that *any* experienced reality, whatever the content, is social and amenable to empirical investigation as social facts.

Put differently, to investigate the *accuracy* of ideas, religious or otherwise, is to investigate reality from within, as taken for granted and experienced by societal members. Durkheim's sociology need not take such an evaluative stance. It would seem more appropriate, in other words, to disregard questions regarding the truth or falsity of specific realities taken on their own terms. This in fact is an indispensable move for capturing a glimpse of reality as social facts.

More generally, when Durkheim says that knowledge is impossible independent of social categories, this should not be read as a philosophical statement about the world for natural scientists to somehow suffer, the way, for example, a philosopher's argument against a "referential theory of truth" might seem to undermine the foundations of science. Durkheim's comments do not correct or contradict natural scientists' visions of the world but make a statement about a different level of phenomena entirely. This in fact is a statement exclusively about the social: *nothing counts* as knowledge about reality independent of social regulation; there is *nothing to know*—better, nothing to *know with*. When Durkheim says that categories are not derivable from the physical universe, this is an extension of that insight; it indicates that collective representations are the media of knowledge and reality-experience and in that sense constitutive of it. This is analogous to pointing out that the sacred energy of the aboriginal totem cannot be derived directly from the plant or animal it represents (Durkheim 1947, pp. 205–6). Nothing counts as the presocial reality that gets coded and put into social categories.

Thus there is a certain Durkheimian distinction between society/reality as experienced from within by the membership and as observable from without by sociologists. By not making this distinction, Parsons (1968b, p. 442) sees Durkheim's distancing from the natural sciences as a retreat from science per se in favor of an idealist conception of the very subject matter natural scientists investigate. To illustrate, any attempt to prove or disprove religious claims through scientific investigations of religious reality would not be Durkheim's social science but a science "from within" society/reality, more like the activities of natural scientists or scientific theologians. Yet Parsons (p. 429) points to the failure of sociology to document religious truth as evidence that religious ideas are not social facts as Durkheim says they are—in saying they are, Durkheim is abandoning empirical science, according to Parsons.

Ethnomethodology recovers this Durkheimian distinction between society/reality as experienced from within and as observable from without, albeit in more explicit form. Most generally, early ethnomethodologists criticized "traditional sociology" for being one more example of that which it set out to study and for thereby missing the phenomenon of interest (see Zimmerman and Pollner 1979; Zimmerman and Wieder 1970). Instead of "going native" in this manner, ethnomethodologists recommended suspending belief in the very existence of society as an orderly phenomenon and examining instead the artful practices whereby people make order appear familiar and obvious on an ongoing basis. This transformation in topic, from society as factually ordered to ethnomethods as topics in their own right, is what characterizes ethnomethodology as a social science.

Ethnomethodologists have been most explicit in their topical transformation in relation to social order (see chapter 6), especially, as we have seen, when it comes to folklore that society is rule-governed. However, in light of the society/reality equivalence, we would expect this analytic bracketing to apply simultaneously to members' reality in general, whatever its content. We have seen this principle in operation in the studies described above. For example, Garfinkel and his colleagues (1981) were not the least bit interested in features of the pulsar, and in fact their study in no way assumes, requires, or depends upon the pulsar's very existence. No more do they deny its existence; the sociology they employ is external to natural astronomical discourse and independent of it. Ethnomethodology is indifferent to whatever ontology astronomical discourse requires, documents, proves, or disproves. Likewise, in investigating the SPC, Garfinkel (1967, pp. 11–18) was utterly indifferent to how anybody died (or whether anybody died), focusing exclusively on investigators' methods of producing an adequate what-really-happened for any given case. Indeed, Pollner (1987) was indifferent to the very existence of reality per se in his study of the methods of its production. This same topical transformation and methodological stance vis-à-vis members' topics and members' world inhabits ethnomethodological studies generally.

Notice that without this topical transformation, and looking at reality from within the moral universe members take for granted, society appears to be "just another thing," one *piece* of general reality, one of many contributing causes to human behavior, an entity that exists in the objective world *in addition to* such things as genetics, natural environment, and so on. This is the same objective world presumed to contain pulsars. Parsons apparently adopted this world as a methodological premise of his sociology. There is a kind of collusion between sociologists and natural scientists implicated in this policy. By necessity, Parsonian sociology views the natural world *from within* the society, designating yet another aspect of it, society-qua-structured-entity. Functionalists see the structured entity, therefore, from within the society, indicative of a more general collusion between sociology and societal members. Functionalists describe a society of institutions, classes, roles, stable rules, organizations and bureaucracies, races, genders, and so on much the same way as societal members do.[6]

Unwittingly, perhaps, social constructionists have pursued Durkheimian insight by demonstrating that functionalism's structural entity is no more independent of human activity than any other aspect of reality (cf. Collins 1985, p. 125), that structures like races, organizations, classes, genders, roles, and social types are not empirically there for sociology except, once again, as embodied practices (Banton and Harwood 1975; Miles 1982; Bittner 1965; Garfinkel 1967, pp. 116–85; Hilbert 1981, 1987; Zimmerman and Pollner 1970). No one ever "sees" any of these structures, no one ever "sees" the society, any more than anyone ever "sees" total reality. But members continually document society's structured status for themselves and for each other, for example in formal documents, data, and research findings that were in turn created by people working in concrete settings (Cicourel 1964, 1968; Cicourel and Kitsuse 1963; Smith 1974). When viewed from the outside, these structured entities are managed accomplishments no less than the pulsar. Yet a dominant trend in American functionalism has been to take the structured entity for granted anyway. Again this can be understood as functionalists' having "gone native" or as producing refined versions of what members themselves say about their social world, rendering sociology of this sort a folk science or a science from within the order that it is allegedly studying (Zimmerman and Pollner 1970).

A major consequence for functionalist understanding is that the Durkheimian equivalence of reality and society appears to make members' reality in general equal to the structured society that functionalists describe and take for granted as part of that reality, an absurdity apparently derived from Durkheim. No wonder Parsons rejected the equivalence. And no wonder functionalist versions of Durkheim divide his work into two periods, generally focusing on the normative aspect and either disregarding or making only passing reference to the alleged idealism. And it is in part the success of such renderings in academic circles (but see Giddens 1971, pp. 105–7; Pope 1973; Warner 1978) that would allow or even require many social constructionists to leave Durkheim entirely and to strike new ground inspired by more recent developments in philosophy. Thus does ethnomethodology seem radical when it might otherwise be seen as sociological to the very heart of the discipline's origins.

5

ANOMIE

In previous chapters I have shown how sui generis society is simultaneously objective reality regulated by and within itself by its membership. This is to say that whatever members do to sustain a sense of stable society is also the very activity that sustains the impression of an inherently stable and objective reality. These are social facts for Durkheim, and they are accomplishments of and coterminous with members' artful practices for ethnomethodology. An additional implication I have barely touched on so far takes center stage in this chapter: wherever artful practices fail or promise to fail to reproduce membership and social order, there also is the imminent collapse of objective reality and subjective experience.

The failures to which I refer are empirically captured in some of Garfinkel's "breaching experiments." More often his studies reveal the practices necessary to prevent such failures. In describing both the failures and their routine prevention, these ethnomethodological investigations also pick up essentials of Durkheim's anomie theory. Anomie theory was largely dropped by Parsons, but it was picked up again and appropriated by one of Parsons's most prominent colleagues, Robert K. Merton, to accommodate functionalist theorizing (see Hilbert 1989). Because of the resultant common conception of anomie as "normlessness" or as somehow causing deviance, I shall be contrasting Merton's anomie theory with Durkheim's as a way of highlighting those aspects of Durkheim's theory that went comparatively underground. Once again those aspects of Durkheim's theory that were driven out by functionalist theorizing are the very ones that ethnomethodological studies resurrect.

DURKHEIM'S ANOMIE THEORY

In essence Durkheim's anomie theory designates situations in which society's ability to regulate is reduced to a state sufficient to be called pathological. This includes abrupt social changes and rapid evolutionary changes that outstrip the development of regulative morality (Durkheim 1951). The pathological status of anomie is reflected in individual consciousness as a state of anxiety, a sense of moral groundlessness, with dire consequences that in extreme cases can lead to suicide (pp. 241–76). Anomie's most essential referent, then, is a situation that runs roughly opposite to that of a healthy social organism. Its limit, or total anomie, would be precisely the absence of any sort of society whatsoever: a dead social organism, to push the bio-analogy a bit. This is consistent with Durkheim's society/morality equivalence. Morality does not simply cause society, as though without morality only a chaotic society would remain. Society *is* moral.

Interpreters of Durkheim will inevitably find anomie as the opposite of their versions of Durkheimian morality, for whatever routinely happens in a healthy society is not happening, or not happening well, in times of anomie. For functionalists who saw Durkheim's collective conscience as a body of norms, anomie became, predictably, "normlessness." Accordingly, Merton claimed to have drawn upon Durkheim's anomie theory in his theory of normlessness (Merton 1968, p. 189; cf. Clinard 1964, p. 7; Coser 1971, pp. 132–33). Merton saw normlessness not as a literal absence of norms but as a circumstance in which norms cannot work, specifically a structural breakdown between two functionalist systems—norms and values. As I indicated in chapter 1, norms and values derive from the bedrock of Parsons's action theory as governing the means and ends of action respectively. For actors, a structural breakdown between norms and values makes conformity impossible and yields several available logical action alternatives in terms of the acceptance or rejection of means and ends (innovation, retreatism, ritualism), which in turn manifest themselves as conventionally recognized forms of deviance, such as crime, mental illness, drug use, and so on (see chapter 9 for an extended discussion of Merton's anomie theory).

Thus for Merton anomie is a normative-structural breakdown that causes behavioral deviance. This impression, as well as the impression of a Durkheim-Merton continuity, is sometimes maintained in the area of deviance theory, where the conventional wisdom is that Merton expanded Durkheim's anomie theory from an explanation of one kind of deviance (suicide) to account for a wide variety of deviant behavior (Cohen 1968, p. 148; Coser 1971, p. 133; Nisbet 1974, p. 209; Thompson 1982, pp. 120–21). More cautious renditions would have it that Merton and Durkheim offer differing analyses of the same general phenomenon, one having something to do with the breakdown of society.

Ironically, however, Durkheim's anomie theory can best be apprehended by contrasting it with Merton's rather than looking for continuity. If there is a similarity to be found between these two theorists, it is in their commitment to viewing deviance as outcomes and consequences of prevailing social regulation, as opposed to deriving from peculiar or individualistic traits of offenders. Durkheim was clear that deviance—or, in his term, crime—is a *normal* phenomenon arising from the way in which society self-regulates: "The principle of rebellion is the same as that of conformity" (Durkheim 1953, p. 65). Likewise for Merton: his announced topic in "Social Structure and Anomie" was the sense in which social structures exert "definite pressure" on certain people "to engage in nonconforming rather than conforming behavior" (Merton 1968, p. 186).

But here the similarity ends. For Durkheim, crime is not only normal but healthy (Durkheim 1938, pp. 70–75), for it is a primary means the sui generis society has for protecting itself against the withering away of the collective conscience, that is, its own withering away. As we have seen, no concrete individuals *are* the collective conscience or personify it or embody it in any way; it transcends all of society's members. Thus its unavailability to societal members in direct experience would reduce its availability to consciousness. This does not happen because of the recognition and punishment of whatever the "outermost" extreme behavior happens to be (pp. 67–70). Crime cannot therefore be eliminated, since whatever behavior is eliminated, something would still be the "outermost" extreme. But more important, it is through the ritualized recruitment of criminal behavior from the fringe that the collective conscience is recognized, reaffirmed, and celebrated (Durkheim 1933, pp. 85–103). These celebrations of morality are functionally equivalent to the transcendent ritualistic phase of aboriginal life (Durkheim 1947).

Merton tends more or less toward silence on the matter of crime's desirability or its status as healthy and necessary for the Parsonian normative order. Even its inevitability is in doubt. The functionalist system is found to be functioning at less than full efficiency (Merton 1968, p. 434), but this seems to be more a factual claim than a theoretical necessity. Moreover, Merton makes no direct suggestion that without "normlessness" and the deviance it causes, society would face an even worse crisis. The main crisis for Merton is the very breakdown of normative order (anomie itself) and the consequent deviance and social problems (see Merton and Nisbet 1971). While for Merton, given that breakdown, deviance is normal, he does not say that it *must be* that way or that a smoothly functioning system with normative ends meeting cultural goals for everybody concerned is either a theoretical impossibility or a precipitant of even worse trouble—that is, worse trouble than deviance.

When Durkheim writes of anomie, he is clearly indicating a crisis of far greater magnitude and scope than mere deviance. When he says that crime is normal, part of what he means is that it is a hedge against this crisis (Durkheim 1933, pp. 85–103). This crisis, moreover, is not at all normal or healthy; anomie is pathological (p. 353). Anomie is a tendency toward social death. In its extreme it indicates the death of society, which is to say no society whatever, not even a disorganized one. Anomie is the dropping away of exterior and constraining moral regulation. Within its terms, which is to say no terms, compliance and deviance are equally impossible precisely because there is nothing to comply with or rebel against, no standards, no social currents judging, and no one being judged. It is, in its logically pure form, a state of no reality, a nonprovision of categories for experiencing the objectivity of perception and experience. Anomie is the absence of all that society provides in the way of reality and objectivity; it is a nonstate. This is neither normal nor healthy, and movement in its direction results in a statistical increase in suicide.

Anomic suicide, in fact, becomes the physical manifestation of psychic death reflecting the death of society, culture, and moral reality. It cannot therefore be deviance that Durkheim was trying to explain in his analysis of anomic suicide (see Hilbert 1986, 1989). Anomic suicide neither anticipates an "expanded" Mertonian anomie theory nor displays the same Durkheimian features reserved for crime. Though anomic suicide can be seen as a natural consequence of anomie, and in that sense normal, it is neither inevitable nor healthy. It is not one more hedge against anomie; it is a consequence of anomie—one might even say, *the* behavioral consequence. It has no functional role in maintaining the integrity of the social organism; it is in fact caused by the withdrawal of this integrity. Here is precisely the pain and anguish that the recruitment of deviance functions to protect people from.

When Durkheim speaks of crime as preventing anomie, he is not saying, strictly, that crime itself prevents anomie, that not enough crime would cause anomie, or that anomie is prevented by any specific activity designated as crime. Specifically it is the *recruitment* of crime—the ritual of labeling and punishing it—that works against anomie. Similarly the severity of crime is not inherent in the act itself or in its frequency, but rather it is indexed by the seriousness with which the judgment is undertaken and the severity of the sanction. So it is ritual social practices that prevent anomie, and they can be expected to generate crime as needed with whatever severity required.

The distinction between anomic suicide and deviance is apparent by contrasting Durkheim's treatment of the former with his treatment of egoistic and altruistic suicide. Both of these latter two are expressed as manifestations of the content of collectively enforced morality, compatible with Durkheim's treatment of crime. They have the character of arising from social conditions within an otherwise healthy (nonanomic) social organism, one displaying the twin features of exteriority and constraint. Both egoistic and altruistic suicide are products of social control (cf. Giddens 1971, p. 85). With egoistic suicide, the collectively enforced morality is one of heavy moral individualism (Durkheim 1951, p. 360—"Our very egoism is in large part a product of society"), so much so that individuals in trouble have no choice but to rely upon their own efforts, whether up to the task or not. Failures in handling difficulty, together with heavy proscriptions against seeking help, may lead to suicide (pp. 152–216). In the case of altruistic suicide, the collectively enforced morality is one of extreme moral collectivism, wherein there is little sense of individuation, and consequently the individual's personal survival is secondary to the survival of the group, hence suicide when the occasion warrants it (pp. 217–40). Neither of these types of suicide is more individualistic or group oriented than the other. Each has its origins in a collective conscience. Stated differently, the distinction between the two is not that of underregulation versus over-regulation but rests instead upon the kind of collectively enforced morality that prevails.

Anomic suicide, once again, happens when moral philosophy per se is on the wane. Society, morality, reality, and all of the furniture of Durkheim's sociology are receding from the individual. There are no standards and therefore no place to stand, nothing to conform to. Likewise there can be no rebellion and no deviance. The only response is to respond in kind: individual death.

The distinction between anomic suicide and the other two kinds is useful for understanding anomie and the role of ritual practices in its prevention. There have been some tendencies to confuse anomic and egoistic suicide (e.g. Johnson 1965) for the simple reason that they occur together in real life, an empirical fact which Durkheim notes at various points in *Suicide* (see e.g. Durkheim 1951, pp. 323, 382; also Pope 1973, pp. 402–5). It stands to reason that rapid social evolution, which leaves anomie in its wake, would result in egoistic as well as anomic suicide and that the two would be difficult to distinguish in actual cases, particularly since the transition from mechanical to organic solidarity is an evolution toward a morality of increasingly radical individualism. But the empirical melding of the two does not make them the same thing (Durkheim 1951, p. 258). The distinction between egoism as a dysfunctionally extreme moral individualism and anomie as an absence of morality is a theoretical distinction. In that regard the two fill distinctive analytic spaces within Durkheim's overall work (see Giddens 1971, pp. 84–85).

In light of this distinction, there is no conceivable way that anomic suicide could be anything like Merton's categories of deviance. The best we could hope for is a similarity between Merton's categories and Durkheim's crime (including egoistic and altruistic suicide). Both, for example, arise from specific forms of social regulation that produce individual problems that individuals by necessity solve in socially disapproved ways. Yet even this similarity is misleading, not only because Merton calls the dysfunctional regulation "anomie" but because he makes no provisions for the necessity of deviance. Having used up "anomie" in the labeling of the dysfunctional regulation, he is left with nothing that deviance could function to prevent. Similarly missing from his formulation is Durkheim's astute observation that whatever specific behavior is abolished, something would still be at the "fringe" and would therefore be recognized and punished as crime; something would still function as a hedge against anomie.

Strictly speaking, Merton does not need this emphasis on "fringe," since he does not address anomie as a potential crisis beyond the problem of deviance. Yet there is another difference embedded in this missing observation. Merton knows beforehand what deviance is, or what constitutes nonconformity: drug addiction, mental illness, that type of thing. Here his ideas are consistent with Parsons's model of social conformity discussed in chapter 3. Durkheim, by contrast, does not declare that certain specific acts and not others will inevitably be crime. Crime is a matter of behavior recruited by society from the "fringe," hauled to the center for trial and punishment in juxtaposition with the collective conscience as an ideal moral standard. This ceremony carries the message throughout the society that this collective morality is alive, that it exists, even though literally no one fulfills its mandates completely. Thus while Durkheim maintains that crime is socially disapproved behavior, what counts as a member of that category depends on what kind of behavior prevails. What counts as crime would not do so if other more extreme behavior were more common than it is. In short, the specifics of what crime is in a given society and era are matters of what that society hauls into court. Merton, again, sees deviance as a matter of nonconformity with functionalist norms. In that sense, while its cause may perplex sociologists, its very identity is nonproblematic for objective observers. In a manner consistent with Parsons's factual order, Merton sees both patterned behavior and exceptions to these patterns as given in the world to disinterested scientists; the categories of conformity and nonconformity are clear and pretheoretical: in the very way he sees objective social order, he also sees deviance, and he therefore sets out to explain this deviance.

But anomie for Durkheim is a crisis above and beyond deviance, and it cannot cause deviance. Deviance is instead necessary for the prevention of anomie and an integral part of moral life. Indeed consideration of Durkheim's anomie theory in light of all he has to say about society, morality, reality, and subjectivity is quite revealing concerning anomic crisis, for it suggests that utilitarian theories of behavior placed utilitarian actors in a position far more tenuous than even Hobbes or Parsons imagined. For Parsons, the ends of action are random for utilitarian actors, thus setting up the problem of order. But if Durkheim is right, not only ends would be random but also means (cf. Giddens 1971, pp. 91–92), as well as ideas, subjective experience, objective reality, and thought. All of this would have to be "random" in the sense of constraint-free. There would be no right or wrong, correct or incorrect, rational or irrational ways of doing any of these things; thus doing any of them would be impossible. There would be no criteria of correctness, no way to determine patterned versus nonpatterned, conformity versus deviance, order versus chaos; none of these would be possible. In short, individuals would not be social, would not be human in the sense of being capable of doing what humans do, and could not be "rational" even in the limited utilitarian sense, since there would be nothing about the natural environment to impress actors with subjective content. This then is "pure anomie." Certainly there would be no deviance in such a world.

ETHNOMETHODOLOGY AND ANOMIE

A number of ethnomethodological principles and findings discussed so far militate against a functionalist rendering of Durkheim's anomie theory. Focus on empirical material, for example, will not allow the positing of an unseen normative structure whose breakdown causes a corresponding behavioral breakdown. Worse, indexicality and reflexivity deny us clear categories of conforming and deviant behavior necessary for recognizing behavioral disorder in the first place. Finally, lack of empirical evidence that rules are necessary for order production suggests that "normlessness" can be a natural condition even among people for whom social order is a fact of life, as in the instance of the police in Bittner's (1967) study.

Notice that none of this is a major problem for Durkheim, who did not necessarily equate morality with rules and who saw deviance as a ritually generated activity in the prevention of anomie. If we pursue this line ethnomethodologically, if we pursue anomie with a commitment to empiricism and in light of reflexive sui generis order, we should recover the very analytic spaces for anomie contained in Durkheim's theory. We should find anomie as distinguishable from deviance, not as a cause of it, but as something that deviance recruitment serves to contain or prevent.

Extending the thesis, if we allow that constraint is embedded in the activity that it constrains, that the activity is empirical and exterior to every social actor, and that the activity is what constitutes both social order and objective reality, then anomie should reemerge as trouble within those artful practices. It should reemerge as trouble exterior to individuals that nevertheless is trouble *for* individuals, robbing them of their ability to construct order and reality and of their subjective experience of either. Individuals would be, in anomic circumstance, strictly reality-less. This should, moreover, include the hypothesized result: anomic anxiety, or anomia.

But of what could such trouble consist? If indexicality forecloses on "core meanings" within the collective conscience, and if conformity is a matter of artfully reproducing cultural resources as having intended "all along" their application in specific cases, then what could possibly prevent anyone from using such resources?

Notice that this is not to ask why a resource cannot be applied in a specific way, or more generally why it can be applied only in certain ways and not others, for such is the very nature of social constraint. I am not simply asking, "Why won't any account do?" for answers to this question have already been found as observable in social practices in their course: not just *any* account will do because members will not allow it; not just *any* application of a word, concept, rule, assumption, folk theory, idealization, or cultural resource counts as a correct application or as a correct documentation of "underlying intent" because members will not allow just any application to count as correct. These matters are not decided in advance or contained in the logical structure of cultural resources but instead are created in the course of members' use of such resources. This is the constraint any individual bumps up against in the use of culture, thereby producing the impression that culture provided proper recipes in advance of their application. But the question of anomie pushes the equivocalness of cultural resources to new frontiers, for here the question becomes, How is it possible that cultural resources might not be useful for any purpose at all; that is, how might it be that they could not be used either correctly or incorrectly?

To clarify this issue, it helps to consider how one might learn to apply a newly encountered word with which one is completely unfamiliar. Asked, for example, to check outside to see if there are any *quarms* today, one would find the task essentially impossible without a definition of the word. Note that a definition would itself have to be composed of familiar terms in order to be useful; in that regard the definition could stand as loose instructions for the use of "quarm." But if one were told, " 'Quarm' *has* no definition," one would be unable to complete the assignment, for such would be tantamount to saying that "quarm" has no use. Notably, though, equal results obtain if one were told, "Quarm has any definition you choose; you don't even have to keep the same definition from one application to the next; you have total freedom." That is, "quarm" means anything. Under these circumstances, one would be equally incapable of fulfilling the task. In either case, the impossibility derives from the absence of enforced criteria for correctly versus incorrectly completing the task. *Any* use (or any account will do) fairs no better than *no* use (or no account will do). Neither provides constraint upon artful practices necessary for practical work. Thus in the context of this hypothetical, "quarm" is truly anomic, especially when entangled with a perceived mandate to go out and *use* it, which must mean to *use it correctly*.

Thus it is an indelible feature of sui generis moral order that it sustains the constraint of competent membership and competent reality production by allowing the usefulness of equivocal resources congruent with the managed disallowal of just any application counting as competent. The line between correct and incorrect use will not be derived from the analytic structure of the resources, more generally the collective conscience, but is observable in members' regulating activity. In this way, no one is "free" to trade on ambiguity for just any purpose whatsoever, nor can anyone complain that, barring that, a resource is utterly useless because of its ambiguity.

Theoretically, then, members' task of having to sustain this certain-use-and-not-others premise is identical to the way Durkheim says they maintain the collective conscience in the absence of any clear example of its fulfillment: ritualized recognition of extreme cases as falling outside proper parameters such that the impression of parameters, as well as "core meaning," can be maintained. Any conversation, for example, could be a locus of such ritual, especially where matters of clarification, repetition, correction, definition, and so on are called for. Or in the case of rules, wherever there is a call for justification in terms of "underlying intent," wherever clarification is sought, and especially wherever violations are determined to have taken place, here also is a Durkheimian event, a ritualized reproduction and reclarification of the transcendent premise, that of core meaning and correct use as conformity with that core meaning.[1]

EMPIRICAL STUDIES OF ANOMIE-PREVENTION PRACTICES

Many of Garfinkel's "breaching" experiments are interventions in social life to make trouble that members by necessity have to repair: order is "destroyed," in a sense, by the experimenter so that one can see what members will specifically do to restore order. Such restoration constitutes a ritualistic reproduction of order. Anomie would be either nonengagement of these methods or their failure.

In the vast majority of Garfinkel's interventions, subjects were able to restore order quickly. Where certain patterns were disrupted, alternative patterns were sketched by drawing upon alternative repertoires of cultural resources. When the range of acceptable conversational distance was perceivably violated—for example, by experimenters moving toward subjects to where their noses nearly touched—the scene was immediately reconstituted as one involving sexual themes, an uncomfortable reality for both subjects and experimenters, one that experimenters were not then fully able to reconvert back to a less embarrassing reality, even in the revelation that the whole thing was, after all, an experiment (Garfinkel 1967, pp. 72–73). Such is the power of enforced reality.

Some of these experiments (Garfinkel 1967, pp. 42–44) required experimenters to live with an atypical degree of attention to the fact that since any occasioned use of a cultural resource is not in strict conformity with anything else, it is always possible to find fault with occasioned use for its failure to come up to literal clarity. It is therefore endlessly possible to ask for further clarification, even for such deceptively simple declaratives as "I had a flat tire," in a fruitless search for precise meaning. Experimenters who adopted this strategy of "No account will do" were met with rebuke from their conversational partners, rebuttals that often contained ritualistic reclarifications of otherwise unthematized organizational assumptions. Simple declaratives like "You know what I mean," repeated with enough emphasis and punctuated with accusations like "What's the matter with you? Are you sick?" or "Drop dead!" or "What a crazy question" (pp. 42–43) can be heard as reestablishing an untested and untestable premise of commonly known "core meaning," underscored by labeling as deviant anyone systematically doubting the premise. In one case very pointed reference was made to what Garfinkel in earlier discussion calls the members' method of "let it pass" (p. 3), or the dictum *not* to ask for literal clarity: "What came over you? We never talk this way, do we?" (p. 44). Here, then, is Durkheimian deviance-recognition in brief—ritual that reproduces and sustains social order.

Thus a characteristic repair work is necessary to avoid the problem of anomie. In one study, such repair work was engaged by subjects to save the Reality Thesis itself (Hilbert 1977). I hypothesized that students asked to simulate jurors searching for a "what really happened" in light of five hopelessly contradictory eyewitness accounts of an event would, in finding the task not only impossible but beyond the horizons of solvability, encounter something of the "anomic terror" (Berger and Luckmann 1967, pp. 102–3) that accompanies the awareness that one's efforts to find reality are useless, that any attempt is as good as any other, that any account will do. The "five eyewitness accounts" actually had not been derived from a core event and in fact had nothing to do with each other. They were arbitrarily selected stories solicited independently from five people who had been asked simply to write several pages describing an event, real or fictitious. These five stories covered such diverse topics as a sensitivity training session, the loss and recovery of some important documents, a water skiing accident, the creation of a new biology laboratory, and a fall into a ravine resulting in paralysis. Instructions directed students to resolve these "contradictions" in a judgment of "what really happened" as an optional coursework assignment with potential toward a final semester's grade. Student responses took the form of short essays (Hilbert 1977, p. 27).

While the logic of the assignment had the potential of forcing the documentation of a contradictory event, thereby a contradictory reality and a breakdown of the Reality Thesis, this did not happen. Instead students were able to use the assignment as accountably "nonsense" (i.e. a deviant assignment) to redocument the Reality Thesis assumption of an objective, internally consistent, and recognizable reality in which cases of "nonsense" such as this could be expected. Moreover, students demonstrated that confusion in the present context was confusion limited to "nonsense," specifically to the assignment, and not the global confusion otherwise hypothesized. According to students, this expected nonsense could be further expected to cause exactly the confusion they were experiencing.

More specifically, students employed "nonsense" categories as cultural resources for organizing, identifying, and explaining the task itself, and they did so in ways identical to their employment of any other kind of cultural resource, the documentation of any other kind of reality. They used the essentially equivocal "nonsense" category to recognize its indexical instances; that is, they used and glossed vague criteria for "nonsense" together with idiosyncratic features of the assignment to produce a sense of "core meaning" within the "nonsense" category. Students were able to make a case for the assignment as *nonsense in reality* as opposed to an assignment capriciously called nonsense as an excuse for giving up on it.

For example, one account read, "A bay cannot be related to a drainage sewer or a laboratory to a ravine," an expression whose truth was allowed to count as obvious for these purposes but which nevertheless might be quite the opposite of obvious in some other imagined context.

Students further maintained a sense of discoverable reality by allowing for an "ultimate explanation" for the nonsense assignment, by expressing interest in learning what the purpose after all was, by speculating on the instructor's intent or deviant frame of mind and so on. The question Why nonsense here and now? was itself preserved as sensible and potentially answerable, a question whose answer would eventually fit in with everything students already knew about reality and its features (Hilbert 1977, pp. 27–29). Moreover, students' idealized sense of what "nonsense" and categories like it *mean*, as opposed to why examples would come up now and then, enabled them to abandon the assignment as one worthy of their attention. Their accountable arguments that *nothing really happened* (as opposed to "something happened that we don't know about" or "something happened that is impossible" or even "this event the assignment leads us to is contradictory and therefore didn't happen") permitted them to ignore the assignment in socially responsible ways that fit in with students' reasoned ways of living in a familiar world (pp. 29–30; see Hilbert 1986, pp. 10–11).

Thus the collective conscience provides resources that can be used not only to document and create a sense of conformity, reality, and constraint as deriving from these same resources but also to prevent any dysfunctional insight into these very practices. At precisely the point where members might see their world and their stable culture as an ongoing and contingent accomplishment of their own artful practices, here also they can mobilize resources for isolating the potentially troubling insight as unusual or strange, in any case as *exceptional*, in such a way that feeds back directly into the assumptions that would otherwise be disrupted. Like a religious dogma or a neurosis, these assumptions assimilate challenges to their internal integrity and their status as independent of members' artful work. This is so whether we are talking about the recognition of nonsense to save reality, of incompetence to save competence (Bittner 1967), of deviance to save conformity, of social problems to save social order (Spector and Kitsuse 1977), or any variations of these. Thus do societal members generally protect themselves from "ontologically fatal insight" (Pollner 1987, pp. 106–8). Here we have closed ranks with one of Durkheim's most profound insights: the necessity of deviance-recognition in the prevention of anomie.

WHEN SOCIAL PRACTICES FAIL: STUDIES OF FULL-BLOWN ANOMIE

As I indicated, anomie is a circumstance where any account will do or no account will do, such that there is no constraint upon the application of cultural resources and nothing counts as socially accountable use. When ritual repair is unsuccessful, we would expect massive anxiety in individuals whose competent use of anomic resources is required. In this section we consider two cases of anomie. One of these is an experimental setting under the principle of "No account will do" (and no repair is possible). The second is a natural setting relative to people in chronic pain, where the operative principle is "Any account will do" (and no repair is possible).

The experimental setting is one of Garfinkel's (1967, pp. 58–65) breaching experiments in which he prevented repair by not allowing subjects to turn the situation "into a play, a joke, an experiment, a deception, and the like" (p. 58). By actively and continuingly sabotaging subjects' sense-making practices, Garfinkel effectively withdrew reality from subjects in ways that would not allow them ritual recovery. And he produced the expected results: profound and marked anxiety.

Twenty-eight premedical students were separately introduced to a setting in which the experimenter identified himself as "a representative of an Eastern medical school who was attempting to learn why the medical school intake interview was such a stressful situation" (Garfinkel 1967, p. 58). For a full hour each student talked with the "representative" about intake interviews and what kinds of events they are. Credibility having been established, the student was then asked if he or she would like to hear "a recording of an actual interview" (p. 58), whereupon the student heard a recording of a fake interview in which the "applicant" performed in a manner that ran roughly opposite to what one would expect from a successful and reasonably competent applicant. The student was then asked to assess the applicant. The "representative" responded to this assessment drawing upon "facts" from the applicant's official record, including performance information (biographical information, family background, academic achievements, charities) and characterological information supplied by "Dr. Gardner, the medical school interviewer," "psychiatrically trained members of the admissions committee who had heard only the recorded interview," and "other students" who had heard the interview also (p. 59). All of this information was contrived and created in the course of the experiment to document a successful and highly articulate applicant based on facts alleged to be in the applicant's record all along. The details were created in such a way as to directly contradict the student's every point regarding the applicant, moreover to contradict his or her every attempt to resolve this very contradiction. The essential contradiction extended to what "other students" (other premedical students just like the subject) had thought of the applicant. Following this exchange, the student was invited to hear the recording again and to reassess the applicant.

Garfinkel was in effect stealing social accountability in the very process of its accomplishment, withdrawing reality from subjects even as they were creating it. What students who were taken in did not know was that here was a situation in which "no account would do"—that is, nothing counted as correct perception. Their inability to arrive at this conclusion was no doubt tied to the "seriousness" of the situation as presented, which is to say the seriousness of intake interviews in the lives of premedical students and the potential hazards of social incompetence in an encounter with a medical school representative. The stakes thus were higher for these subjects than they were for the students discussed in the last section. Premedical students needed to know the nature of the situation they were in and could not write it off as "nonsense." Yet Garfinkel's experimental tactics withdrew the possibility of such knowledge and with it objective experience of relevant reality. Subjects' inabilities to reject the situation as serious, to "leave the field" in Garfinkel's (1967, p. 58) terms, did not allow them to repair the experience. For students taken in, the situation was neither meaningful nor, strictly speaking, meaningless, as even that alternative— and final—normalizing strategy was beyond their horizons.

Subjects varied with respect to how far they were taken in, and three were not taken in at all (Garfinkel 1967, pp. 63–67). Of those who were, dramatic anxiety was evident as they approached the point where resolution seemed hopeless or otherwise not forthcoming. Transcripts reveal students profoundly disturbed, in the throes of questioning their own abilities to judge people and situations, sometimes raising comprehensive doubts about themselves as persons (pp. 60–63). Of the seven most profoundly perplexed, Garfinkel (p. 63) says, "Their suffering was dramatic and unrelieved." Two of the three who had acted on the conviction that the interview was a hoax and who thus showed "no disturbance" during the course of the experiment displayed "acute suffering" when the interview appeared to be over with no confirmation of their suspicions forthcoming (p. 63).

This kind of suffering is anomic in that its nature and origins cannot be derived from individual psychology. Its cause is located outside of individual consciousness, here in the essential lack of social accountability that subjects could not be aware of but nevertheless could not help but "experience." Quotation marks around "experience" indicate that the object of subjects' experience was not known or recognizable to them; indeed its status as an "entity" in their lives lay beyond their consciousness. In that sense the experience was "content-free" or "reality-free" because there was nothing for them, in their terms, to experience. Their disorientation was unaccountable in that all attempts to account for it were similarly disorienting. Their suffering was not derived from social conditions but rather from the withdrawal of social conditions—that is, the terms with which to document and recognize social conditions. Subjects were alone in ways that move far beyond the most extreme kind of moral individualism, and in terms of reality they were "nowhere" in ways that transcend the most extreme nihilistic philosophy.

Upon learning of the deception, subjects expressed relief, "ten of them with explosive expressions" (Garfinkel 1967, p. 64). Unanimously they declared their abilities to return to their former views, although it is indicative of Garfinkel's success that seven subjects needed to be convinced that the news of deception had not itself been manufactured to relieve them of their damaged self-images (p. 64). One would expect this return to familiar settings, here the world of social-psychological experimentation, to precipitate a return to reality and an end to anomic suffering.

However, even this final return to "normal reality" is not possible for the subjects of the second example, chronic pain patients (Hilbert 1984). Here in natural settings, chronic pain sufferers were experiencing troubles beyond the troubles of physical pain or related pain psychology. These troubles are identical in many respects to the troubles of Garfinkel's premedical students. Ultimately they are worse in that pain patients cannot experience relief when the announcement comes that the experiment is over.

The trouble for chronic pain sufferers is this: pain is an ongoing, incorrigible "fact" for them, yet sufferers cannot conceivably experience pain as a fact in the social sense, that is, as an item of knowledge (Berger and

Luckmann 1967). Sufferers cannot know their pain, know what it is, know its nature, experience its identity as an objective cultural object, even as they require and search for these very certainties. Their inabilities to describe and experience do not lie either in their skills and talents as persons or in the nature of pain itself but rather in the culture around them which provides neither the resources nor the social constraint for conceivably accomplishing the task. In that sense, culture is anomic for the practical concerns of these sufferers. While most sufferers confront these troubles from time to time, the problems are most severe among sufferers without benefit of each other's counsel in the creation of what Kotarba (1983a, p. 4) calls "chronic pain subcultures."

The process whereby sufferers arrive at an "any account will do" juncture in their lives is long and harrowing (see Hilbert 1984, pp. 366–73). Generally it involves the failure of all culturally idealized and socially regulated methods of identifying sufferers' experience and what it is an experience of. Beginning with the gradual inability to identify it as *pain*, specifically pain as a cultural object or "normal pain," which contains as part of its experience the expectation of relief, sufferers search for accounts as to why their experiences are not conforming to routine. The search is, then, a search for something to experience. It most often includes a search through the medical establishment for diagnosis and cause, a search often more frantic than the attendant search for relief and cure. The journey is marked by self-doubts, doubts about one's sanity and ability to experience one's body correctly, doubts that are often encouraged by the same medical establishment (or other social spheres) that sufferers consult to find meaning. Where solutions are generated, as with a medical diagnosis, relief is dramatic, even though it may have nothing to do with pain reduction or the promise of a cure. Indeed one subject reported that she had been so "delighted" by the news that the problem had been at last found that she had not heard what the diagnosis was. In some cases the mere label "chronic pain syndrome," as a medical condition in its own right, can reduce sufferers' anxiety. But for those who turn up repeatedly negative diagnoses, the very search for meaning is itself a deepening of anomic dread, an increasing emersion into anomic circumstance.

Many sufferers thus arrive at a place where they abandon social methods of reality discovery entirely, turning inward to discover pain reality on their own. This withdrawal is inadvertently encouraged by the wider pain culture, which promotes notions of pain as a private reality that only the person in pain can ever truly know. This view in fact is promoted in professional pain literature (Fagerhaugh and Strauss 1977, p. 24; Kotarba 1977, p. 261; Pace 1976, p. 1; Sternbach 1968, p. 1). The general understanding is that no one can feel, understand, or experience the objective character of someone's pain except the person in pain. Each person presumably has private access to the objective organization of his or her own private pain: its intensity, its character, its fluctuations, any and all patterned dimensions to pain. Under this model, pain ceases to be an object of shared understanding; it ceases to be a cultural object. Instead it is private. Sufferers turning inward could supposedly study their pain and gather information about it. That way they could obtain knowledge of it, understand it, and describe it, if only for themselves, and thereby find meaning.

Yet notice that such efforts require cultural resources without constraint on their use. The only standard for correct use must come from the individual who is using them, the individual radically conceived, not a societal member. Here we are dealing largely with the human bio-organism struggling to be a member. Constraint from the outer social world cannot even be imagined because of the essential privacy of pain experience. Even "taking the role of the other" is impossible. Like measuring one's height by placing one's hand on one's head, the pain searcher is here without possibility of constraint in the search. A continual, private constraint can be withdrawn or changed, or the change can be called the "same," or "sameness" becomes "difference," or something can be the same and different simultaneously without fear of contradiction, according to however the individual chooses to call things or, more properly, however the individual calls things. For if there is a "choice" or "freedom" here, it is choice without constraint, without the possibility of being correct or incorrect, of being consistent or inconsistent with earlier decisions—in short, of being accurate or inaccurate renderings of pain reality.

Thus it is theoretically predictable that such private searches would fail (Hilbert 1984, pp. 373–76). Sufferers describe their failures as searching for patterns that dissipate in the finding, as intuiting patterns with unlimited variables and exceptions, as hypothesizing patterns they cannot check up on, and so on. Sometimes sufferers give up in the attempt with the conclusion that pain is too random or complex for description. A sociological understanding of this failure finds randomness not in pain but in sufferers' descriptive work. Attempts to describe an objectively arranged internal reality provide no criteria for correct or incorrect description. In short, any account will do or will not do, according to whatever sufferers feel like saying—that is, whatever sufferers say. Correct description, and with it objective knowledge and reality, is impossible precisely because nothing (or anything) counts as correct description. There is no constraint (cf. Becker 1953; Schachter and Singer 1962; Kopel and Arkowitz 1974; Zborowski 1969).

Thus sufferers' private pain vocabulary is anomic. It expresses pain but is no more descriptive of it, no more true or false, than "ouch" (cf. Goffman 1981, pp. 105–6). Sufferers requiring anomic vocabulary to do the work of description will find the task impossible in ways that are unavoidable. Indeed, even the sufferer's professed knowledge that he or she is in pain is more like a symptom of pain than a description of internal affairs. This does not mean that such professed knowledge is false; it is just that it could not be true or false. It is without criterion for its own verification. Sufferers searching for verification, for reality, will only turn up endless paradoxes (cf. Sauerbruch and Wenke 1963, p. 73).

In sum, pain sufferers have troubles that transcend pain. These troubles are anomic in that they do not derive from culture or social activity but instead are manifestations of culture withheld, from social nonparticipation, from radically receding membership. Sufferers have puzzles to solve but are falling away from culture, in whose terms it is possible to solve anything. Even "meaninglessness" does not capture the object of their experiences, for they are, strictly speaking, not experiencing anything. There is nothing, no objective phenomenon, for them to experience. They are losing reality.

SOME ADVANTAGES OF DURKHEIMIAN-ETHNOMETHODOLOGICAL ANOMIE THEORY

The advantages of these interpretations of Durkheimian anomie are both substantive and theoretical (see Hilbert 1986, pp. 14–17). Substantively, pain researchers are well familiar with a high correlation between chronic pain and clinically diagnosed personality disorder, particularly depression (Brena 1978, p. 8; Pace 1976, p. 13; Merskey and Spear 1967; Shealy 1976; Sternbach 1974; Unikel and Chapman 1978). Clinicians hold that personality disorders either cause pain or cause patients to exaggerate pain; thus proper treatment is one or another form of psychotherapy (Biggers 1978; Brena 1978; Pace 1976; Sternbach 1968, p. 117; Szasz 1968; Unikel and Chapman 1978). While continued controversy over the direction of causality may generate epidemiological research (see Kotarba 1983b, pp. 687–88), the formulation presented here provides a clear sociological theory that would predict symptoms of anxiety and depression as a complication of chronic pain, no matter how benign a clinician thinks the pain is, so long as the sufferer perceives pain as sufficient for raising questions as to its cause or identity. Durkheim's view is supported by Kotarba's (pp. 685–87) finding that thoughts of suicide are a recurring theme in the minds of chronic pain sufferers, a theme Kotarba ties to sufferers' loss of cognitive control. While actual suicide attempts appear rare (p. 686), Kotarba found that the suicide theme is sometimes mitigated by sufferers' resorting to alternative cognitive systems regarding pain, meaning systems that allow for the abandonment of the search for an objective understanding of one's condition in favor of a new social understanding that accounts for the very existence of the unsolvable puzzle. Thus do religious, mystical, and other metaphysical understandings of suffering relieve sufferers' anomic dread.

There are also some very distinct theoretical advantages in an ethnomethodological understanding of Durkheim's anomie theory, for it addresses, answers, and clarifies a number of specific questions and doubts raised about anomie in the general literature. Some of these issues involve (1) the measurement of anomie as something outside of individuals; (2) the identity of anomie as something other than collective psychological distress (anomia), even though that is what it amounts to in some of its more famous measures (Seeman 1982, p. 84; Schacht 1982, pp. 73–80); (3) the status of anomie as empirical; (4) the problem of indexing anomie by using individuals as informants (Johnson 1960) and the related problem of "false consciousness" (Seeman 1982, pp. 126–27); and (5) anomie as lack of consensus among members of a collectivity (Jessor et al. 1968)—whether that underestimates the benefits of cultural heterogeneity (Seeman 1982, p. 126), or whether it presupposes a fictitious unified system of goals and values which may not exist even in the best of times (Schacht 1982, p. 72; Clinard 1964, pp. 55–56).

A Durkheimian ethnomethodological anomie theory answers these doubts in several ways (see Hilbert 1986, pp. 15–17). Most generally, it returns anomie to sociology as an empirical phenomenon, at worst the absence of constraint that would be empirical if it were not absent, something that can be diagnosed by sociology external to individuals and independent of individuals' perceptions of it or experience of it. Indeed, anomie can be diagnosed independently of its psychological counterpart, anomia, which then becomes a predicted consequence of anomie as opposed to an "index" of it. Anomia, furthermore, need not be the experience of anomie but rather contentless experience. Anomie is the withdrawal of social accountability, society, and reality, the reduction of the universe external to individuals, thereby resulting in a reduction of subjective experience.

Finally, Durkheim indicates a diversification of reality and experience in an emerging organic solidarity, making "lack of consensus" beneficial in a sense. Yet there evolves a new kind of unifying moral consensus, moral individualism, which finds expression in organic solidarity as a commitment to circumstantial social competence, specialization, and situated rationality—a sort of divvying up of reality into specialties with a view of overarching, comprehensive reality as objectively organized and ultimately self-consistent, albeit presently unknown by specialists either individually or collectively. It is not generally these underlying and unifying commitments that are addressed in measures of consensus. In any case, anomie need not be indexed by "disagreement" over commitments in the first place but only by the withdrawal of the social accountability within whose terms it is possible to live these commitments and to document their status.

6

INDIFFERENCE TO ORDER AND IDEAS

In volume 2 of *The Structure of Social Action* Parsons claims that Max Weber's sociology implies a voluntaristic theory of action resembling Parsons's own theory. He makes this argument less directly than he did with Durkheim, tending more to establish a convergence between Weber and Durkheim and thus indirectly to his own action theory. Naturally this means tying Weber to Parsons's reading of Durkheim. The claim that Weber implied Parsons's theory cannot therefore fare better than that reading; nevertheless Parsons does provide some direct argument for the implication.

I began the discussion of Durkheim and ethnomethodology in chapter 2 with a rejection of Parsons's normative order in both its empirical and its analytic aspects: it cannot be seen and cannot work even in the abstract. Consideration of Garfinkel's indexicality and reflexivity in conjunction with Durkheim's society/morality equivalence and sui generis principle led indirectly to a rejection of Parsonian factual order as well. Instead, society in both its moral and factual manifestations emerges as one fully self-contained incarnate order.

The critique of normative order is not the only ethnomethodological route toward rejecting factual order. Ethnomethodologists have also made the case directly. In fact the suspension of belief in factual society was a cornerstone of early ethnomethodological research policy. By no mere coincidence, bracketing factual order in this way was simultaneously bracketing normative order.

Yet the rejection of factual order on its own terms is inherently interesting as we begin to pick up Max Weber's work, for Weber also argued against the assumption of purely factual social phenomena. Indeed Parsons had to ignore Weber's counsel against reification in order to derive action theory from Weberian sociology. Thus once again a suppressed classical theme is recovered in ethnomethodological reaction to Parsons's theory, even though Garfinkel did not deliberately set out to rediscover these aspects of Weber.

WEBER ON ORGANIZATION AND REIFICATION

An initial assumption of an objective domain of social facts is quite compatible with Durkheim. In essence it is compatible with Garfinkel too. For Garfinkel, however, this objective domain is to be found in "the concreteness of things" (1988) rather than as products of formal a priori theorizing. Ethnomethodological criticism of Parsons, therefore, is not directed to his premise that the job of sociology is to describe and account for social phenomena empirically before us. Accordingly, I am not particularly critical of Parsons simply for using the term "factual." My argument, rather, is against *what* Parsons says is factually before us. His initial phenomenon— factual social order as patterned human behavior—is an assumption borrowed from common-sense reasoning; upon that premise Parsons builds his logically deduced normative order. But the more general objective of sociological investigation into social facts is as it should be.

This general objective is as it should be for Weber too. Though coming from an idealist tradition, Weber did not deny the existence of factual behavior; indeed he was concerned with social order in its most institutional manifestations, including capitalism as a defining feature of modern Western society. However, a look beneath the surface of Weber's many substantive discussions to the theoretical orientation informing his work reveals that one cannot blithely assume that what Weber takes to be existentially present is the same "factual order" that Parsons postulates, particularly with its analytical detachment from subjectivity. This is revealed particularly in Weber's many warnings against *reification*, which for him is every bit as distorting of social phenomena as psychological reductionism is for Durkheim.

In general, reification is the positing of organizational structure as analytically capable of existence independent of the human activity that gives rise to it. Weber categorically warns against this tendency early in *Economy and Society*, where he identifies the "functional frame of reference," the treatment of organic wholes as the context in which individuals act, as a convenient, even indispensable, perspective "for purposes of practical illustration and for provisional orientation" but one whose utility vanishes "if its cognitive value is overestimated and its concepts illegitimately 'reified'" (Weber 1978, pp. 14–15; cf. Pope, Cohen, and Hazelrigg 1975, p. 418; Cohen, Hazelrigg, and Pope 1975, p. 230n; Collins 1986, pp. 44–45; Giddens 1971, pp. 150–51). Another revealing passage immediately precedes:

> These concepts of collective entities [a state, a nation, a corporation, a family, or an army corps] which are found both in common-sense and in juristic and other technical forms of thought, have a meaning in the minds of individual persons, partly as of something actually existing, partly as something with normative authority. This is true not only of judges and officials, but of ordinary private individuals as well. Actors thus in part orient their action to them, and in this role such ideas have a powerful, often a decisive, causal influence on the course of action of real individuals. . . . Thus, for instance, one of the important aspects of the existence of a modern state, precisely as a complex of social interaction of individual persons, consists in the fact that the action of various individuals is oriented to the belief that it exists or should exist, thus that its acts and laws are valid in the legal sense. . . . Though extremely pedantic and cumbersome, it would be possible, if purposes of sociological terminology alone were involved, to eliminate such terms entirely, and substitute newly-coined words. This would be possible even though the word "state" is used ordinarily not only to designate the legal concept but also the real process of action. (Weber 1978, p. 14)

The cumbersome project envisioned here would be that of systematically replacing common-sense collective concepts with newly minted sociological concepts, a project Weber never undertook. But it is important to keep this proposed project in mind when examining Weber's vocabulary of aggregate behavior, including "society." Notably, Parsons never went forward with the project either, using "society" in much the same way common-sense actors do, to refer to the patterned, factual, large-scale behavioral order that surrounds us.

To clarify the distinction between sociological and common-sense usage of collectivist terms, consider another concept that figures prominently in American functionalist theory, that of "social organization." Generally there is no thematic distinction between the everyday common-sense use and the functionalist use of this concept in terms of the very recognition and identity of what it refers to, though functionalists may then proceed to provide a refined vision of the phenomenon. But for Weber, social organization does not have an independent, objective existence for the scientist apart from a subjective orientation of its membership. Early in *Economy and Society* he tells us that a social organization is a *social relationship* "which is either closed or limits the admission of outsiders . . . [whose] regulations are enforced by specific individuals" (Weber 1978, p. 48). A social relationship is "closed" (for example) when, "according to its *subjective meaning* and its binding rules, participation of certain persons is excluded, limited, or subject to conditions" (p. 43, emphasis added). But what is a social relationship? Weber introduces the concept as follows:

> The term "social relationship" will be used to denote the behavior of a plurality of actors insofar as, *in its meaningful content*, the action of each takes account of that of the others and is oriented in these terms. The social relationship thus consists entirely and exclusively in the existence of a probability that there will be a *meaningful* course of social action—irrespective, for the time being, of the basis for this probability. (pp. 26–27, emphasis added)

This definition of social relationship as probability (see Giddens 1971, pp. 151–54; Coser 1971, pp. 224–26) points to a simultaneity of subjective orientation and behavioral consequence in social organization (Hekman 1983; cf. Wrong 1970, p. 25). It leads Weber to say of such seemingly incorrigible institutions as "a state, church, association, or marriage" that their very existence

> consists exclusively in the fact that there has existed, exists, or will exist a probability of action in some definite way appropriate to this [subjective] meaning. It is vital to be continually clear about this in order to avoid the "reification" of those concepts. A "state," for

example, ceases to exist in a sociologically relevant sense whenever there is no longer a probability that certain kinds of meaningfully oriented action will take place. . . . It is impossible to find any other clear meaning for the statement that, for instance, a given "state" exists or has ceased to exist. (Weber 1978, p. 27)

In light of these Weberian qualifications, it would be difficult to maintain the Parsonian claim that factual social order presents an incorrigible existence at the outset for empirical science. To be sure, Parsons explains this order as an outcome of subjective orientation—subjectivity causes behavior in this sense—but he nevertheless provides for the possibility of scientifically *observing* this factual order independently of considerations of subjectivity. Indeed it was *observed*, says Parsons, long before sociology came on the scene; this is the order that Hobbes and Locke saw, and subjectivity is not a feature of it as it exists factually before us. Moreover, the factual order, when explained in Parsonian fashion, retains the very identity it had prior to the explanation. Parsonian insight does not therefore change or affect the nature of the phenomenon; it simply explains it. The preeminently existential status of organized behavior means that Parsonian sociology does not, and cannot, require the replacement of common-sense organizational concepts with sociological ones, the project Weber alludes to. Indeed this factual status can be maintained only through the very activity Weber warns us against: reification.

ETHNOMETHODOLOGICAL INDIFFERENCE TO FACTUAL ORDER

Though ethnomethodologists have not expressly grounded their work in Weberian theory, their investigations have derived from a methodological stance disavowing the factual status of structural organizational phenomena. They make their case in response to functionalist preoccupation with structure, arguing that such preoccupation reifies structure as existing independently of the human activity that produces it (see Maynard and Wilson, 1980). That is, the assumption of factual order provides for social structure the possibility of independent existence similar to allowing the existence of sonatas or paintings independent of composers or painters or their artful work. This is an error, wrote early ethnomethodologists; indeed ethnomethodology was known for its antireification stance almost at the outset. An empirical social science is committed to examining human activity as it visibly occurs, not the products of that activity as "natural" phenomena for science.

One of the clearest statements of this methodological policy is contained in Zimmerman and Pollner's (1970) "Everyday World as a Phenomenon." Here the authors treat the assumption of structured behavior as a *belief* of the membership—in Weber's terms, a subjective orientation to a presumed order—recommending as an empirical topic "the ways in which members assemble particular scenes so as to provide for one another evidences of social order as-ordinarily-conceived" (p. 83). This assumption of structured social order is omnipresent throughout the society, and it never, as a practical matter, comes up for critical review. The embeddedness of this assumption in the very society under study makes both the assumption and the activities whereby it is sustained and reproduced phenomena for science. Zimmerman and Pollner fault "traditional sociologists" for sharing in this assumption. By participating in the society in question, traditional sociologists become one more example of the phenomenon they wish to study. Such an error masks concrete social activity, concealing it from the scientist's field of observation.

For example, Zimmerman and Pollner compare traditional sociologists' version of the causes of juvenile delinquency with that of policemen, pointing out that differences and disagreements in professional outlook are dependent upon a preliminary and unthematized background agreement located in native culture: "They have no trouble in agreeing that there are persons recognizable as juvenile delinquents and that there are structured ways in which these persons come to be juvenile delinquents" (Zimmerman and Pollner 1970, p. 81). The error consists of using an unquestioned native assumption to generate a phenomenon (topic) of investigation, an assumption which ordinary societal members use as a resource for the production of social order as-ordinarily-conceived. In other words, the error consists in sociologists' using this assumption as an unquestioned and already apparent resource for their investigations the same way ordinary members do. Zimmerman and Pollner call this error a "confounding of topic and resource" (p. 81).

Later in the essay the authors offer a more direct line of argumentation against incorporating the assumption of factual social structure into social science. Their characterization of presumptive structure as an "occasioned corpus of setting features" (Zimmerman and Pollner 1970, pp. 94–99) indicates its status as a product of members' artful work and as a contingent accomplishment: "The occasioned corpus is a corpus with no regular elements, that is, it does not consist of a *stable* collection of elements" (p. 95). Or again: "For the analyst, particular setting features are 'for the moment' and 'here and now' " (p. 96).

Thus there is nothing generalizable from one presumptive structure to another or from one situation to another. Social structure as conceived and experienced by societal members, as recognizable because of its repetitive, patterned, standardized quality, simply does not exist for empirical science. No two restaurants are identical, for example, nor are any two events or behavioral displays occurring within a restaurant empirically identical. The structure can be experienced and recognized only "from within" by members of the presumed order. This is to say that they make it happen, they make it be seen that way, through mobilization of common-sense assumptions and categories for classifying this or that as instances of presumed underlying structure. Through these kinds of practices members can see at a glance what is happening in a restaurant as typical restaurant behavior, as something they have witnessed before, as something they "were already" familiar with prior to its occurrence. Even the simple casting of the setting as "after all, a restaurant" may be sufficient work for constituting recognizable stability.

The crux of Zimmerman and Pollner's research recommendation is that these structure-making practices can be investigated in their own right, without regard to the truth or falsity of what they produce in terms of structure: "The occasioned corpus is thus conceived to consist in members' methods of exhibiting the connectedness, objectivity, orderliness, and relevance of the features of *any* particular setting as features in, of, and linked with a more encompassing, ongoing setting, typically referred to as 'the society' " (Zimmerman and Pollner 1970, p. 99). This "society" as an already available phenomenon is exactly what Parsons takes for granted as the objective starting point for sociology.

The concept of "occasioned corpus" requires that members, as they make new constructions, necessarily deconstruct old ones or restructure them in accordance with new structures such that the old and the new can be seen as equivalent, as a repeated event, or as documenting a single and familiar pattern. Thus Zimmerman and Pollner (1970, p. 95) include in the proposed phenomenon "the ongoing 'corpusing' and 'decorpusing' of elements rather than the situated retrieval or removal of a subset of elements from a larger set transcending any particular setting in which that work is done." In other words, any setting, any structure, any social order can be transformed by ethnomethodological research policy into empirical phenomena. This transformation is deeply resonant with Weber's musing on the possibility of replacing all structural concepts with newly coined sociological ones. More resonant still is a recent device of Garfinkel's wherein he uses ordinary structural concepts followed by an asterisk, for example "order*," which in this case is short for "(order*)-in-and-as-of-the-workings-of-ordinary-society," that is, as a practical achievement (Garfinkel 1988, p. 103).

THE IMPLICATION FOR NORMATIVE ORDER

Though ethnomethodologists did not express it this way, their suspension of belief in factual society by necessity included a suspension of belief in normative order. This is predictable on a variety of fronts. For one, we have seen how Durkheim's sui generis principle will not allow a bifurcation of society into separate factual and moral parts; therefore to abandon the assumption of factual order is simultaneously to abandon belief in normative order. Second, we have seen how Garfinkel recovers this society/morality equivalence and how the factual/moral society is generated from within by its membership through social practices; to suspend belief in factual/moral order would be to cease producing it in normative and morally accountable ways. These two observations converge with Weber's claim that human action as it visibly occurs is a probability of behavior in accordance with a subjective orientation, most basically a belief in the existence of social order. To abandon factual order is also to abandon ideas about what causes it, including theories that it is rule-governed. This is so with regard to society as a whole, to classes, states, churches, or to the many varied forms of social organization, including, as we shall see, bureaucracy. Thus Weber's version of organization turns out to be a simultaneity of organized behavior and ideational cause (Hekman 1983). There is, then, a merging of subjective ideas about organization and behavior within that subjective orientation.

Here, then, is a crucial link to the concerns of ethnomethodology: In their efforts to distance themselves from common-sense assumptions, in their methodical refusal to reify social structure, ethnomethodologists by necessity and at the same time had to distance themselves from dominant ideas about structure, including its nature and cause. Again, this is inevitable, given the phenomenon of reflexivity, the Durkheimian equivalence of society and moral regulation, and Weber's comments about the relationship between reification and ideas about structure. If Parsons's allegedly separate orders are truly one sui generis order, then to abandon one is to abandon the other; they are one presumed thing. Moreover, at least in contemporary Western society, factual social order *means* a produced-by-rules order; this is a common-sense formula of our time. As we saw in chapter 3, rules are used by members not simply to explain the order they take for granted but also to produce it as a factual matter in the first place. Thus to abandon Parsons's factual order as a reified entity is to abandon his normative order as well and also to abandon any ideas about the connectedness between the two orders.

Members' method of "corpusing and decorpusing" setting characteristics (Zimmerman and Pollner 1970) is therefore social activity that produces behavior-in-accordance-with-rules. Since this production work is the phenomenon of ethnomethodological study, it would be an error for analysts simply to do the production work, to produce social order themselves, or otherwise to buy into common-sense formulas of behavior, rules, and their interrelatedness. As Zimmerman and Wieder characterize this commitment to ethnomethodological investigation:

> The first step is to *suspend the assumption that social conduct is rule governed* [emphasis added], or based in and mounted from shared meanings or systems of symbols shared in common. The second step is to observe that the regular, coherent, connected patterns of social life are *described* and *explained* in just such terms, or close relatives of them, by laymen and professional sociologists alike. The third step is to treat the appearances of described and explained patterns of orderly social activities as *appearances* produced, for example, by and through such procedures as analyzing an event as an instance of compliance (or noncompliance) with a rule. To take these three "steps" is to leave the problem of order altogether as the analyst's problem. (Zimmerman and Wieder 1970, pp. 288–89)

Notice that to take these steps is not to argue with common-sense ideas or to say that they are false but only to assert that the objects that common sense presupposes and produces are not objects for science; something else is. Indeed, the objective status of what members perceive as real phenomena is not denied as ethnomethodologists turn to the artful practices that produce and sustain that objectivity. To suspend belief in a rule-governed order is not to argue that it is false. Stated most forcefully, Zimmerman and Pollner (1970, p. 98) write, "Every feature of the world of everyday life is maintained intact." This means that the transformation of topical concerns renders their objectivity irrelevant for sociological analysis. Only when they are proposed, hypothesized, or otherwise assumed to be "objective for science" (as they are by American functionalists) could they become objects of professional dispute.

One of Garfinkel's most celebrated case studies, the case of Agnes, illustrates the simultaneity of producing social structure and ideas about rule-governed behavior (Garfinkel 1967, pp. 116–85). The study concerns a subject who was born and raised until the age of seventeen as a boy, though having developed secondary feminine sex characteristics by age twelve. At age seventeen she moved to a large city and assumed a female identity. This she sustained until age twenty-one, when she underwent what is conventionally known as a sex-change operation. During her "passing" years, she was successful in accomplishing female identity in the most trying of circumstances, including those in workplace environments, group dates, life with a female roommate, and a romantic relationship with a boyfriend whose proddings toward sexual intercourse pressured her toward eventually revealing the nature of her anatomical problem.

Throughout Agnes's performance she was successful not only at being recognized and treated as a woman but also at sustaining the following common-sense notions about gender: (1) sex is a natural biological status one has no choice over; it is fixed and cannot be changed; (2) differing behaviors are appropriate to different sex statuses; (3) these behaviors are rule-governed, such rules being learned during the formative years; (4) anyone who deviates from these common-sense notions or otherwise tries to flout them, either by biological or surgical intervention (transsexuals) or by acting or dressing inappropriately for one's gender (homosexuals, transvestites), is sick and someone to be avoided; and (5) Agnes was none of these but a perfectly natural, normal woman. Her success in doing this extended to medical and psychiatric settings where society's recognized experts sought certain knowledge of "what she was" and what was to be done with her. The details of her success are fascinating and deserve a reading; they are far too massive to reproduce here. The point, however, is that even as Agnes worked to sustain the structured world of naturally sexed people, she was simultaneously sustaining common-sense impressions of rule-governed behavior and related notions of conformity versus deviance.

One irony of Agnes's success is that if the reality she worked to sustain were "true" in a scientific sense, then her very success would have been impossible. For example, if feminine behavior truly depended upon rules for its production, then Agnes would have been unable to produce such behavior without having first learned the rules to follow. Instead, she learned by doing, becoming a "secret apprentice." She was able to be strategically feminine in order to learn what she needed to know about femininity, including what it was about past and present performance that made it feminine.

These considerations illuminate the transparency and accomplished nature of the world Agnes produced; yet the products of her ongoing work are roughly equivalent to the principles of Parsonian theory and functionalism generally: sex is an ascribed status, gender roles are learned during the socialization process, and the result is structured gender behavior. To summarize the functionalist view, structured gender behavior is possible because of socialization into gender roles—whatever else happens can be recovered by theories of deviance. That these same principles are both products and premises in Agnes's work points out their accomplished character. Garfinkel's point is that Agnes provides a uniquely visible example of what "anyone" does to sustain the reality of these principles. Her exaggerated expertise in what happens routinely is analogous to the linguist's privileged expertise in a language that native speakers nevertheless speak fluently. Such expertise is also what Parsonian functionalists must necessarily mobilize in the formal maintenance of these very same suppositions.

If, as Weber has it, social organizations are belief-objects for subjective actors, then it is only natural that ethnomethodological indifference to those objects is simultaneously an indifference to the accuracy of actors' ideas. In a society in which actors routinely believe their stable action to be in accordance with rules, it follows that to disavow stable action is to disavow formulas concerning how action comes to be stable, here the rule-governed model of society. But there is no inherent reason to expect actors to subscribe to that formula in the first place. Indeed, for Weber this is only one type of subjective orientation toward action. Weber's general methodological stance includes a rejection of reified belief-objects, regardless of the character of the belief. Likewise, ethnomethodological indifference includes a suspension of whatever beliefs about social structure dominate in a given place and period. It is to this broader area that we now turn.

TYPES OF SUBJECTIVE ORIENTATION
TO ACTION AND LEGITIMACY

Beliefs and action are so tied up together that Weber types and characterizes action according to the kinds of subjective orientations that give rise to it. For example, *instrumentally rational* action is "determined by expectations [concerning the behavior of objects and other people] . . . used as 'conditions' or 'means' for the attainment of the actor's own rationally pursued and calculated ends" (Weber 1978, p. 24). *Value-rational* action is "determined by a conscious belief in the value for its own sake of some ethical, aesthetic, religious, or other form of behavior, independently of its prospects for success" (pp. 24–25). *Affectual* action is carried out under the sway of an emotional or feeling state (p. 25). Finally, *traditional* action is "determined by ingrained habituation" (p. 25). This final type of action varies with respect to the degree of consciousness actors have concerning their own behavior. In one extreme it shades into value-rational action; in the other it shades into nonmeaningful action. The latter is characterized by its specific lack of ideational content, for example an accidental event such as "a mere collision of two cyclists" (p. 23). The point is that action, even this nonsocial kind distinguished as subjectively empty, is characterized by virtue of the content and style of the subjective orientation that goes into it (see Collins 1986, pp. 42–44; Giddens 1971, pp. 152–53).

Notice the similarity between Weber's description of rational action—with its orientation to conditions, means, and ends—and Parsons's own bedrock assumptions about action-in-general reviewed in chapter 1. This similarity suggests that Parsons's orientation toward action is a rational orientation. The similarity becomes more pronounced, as we shall see, when it comes to ideas about the facticity and cause of social organization, a point I will elaborate on in chapters 8 and 9. For now I note the additional similarity between the functionalist model of action and the orientation toward behavior shared by common-sense actors in Western rational society—for example the functionalist theory of gender roles and the model of sex and gender Agnes worked so hard to sustain. By contrast, ethnomethodology not only disavows this model along with a rational orientation generally but, in its indifference to organized society per se, necessarily disavows the affectual and traditional orientations as well.

Another well-known dimension of Weber's work is sometimes referred to simply as his societal typology. Given Weber's ideational qualification concerning social organization, we would expect the same qualification regarding the entity "society." Indeed his interest in legitimacy derives from the stabilizing effect the belief in society has on human activity—that is, a belief in the existence of a legitimate social order. The stabilizing effect derives from the fact that such beliefs provide the necessary warrant for certain behavior as opposed to other behavior, together with ways of seeing that behavior as in accordance with what it should be in accordance with (see Giddens 1971, pp. 154–55). Legitimate social order *means* that to which one should submit oneself, with which one should conform, or, lacking that, at least something one would be better off conforming with. Thus we see in Weber ties between legitimacy and authority, the latter being the basis upon which a legitimate order, or its "leader," can make its claim to legitimacy.

Hence Weber's tripartite typology: *rational, traditional,* and *charismatic.* They are, as stated, three types of subjective orientation to legitimacy and authority. Weber introduces each of these three types in subjective terms in his preliminary remarks about the typology ("The Three Pure Types of Authority").

1. Rational grounds—resting on a belief in the legality of enacted rules and the right of those elevated to authority under such rules to issue commands. . . .

2. Traditional grounds—resting on an established belief in the sanctity of immemorial traditions and the legitimacy of those exercising authority under them. . . .

3. Charismatic grounds—resting on devotion to the exceptional sanctity, heroism or exemplary character of an individual person. . . . (Weber 1978, p. 215)

The subjective dimension of authority is easy to lose sight of throughout Weber's rich and detailed case studies of the styles and variations of the three types, so he periodically recalls it to the foreground during discussions that might otherwise tend to mislead.

In general, it should be kept clearly in mind that the basis of every authority, and correspondingly of every kind of willingness to obey, is a *belief*, a belief by virtue of which persons exercising authority are lent prestige. (p. 263)

Reminders like these are nonsystematic, but they should not be ignored. Common tendencies toward thinking of the three types as types of societies, as structured entities, might well account for Weber's musings concerning the cumbersome task of replacing common-sense organizational concepts with newly coined sociological concepts.

WEBERIAN INDIFFERENCE TO THE ACCURACY OF SUBJECTIVE ORIENTATIONS

One could operationalize Weber's proposed replacement of common-sense organizational concepts as the systematic bracketing of subjective orientations to social order, whatever their content. This is the essence of ethnomethodological indifference. Support for ethnomethodological indifference can be taken directly from Weber. Here I call attention to what could be termed Weber's *distancing* from the substantive content of ideas. For Weber, scientists had to make value decisions in selecting topics for investigation, but this did not mean that value-neutral knowledge about a given topic was impossible (cf. Giddens 1971, pp. 138–41). Thus it should be possible to examine prevailing ideas of an era without regard to the truth or falsity of those ideas. The scientific attitude toward those ideas is neither to embrace them nor to deny them, neither to sustain them nor to correct them, but rather to examine their role in human history. All concerns pertaining to their accuracy are therefore irrelevant from a sociological point of view.

As I suggested above, Parsons did not distance himself from Weber's ideational modes and in fact expresses one of them, the rational subjective orientation. This explains his belief in the reified objects of Western society, including structural institutions and "the society" in general as factual order. I am not saying that Parsons *derived* his subjective orientation from Weber's work, but that his sociology expresses and exemplifies what Weber called rationality. That Parsons would embrace rationality as opposed to traditional or charismatic ideas is not surprising, given his membership in an advanced, bureaucratic society. Nevertheless it was this deep embeddedness in a common-sense era that ethnomethodologists worked so fervently to overcome. In the process they inadvertently revealed how sociology might proceed when we extend Weber's distancing principle to all three subjective modes—that is, subjective orientation per se, rationality included.

Thematic emphasis upon this distancing principle varies among secondary discussions of Weber, but it is almost always recognized when analyzing cultures radically different from our own. It is commonly known that Weber's discussion of charisma does not itself attribute supernatural qualities to religious leaders; all that matters is that people make such attributions (Giddens 1971, p. 160). Perhaps this is emphasized because it might otherwise seem strange that charisma could be a topic of scientific investigation at all. In any case, less often is it stated that this disinterest applies to traditional orientations as well; "tradition" comes closer to our everyday vocabulary and is something most Westerners can relate to. Still less often is it stated how this Weberian distancing is to be applied to rational ideas. Western society approaches this latter type, and there is a tendency in Western sociology to embrace rational ideas as a correct rendering of the workings of society. This tendency perhaps runs more strongly than the equally misleading tendency to discredit charisma. Either of these is in error.

Yet the error is not, for the most part, Weber's error, although there is room for confusion along these lines which I shall touch on below. But Weber does not, at this level of analysis, differentiate between types of ideas according to their relative truth value.

> In spite of their vast differences, "ideas" have essentially the same psychological roots whether they are religious, artistic, ethical, scientific, or whatever else; this also applies to ideas about political and social organization. (Weber 1978, p. 1116)

With regard to legitimacy, Weber sometimes speaks of ideas as deliberate "myths" developed by privileged groups to consolidate and justify their otherwise fortuitous advantage, myths in essence packaged and sold to the public (p. 953) in a manner not inconsistent with Marxian "ideology" (see Collins 1968, 1980). Thus there is no basis for evaluating ideas as to their accuracy, much less their relative accuracy in terms of each other.

In a way, the increased clarity of distancing relative to foreign cultural idioms is a reflection of Weber's own varied emphases to the recommendation. Weber too is most clear about distancing when discussing charisma: the objective status of the charismatic leader's supernatural authority and other special qualities is totally irrelevant to scientific investigation; all that matters is how the leaders are regarded by their followers (Weber 1978, pp. 241–42) and how successful they are in convincing their followers of their extraordinary powers (cf. Parkin 1982, p. 84). Likewise with traditional authority: whether commands have really been "valid of yore" or can be derived from "precedents and earlier decisions" is irrelevant for scientific purposes; all that matters is how the commands are regarded and how successful the leaders are in convincing their followers that their commands are indeed in accordance with age-old rules and powers (Weber 1978, pp. 226–27; cf. Parkin 1982, p. 81).

But when Weber comes to rational-legal authority, he is less clear on what this analytic distancing would entail. There is no indication, however, that we are to abandon distancing when examining this subjective mode. His introduction to rational-legal authority, as noted above, is stated in categorically subjective terms. As we shall see, bureaucracy is introduced this way too. Thus rational-legal is a mode of subjective orientation to legitimate order no less than the other two, and no less than for the other two, the truth value of rational ideas is irrelevant for sociological analysis.

Weberian distancing from rational-legal orientations can be gleaned from Weber's more substantive discussions, for example his sociology of law. Here he distinguishes between legal reasoning and sociological reasoning. Legal reasoning is concerned with, for example, "whether a rule of law does or does not carry legal authority," that is, whether something is legally correct, whether a legal relationship factually exists (Weber 1978, p. 28). Sociological reasoning is concerned strictly with the *belief* in legal authority as held to by societal members, the subjective acceptance of a determination that a rule carries the full force of legal authority, together with the probability of appropriate action (p. 28). For sociologists, in contrast with legal scholars, the law does not prescribe or enforce what is legal. What provides legality is subjective respect for the interpretation of law in its course, and here only as subscribed-to beliefs that generate predictable kinds of behavior.

Still, distancing from rationality in general may have been a trouble spot for Weber. This might have to do with a double status of rationality: on the one hand, it is a sociological phenomenon, a historically occurring subjective orientation toward which sociologists are to remain value-neutral; on the other hand, it is a first principle of science, which sociologists are supposed to embrace (see Giddens 1971, pp. 138–41). Weber speaks occasionally of "pure" rationality as conceivable and scientifically deducible and from which behavioral deviations could happen only as results of mixed traditional and charismatic orientations (Weber 1978, p. 6). Having thus embraced the values of rational science, he may have been less successful in analytic distancing than he was with regard to the other two types. Indeed, accentuated distancing from the other two may have been necessary to avoid a tendency to evaluate them negatively. Weber in fact speaks of the special difficulty of understanding subjective orientations that differ from "our own ultimate values" (pp. 5–6). Such values might in the immediate case be embedded in sociology itself, which is in turn rooted in rationality. But if Weber had to resist the tendency to discredit foreign cultures, sociologists today are faced with a complementary bind, suggesting an even greater difficulty understanding their own subjective times, because of their proximity, than the more foreign ones. In any case, sociology, albeit rational, requires a Mannheimian metadistancing from the familiar no less so than the strange.

One way through this thicket is to keep in mind the distinctiveness of sociology with regard to *topic*, as opposed to those of the rest of societal membership. Sociologists, for all of their scientific rationality, are not rational about the same topics that other people are rational about. This is fairly easy to see when comparing sociologists with, say, physicists. It is less easy when we consider that the societal membership also talks rationally about society. But the distinction comes into better focus when we recall that Weberian rational legitimacy is a subjective orientation toward a presumed *order* which sociologists cannot orient to in precisely the same way without reification. Their mere focus on subjectivity—indeed the whole sense of there being a Weberian sociology at all—sets sociologists apart from the membership in terms of topical concerns. As Weber says, "rationalism allows for widely differing contents" (Weber 1978, p. 998).

Ethnomethodologically, the distinction between sociologists' and members' topic is related to the distinction between topic and resource (Zimmerman and Pollner 1970) discussed above. The ethnomethodological topic is the unthematized social practices members engage in when producing and sustaining the reality of their topics (unthematized because these practices are not, for members, topics at all). The error of "confounding" topic and resource is that of adopting members' topic as an a priori factual domain, that is, something about which things can be said and facts gathered. Correction of this error is to turn the production of this commonsense topic into a topic in its own right. The error uncorrected will, as in the case of American functionalism, provide unwarranted credibility to claims about the factual existence of a rule-produced behavioral domain.

So what are the topical concerns of a rational-legal *membership*? Weber does not separate such an order from its typical organizational expression, bureaucracy, so I will take up the discussion again in that context in chapter 8. For now it suffices to say that a rational orientation to legitimacy sees order as an outcome of, and in accordance with, systems of rational prescriptions that are logically consistent with each other and *make sense*, working together to produce a smoothly flowing and predictable society. For bureaucrats, these prescriptions are "policy." To less deliberate members of such an order, that there are rules that produce stability is, at the descriptive level, a matter of common sense. At the prescriptive level, the authority of commands derives from their logical-rational fit with other prevailing rules whose rationality is never in doubt or whose rationality must be rationally discredited in cases of revision or replacement.

7

EMPIRICAL SUBJECTIVITY AND

THE COMPELLINGNESS OF IDEAS

In chapter 6 we saw how both Weber and ethnomethodologists distance themselves from common-sense ideas of an era. What this amounts to for ethnomethodological studies of our own society, one saturated with rational-legal orientations, is the subject of chapter 8. First, however, I wish to lay emphasis upon the commonalities between ideas in general, especially what Weber referred to as their common "psychological roots." I wish to draw out what it is about ideas that makes them so compelling, so believable, to social actors. I begin with Weber's approach to ideas as an empirical science and move on to show how ideas and subjectivity are likewise empirical for ethnomethodology. Indeed, ethnomethodology even examines the problem of intersubjectivity and shared understanding through empirical study. This sets the stage for understanding ideas as compelling to those who subscribe to them by virtue of social practices invariant to the substantive content of the ideas themselves.

WEBER AND EMPIRICISM

Some aspects of functionalist theory most subject to doubt in light of Garfinkel's investigations have to do with how Parsons conceives subjectivity and shared understanding. Indeed Heritage (1984, p. 9) reminds us that part of Garfinkel's dissertation agenda was to examine implications of Weber's work that Parsons overlooked, those having to do with "experience structures." Ethnomethodological investigations yield results devastating for the general Parsonian action model, and they bring us back to a practiced empiricism relative to ideas that Weber recommended and that Parsons abandoned.

In Parsons's theory, subjectivity consists of respect for an internalized normative order consisting of norms and values. Assuming that Parsons is correct in seeing norms and values as capable of prescribing behavior (which we can no longer assume; see chapter 2), then anyone who respects them would voluntarily follow them; this makes social order. In this way Parsons assigns a causal role to subjectivity and seems to be on safe Weberian ground. The problem has to do with the scientific accuracy of the claim that the content of subjectivity is norms and values. Given that normative order is nonempirical (see chapter 2), how could anyone verify its objectivity for science as actors' subjective content? Even if it could be shown that actors themselves believe in the existence of normative order, how could we verify that there really is such a thing and that it in fact causes actors to act the way they do?

These are not trivial questions, since Weber, at least in theory, recommends the *empirical* study of ideas in human history. Though many of the roots of his sociology are in German idealism, Weber does not adopt idealist standards when approaching ideas. Instead, a significant theme in his methodological writings concerns questions of *scientific objectivity* in ascertaining the subjective ideas and motives that stand behind and thereby cause behavior (Weber 1949, p. 74; 1978, pp. 4–13; see Giddens 1971, p. 134). One might well conclude from these methodological writings that Weber's theory of subjectivity is by today's standards limited and underdeveloped (see Alexander 1983, pp. 30–33). Schutz (1962, 1964, 1966, 1967), for example, made definite headway beyond Weber toward a sophisticated understanding of subjectivity. But while Weber's characterization of subjectivity, its inner workings and dynamics, may seem unduly primitive, he is second to none, especially among classical theorists, in appreciating its critical importance in human affairs and moreover the importance of objective renderings of ideas for sociological understanding.

The critical importance of ideas in human history is accented in the way Weber characterized the entire modern era. Capitalism, which for Marx was a specific set of material relations between economic classes, was in addition, for Weber, a set of economic and rational ideas, which he termed the "spirit of capitalism" (see Weber 1976). These ideas have a causal role for capitalism; without them capitalism would never have arisen. There are other requirements as well, including material circumstance in the sense of Marx, but these conditions are not alone sufficient for the development of capitalism. Ideas, then, do not replace material interests and political power as decisive for capitalism but complement them (cf. Giddens 1971; Cohen, Hazelrigg, and Pope 1975, pp. 236–39).

Nevertheless ideas, while not in themselves sufficient, are subordinate to nothing else in order of necessity, as Weber reveals by a systematic review of non-Western civilizations where material circumstances similar to that of precapitalist Europe prevail but where capitalism nevertheless fails to materialize because of the missing capitalist spirit. Capitalist ideas, in turn, do not spring into existence either full blown or as a consequence of other nonideational conditions. They come from other ideas. They have their necessary forebears in the ideas of a precapitalistic religious era, ideas Weber terms "the Protestant ethic." These religious ideas are also fortuitous; Calvinism was a unique combination of ideas found separately in other times and places but which nowhere else are found in precisely this combination (Weber 1976; see Collins 1986, pp. 47–59; Giddens 1971, pp. 124–32). Thus capitalism is an exceptional social development, by no means the rule when it comes to societal evolution.

Yet notice that in all of these studies Weber's emphasis on the importance of sociological objectivity is apparent (Giddens 1971, p. 134). He does not speak of ideas in an abstract or ethereal sense (cf. Alexander 1983, p. 24). He departs significantly from such understandings of "idealism" in his empirical method (cf. Giddens 1971). In the case of the Protestant ethic, he finds subjective orientation in the work and writings of Protestant thinkers; likewise with the spirit of capitalism, he locates subjective orientation in the writings of secular economic thinkers and purveyors of folk wisdom, including Benjamin Franklin. And for his general thesis that the latter has its roots in the former, he locates this transition in an examination of intervening historical documents that reveal a gradual secularization of religious thought (Weber 1976). Thus we have here a theory that is at every turn empirical, not crude idealism or an emanationist philosophy, but one which nevertheless takes the role of ideas quite seriously.

From this we can see several related anomalies when we juxtapose Weber and Parsons. First, Weber does not require that the object of actors' subjectivity (the belief-object) be a real object for science, since the existence of that object is itself contained by, and part of, subjectivity; Parsons requires such an object. Second, the object of actors' subjectivity for Weber is the very social order presumed by actors to be factual; for Parsons social order is not an object of actors' subjectivity, since it exists as truly factual independent of actors' subjectivity, which emerges only as its cause. Third, Parsons therefore posits yet another order, which Weber does not require, to serve as the object of actors' subjectivity: normative order. Subjective respect for that order produces the objective social structures given as first phenomena for science. Finally, for Parsons, therefore, two orders exist, neither of which exists for Weber: factual order, which Weber recognizes and clarifies with his ideational qualification, and normative order, which has no place at all in Weber's sociology.

INTERSUBJECTIVITY AND THE ETHNOMETHODOLOGICAL SOLUTION

Once again, for Weber the objective existence of whatever is believed in is irrelevant for the significance of those beliefs in human behavior. For Parsons, the object of beliefs is in every way critical. Indeed Parsons's hypothesis of normative order seems to be useful in solving one of the profound issues in the history of philosophy and sociology: the problem of shared understanding. If normative order, as a complex system of norms, roles, and values, is an objective entity into which all societal members are socialized, then it consists precisely of that to which all people orient in an attitude of respect and therefore designates the content of their consciousness. Normative order *is*, literally, their shared culture (Heritage 1984). Since socialization is imperfect, different people can access different realms of the collective conscience thus conceived; shared understanding therefore is not global or universal, and there can still be deviance. But this does not alter the terms of the solution: intersubjectivity is possible because of simultaneous objective content, or of varying degrees of overlapping content, between one mind and another. Overlapping content in turn is possible because of the objective source of that content and its access through socialization: objective normative order. The rest of the solution to the problem of social order falls into place as mutually cognitive people play out the behaviors prescribed by their objectively shared normative order. Here is where Parsons claims his origins in Weber: ideas cause behavior.

One intriguing aspect of Parsons, then, is that he requires a scientifically "real" object for subjectivity at all. Another notable aspect is that he allows the objective status of that object to solve the problem of intersubjectivity. The first of these is definitely a Parsonian move because Weber makes no such requirement; the second is a seductive consequence that might otherwise seem unattainable. That is, intersubjectivity might seem theoretically impossible without an objective ideational content that reproduces itself in different people's minds. However, we are once again led to an innovative move on Garfinkel's part which allows the possibility of beliefs operating on their own, without objective ideational content, and which also allows for intersubjectivity. Most important, Garfinkel's work is empirical.

Some of the theoretical groundwork for Garfinkel's move was laid by Alfred Schutz (1962, 1964, 1966, 1967), who understood some of his own work as elaboration, development, and correction of Weber relative to the dynamics and workings of subjectivity. Garfinkel in turn was influenced by Schutz, as indicated by the many references and derived summations scattered throughout *Studies in Ethnomethodology*; the details of these influences, as well as those from phenomenology generally, are spelled out nicely by Heritage (1984, pp. 37–74) in a chapter called "The Phenomenological Input." Briefly for present purposes, Schutz's solution to intersubjectivity includes treating intersubjectivity itself as ideational, as part of a subjective orientation, an assumption or presumptive stance on the parts of everyday social actors. In a manner roughly paralleling Weber's ideational qualification relative to social organization, Schutz disavows intersubjectivity as objectively "true" for science but looks to it as a contingent, lived idealization about and within social life. In its simplest expression, the intersubjectivity assumption allows for differences in subjective content relative to a presumed objective, factual, common domain of real objects, events, and structure because of biographical and other transient distinctions between people. These "differences," however, are covered by the intersubjectivity idealization itself through two related common-sense assumptions: (1) different people orienting toward the same objective phenomenon have selected a common domain of practical relevancies rendering any potentially discoverable differences in perception irrelevant, that is, the selection of relevancies are presumed identical across individuals, and (2) any trivial differences would be erased anyway, were fellow participants to literally exchange places. Thus do people interact meaningfully within a shared world with shared ideas about the world. It should be kept in mind that Schutz does not depend for purposes of his analysis upon any of these ideas being "true." Rather, they are lived assumptions continually tested, retested, and ultimately sustained in practical life in a prospective/retrospective manner. Intersubjectivity is therefore an accomplished intersubjectivity-for-all-practical-purposes, not a working premise for social science.

Several of Garfinkel's experiments illustrate the lived, contingent, practical dimension of the intersubjectivity idealization. In one of these (Garfinkel 1967, pp. 79–94), ten undergraduates were asked to participate in research about a new form of personal counseling. Each subject would provide for a "student counselor in training" some necessary background details in the area of personal life in which he or she would like help. Then the subject would ask a yes/no question of the "counselor" over an intercom. The "counselor" would give an answer, the subject would turn off the intercom and tape-record his or her impressions of the exchange, formulate a new yes/no question, turn the intercom on and ask the new question, receive an answer, turn the intercom off and record impressions, and so on for about ten questions. The "counselor" was actually an experimenter, and the yes/no answers were prearranged randomly. Thus the terms of the experiment seemed to put subjects in interaction with a sentient "other," although there was actually no one there.

Notably, even without the presence of a sentient "other," subjects were able, absolutely on their own, to live in and document the world-in-common with the "counselor"—and to establish intersubjectivity with the counselor. Subjects were able to hear what the counselor had in mind, what kinds of theories and folklore the counselor was bringing to bear upon the problem. They could revise and rearticulate previous understandings of these matters, and they could hear the counselor doing the same thing. They could hear the counselor having changes of mind, for example, and they could see why a change of mind was warranted. Subjects knew motive, intent, reasoning processes, and common-sense knowledge on the part of the counselor; they saw the real world, the structured behavior, the morally valued formulas, the rules, and so on that they shared with the counselor. These understandings were not arrived at randomly but strategically and artfully. They were not constructed in a linear fashion but in a prospective and retrospective fashion that provided for limitless revision and repair. Garfinkel (1967, pp. 89–94) offers over forty specific observations on these matters.

The question that comes to mind, then, is that if subjects are able to document all of this material on their own, how much more so must this be going on in the everyday world in which there routinely *are* "sentient others" to interact with. A demonstration directly related to this question (Garfinkel 1967, pp. 24–31) involved asking participants in a conversation to write down what was said in one column and what they "understood they were talking about" in another. Naturally the second column was more elaborate and contained greater detail, as though the original conversation had been shorthand for what was intended but unnecessary to delineate. Yet this expanded version of the conversation could itself be seen as shorthand for "something more"; hence Garfinkel asked subjects to clarify the expanded versions, and so on. Eventually he imposed on them the task of "finishing" this clarification process to the point that he, as a reader, would know exactly what conversational participants knew regarding the conversation just from reading what was written.

Subjects eventually gave up on the task, complaining that it was impossible. Garfinkel is clear that this impossibility did not consist in the laboriousness or complexity of the task; it was not a task that was simply "humanly impossible" such as jumping to the moon or counting aloud to ten trillion. Rather it emerged as a task that was impossible in principle, more like counting to infinity or attaining the "highest heights" and knowing they are the highest by observation from above. Indeed pursuit in accomplishing the task is the very activity that led to the "more" that remained to be done. In Garfinkel's (1967, p. 26) terms, "the writing itself developed the conversation as a branching texture of relevant matters. The very *way* of accomplishing the task multiplied its features."

On a more theoretical plane, Garfinkel (1967, pp. 28–31) explains subjects' difficulties by dropping a distinction between what was said and what was talked about. He sees the expanded version of the conversations not as reports concerning the underlying and unspoken content of the conversation but simply and solely as attempts to satisfy the terms of his request, which in turn was taken by subjects as a call for instructions as to how to see what was said *as* what was talked about. Thus it was Garfinkel's instructions, not a substantive body of shared understanding, that could be chronically brought into question by pointing to matters of ambiguity and incompleteness. In contrast, the "what" of what is talked about in routine conversation is accomplished in the here-and-now of what is said; linguistic usage is not explainable by common understandings of what linguistic signs refer to or stand for but rather by the here-and-now assignment of what is said to a presumed sphere of clarity, consistency, coherence, understanding, planfulness, rationality—that is, "as subject to some rule's jurisdiction" (p. 30). In summarizing the significance of these findings for a theory of intersubjectivity, Garfinkel notes:

> "Shared agreement" refers to various social methods for accomplishing the member's recognition that something was said-according-to-a-rule and not the demonstrable matching of substantive matters. The appropriate image of a common understanding is therefore an operation rather than a common intersection of overlapping sets. (p. 30, original in italics)

Empirical studies of subjectivity indicate that intersubjectivity does not require an objective ordering of shared subjective content. Rather, shared understanding is an accomplishment of the very same artful practices employed to reproduce and sustain reality, objective social structures, and organizational integrity. This should come as no surprise in light of the discussions of Durkheim's society/reality equivalence, Garfinkel's reflexivity, and Weber's notion of organizations as probability of behavior in accordance with belief in their existence. Each of these theoretical principles suggests an analytic congruence between the methods of production of social structures and the methods of production of ideas relative to those structures. For members, then, ideas are shared because of the objective status of the ordered reality they are about; intersubjectivity is easy for members to explain by virtue of mutual orientation to an objectively given social reality. That members are simultaneously producing reality and intersubjectivity is "uninteresting" (Garfinkel 1967, pp. 7–9) to members, but it is a central phenomenon of ethnomethodological studies.

IDEAL TYPES

It is necessary at this point to briefly consider Weber's use of what he called *ideal types* and Parsons's critique of the concept. This is necessary for two interrelated reasons. First, Parsons disrupts the internal integrity of ideal types to find an "element" that they share in common by virtue of which ideas can be compelling to social actors; this element, paradoxically, is one of the types (charisma). Ethnomethodology, by contrast, can account for this compellingness without disrupting the types themselves. It accounts for the compellingness of ideas directly in the social practices that functionalists gloss out of existence in the production of their reified object. Second, as I shall show in the next chapter, Parsons derives from his critique of Weber the notion that "pure rationality" is an analytic impossibility, which would tend to mollify Weber's worry over nonstop rationalization in the West. Again, ethnomethodological focus on members' methods reveals how "pure rationality" is analytically possible and how Weber could be right in his prognostications. Indeed, I will argue in chapter 9 that Parsonian theory is itself an example of "pure rationality" and rationalization.

It is fairly well known that ideal types are analytic constructs in Weber's work (e.g. Giddens 1971, pp. 141–44; Coser 1971, pp. 223–24). They do not refer to concrete reality and cannot be taken, therefore, as empirical descriptions. They are not "averages" concerning what is in the real world, nor are they hypotheses concerning what might be found there (Weber 1949, p. 90). Rather, they are methodological tools, concepts constructed by the theorist not to capture empirical reality but to compare with it. They are in that sense "fictions," but fictions analogous to the fictions of "frictionless motion" in the physical sciences. They are purified conceptions of some aspect of the social world and formulations of the consequences that would obtain from these abstract pure forces. Actual developments in the concrete empirical world can then be compared with the ideal-typical formulations and examined for their deviations and the case-specific causes of such deviations (Weber 1978, p. 21). Thus while the empirical world always remains the phenomenon of central interest, as exemplified in Weber's many case studies, ideal types are the conceptual tools for understanding that world as an object of broader theoretical interest. This is what Weber is referring to when he talks about the construction of ideal types "not as an end but as a *means*" (1949, p. 92).[1]

Ideal types, for Weber, reflect scientists' interests in what they wish to study about the social world. There is no other way to study the social world, no way to understand it independently of an evaluative decision as to what about it one wants to examine scientifically (Giddens 1971, p. 142).

This does not inhibit objective research, but it is the means by which objective research is possible (Weber 1949, pp. 80–84); it is the selection of topics to be objective about. It does mean, however, that "the most varied criteria can be applied to the selection of the traits which are to enter into the construction of an ideal-typical view of a particular culture" (p. 91). An ideal type is a "one-sided *accentuation* of one or more points of view and . . . the synthesis of a great many diffuse, discrete . . . *concrete individual phenomena*, which are arranged . . . into a unified *analytical* construct" (p. 90). Thus there is no one, true classification scheme for organizing the world (p. 84; Giddens 1971, pp. 141–44).

Parsons works diligently to undermine the integrity of ideal types (Parsons 1968b, pp. 601–24). He draws upon Weber's characterization of ideal types as composites of "individual phenomena" or "traits." According to Parsons, ideal types are one of several kinds of universal concepts which stand in relation to their particulars in differing ways. They are uniquely rigid in that they designate a "fixed set of relations . . . of elements" (p. 616). These elements can vary independently of each other in concrete reality; it is their combination that defines the type (p. 617). The type, therefore, is not only a useful fiction in the sense of Weber but an unnecessary distortion of reality that could be remedied with a focus on the elements themselves. Put differently, type analysis would require a huge array of possible combinations of elements resulting in many types, where element analysis could recover all of these possibilities with a smaller number of concepts, all of this more in keeping with the principle of scientific economy (pp. 618–19; cf. Bershady 1973, pp. 55–64). Parsons holds out for the possibility of a "complete scientific theory" that envisions "all possible concrete types of a class of historical individuals . . . as exemplifying different combinations according to laws, of the same analytical and structural elements" (1968b, p. 624).[2]

In making these arguments, Parsons loses the methodological advantages of ideal types. My point is not to say that ideal types have nothing to do with each other; indeed a major dimension of Weber's work has to do with their interrelatedness, how one turns to the other in historical process, how they are found in various unique combinations in actual cases. Weber is also clear that they never appear in their pure form in the empirical world. But the entire methodological advantage of pure types is lost when one begins to analyze the types themselves, in a strictly methodological discussion, as "mix and match" versions of each other. Eventually Parsons would be led to say, as I shall show presently, that entire ideal types are contained in other ideal types; mutually exclusive pure types become features of each other.

A final point to make about ideal types concerns what they are typifications of. To some extent they are invariably typifications of subjective orientations. The types of action reviewed in chapter 6 are organized around subjective principles that give rise to action, despite their convenient shorthand designation as "types of action." Likewise with ideal types of organization: given Weber's vision of organization and antireification policy, organizations too cannot be distinctively set off from the subjectivity and belief that they necessarily entail (Hekman 1983). As we shall see, this applies to bureaucracy. Parsons, consistent with his commitment to an analytic distinction between subjective ideas and objective behavior, says simply that there are two heterogeneous categories of ideal types: those typifying concrete social systems, and those typifying ideas (Parsons 1968b, pp. 604–5). In this way he sustains the subjectivity/objectivity distinction essential to his theory.[3]

THE COMPELLINGNESS OF IDEAS

Parsons and Weber most assuredly agree that ideas are compelling for social actors. But for Weber it is subjective commitment and belief in ideas that themselves provide their driving force. Parsons looks to something beyond that, something by virtue of which ideas can be compelling, an *element* of the normative system that would evoke subjective respect. For Parsons, again, the normative quality is an element; what, he asks, is the nature of this element?

Parsons's answer to this question begins with Weber's discussion of ideas about legitimacy as though it were a discussion of legitimacy itself as an objective feature of social order. He can do that because of his proposed "element analysis," as I discussed above. Viewed that way, legitimacy is an element which attaches to Parsons's own device—normative order; there is where it commands subjective respect from social actors. On this issue Parsons makes one of his early, bold claims about the convergence between Weber and Durkheim. Equating legitimacy with Durkheim's "moral obligation," he then calls it "a property of an *order*, that is, a system of norms, to which particular actions are oriented" (Parsons 1968b, p. 652).[4]

From this beginning, Parsons needs to account for legitimacy as a real "quality of an order" (1968b, p. 661). Through a long and deeply circuitous route, he eventually settles on *charisma* as the source of legitimacy in general, that is, charisma as a real element in his proposed alternative to ideal type construction. Along the way he connects charisma to the sanctity of traditionalism, morality, and Durkheim's notion of the sacred.[5]

On a substantive level, Parsons defends this claim through a review of the ways religious and charismatic ideas evolve into traditional and rational authority in Weber's many case histories. Parsons correctly identifies a major thrust of Weber's work as the way in which religious ideas shape and affect the destiny of entire civilizations; *The Protestant Ethic and the Spirit of Capitalism* is one such case history. The lesson Parsons draws is that in the case of rational-legal legitimacy, for example, "the quest of the source of legality always leads back to a charismatic element," concluding that "there must always be a source of the legality of [the] order which is, in the last analysis, charismatic" (Parsons 1968b, p. 665). In other words, he takes the historical origins of a system of ideas as the source of the Durkheimian sacred dimension of those ideas as currently subscribed to.[6]

Making charismatic orientation a feature of the rational and traditional orientations defeats the entire methodological purpose of ideal types, that is, *pure* types (cf. Pope, Cohen, and Hazelrigg 1975, p. 425). Again this is not to say that the types occur in their pure form in concrete cases; there they are present in varying degrees and varying combinations, and they merge into each other in concrete historical process. Current Weberian scholarship finds rationalization far more subject to charismatic outbursts than one would glean from Weber's pessimistic forecasts (Lash and Whimster 1987). But at the methodological level, the types must remain pure. Once we abandon that, we have lost the whole notion of ideal types of legitimacy. It makes no sense to speak of pure types as contained by other pure types; they would not be pure then and would have no internal conceptual integrity. By analogy it would be like saying that a hypothetical frictionless machine would require friction to run smoothly. None of these types, therefore, can stand out as the "source" of legitimacy for all three types, nor can one be a feature of the other two.

What it boils down to is that for Weber, legitimacy derives from *belief*, while Parsons searches for it in the entity believed in. Parsons attempts to find legitimacy in the nature of what is believed, in the content of ideas. Taken that way, Parsons could not imagine the source of legitimacy for either a traditional or rational order, though this sacred dimension is more readily apparent in charismatic order because of its ties to religion. Thus he says that the Durkheimian sacred principle is the same thing as charisma and that traditionalism and rationalism both contain charisma. That the Durkheimian sacred principle is operative in all three types is assured, but Parsons, unable to find the same principle in Weber's work, seized upon charisma to rescue the convergence theory in ways not quite compatible with Weber's general methodology.[7]

Parsons makes these moves in part as a consequence of understanding the terms and inner dynamics of Weber's three legitimacy types according to their content, that is, according to their own versions of how and why they work. For Parsons, charismatic ideas *are* charismatic, traditional ideas *are* traditional, and rational ideas *are* rational. These characterizations do not of course mean the same thing for Parsons that they do for Weberian actors; Parsons does not believe, for example, in the supernatural basis of charismatic legitimacy. But he does believe that charisma inhabits charismatic ideas, just as he believes that rationality inhabits rational ideas; these are real "elements." In general, he sees different ideas as compelling for actors in different substantive ways, varying according to their content. These differing sorts of compellingness are tied to formal "elements"; charisma is an element of charismatic orientations, tradition is an element in traditionalism, and rationality is an element of rational-legal orientations. From here Parsons shows why none of these three orientations could be compelling on its own terms, how each shares the elements of the others, in the real world. Rationality alone cannot provide values, essential to Parsons's theory as the ends of action, and traditionalism cannot alone generate sanctity and moral respect; neither could be legitimate, therefore, without the element of charisma derived from a previous era. Neither of these ideal-typical orientations alone, in other words, could be compelling for actors.

But for Weber, a scientific understanding of how ideas work does not differentiate between substantive subjective orientations: ideas have "the same psychological roots whether they are religious, artistic, ethical, scientific, or whatever else" (Weber 1978, p. 1116). We would therefore expect to find that whatever is compelling about charismatic ideas is compelling about rational ideas as well. Neither charisma, tradition, nor rationality can account for the compellingness of their respective subjective modes. It is not the *truth* of ideas, not even as they turn to themselves to characterize their own inner workings or to discredit competing ideas, that makes them compelling, but something else entirely.

ETHNOMETHODOLOGY AND THE COMPELLINGNESS OF IDEAS

One glimpse into this "something else" is provided by Pollner's (1987) investigation into mundane reasoning, particularly his comparison of Azande religious reasoning with rational-legal reasoning in a modern traffic court. The heart of this comparison reveals that the two systems of reasoning, although as radically removed from one another as can be when it comes to matters of substance, are identical in their inner workings, their sustainability, and their compellingness for those who subscribe to them. The compellingness of Azande reasoning is not the supernatural source of either its assumptions or its conclusions, as Azande operating within that idiom might suppose. Neither is the compellingness of rationality due to the rational character of its assumptions or conclusions. And neither ideational mode is compelling because of a Parsonian charisma that inhabits it. Once again, both modes are compelling by virtue of a family of social practices.

Azande reasoning as described by Evans-Pritchard (1937) and as reanalyzed by Pollner (1987, pp. 54–58) includes as a primordial and incorrigible assumption the infallibility of a poison oracle. The poison oracle consists of administering ritually prepared poison to a chicken and interrogating the poison, or *benge*, regarding anything the interrogator seeks knowledge about, for example, the future. The benge's answers come in a yes/no format corresponding to whether or not the chicken dies; the order of this correspondence, which outcome indicates which answer, is decided by the interrogator in the initial consultation with the benge. The accuracy of the outcome can typically be corroborated by the same question later on, reversing the terms of the correspondence.

The intriguing aspect of this ritual is that the infallibility of the oracle is invariably sustained, even when the answers that come in are inconsistent with each other and when answers regarding the future fail to correspond to later events. A rational Western view takes such failures as a discrediting of the supernatural and infallible source of oracle answers (Pollner 1987, p. 54); indeed Evans-Pritchard saw them that way. But for the Azande, such failings only serve to resubstantiate the oracle's infallibility. Wherever Evans-Pritchard queried them using logic that led to rational conclusions, they countered with equally compelling logic of their own (Pollner 1987, pp. 54–55). They saw the contradictions and failings, but these very failings were seen from within a subjective orientation that sustains the oracle's infallibility. At times their response to Evans-Pritchard's inquiries was more like amusement and befuddlement that someone would be asking such absurd questions or questioning such basic truths. Pollner comments that these responses were similar to the way Westerners regard children or others judged marginally competent (p. 55).

The artfulness of Azande reasoning consists in their natural abilities to make "whatever," including failings, stand as documents of an underlying truth. Such failings therefore do not surprise them; they expect these failings and incorporate them into their belief system (Evans-Pritchard 1937, p. 330, quoted in Pollner 1987, p. 55). A variety of normalizing explanations for the failings inhabit this reasoning: "(1) The wrong kind of poison having been gathered, (2) breach of taboo, (3) witchcraft, (4) anger of the owners of the forest where the creeper grows, (5) age of the poison, (6) anger of the ghosts, (7) use" (Evans-Pritchard 1937, p. 330, quoted in Pollner 1987, p. 55). These formulas serve as resources for normalizing events as they occur, especially demonstrating how the very types of things that interfere with the oracle prove how right it inevitably is when these things do not happen. Thus there is a self-preserving quality to Azande reasoning engaged in the artfulness of these accounts. In Pollner's words,

> The incorrigibility of the oracle's infallibility is the gloss (Garfinkel and Sacks 1970) for the practices of the Azande through which the status of incorrigibility is secured and sustained. The incorrigibility of the oracle's infallibility is at once the process, presupposition and product of Azande reasoning practices. It is a process in that the maxim's incorrigibility is assured in no other way than through the *artfulness of Azande practices* of the formulation of accounts, which explain the discrepancy between oracle verdicts and the actual fall of events. Simultaneously, the doctrine is a presupposition of the Azande practices in that the field of possibilities from which explanations are selected are predicated on the oracle's infallibility. All of the candidate explanations from which the Azande choose are uniform in their respect for the integrity of the oracle: they locate the source of the discrepancy in conditions which leave the oracle's validity unquestioned and intact. Finally, in the ways that the incor-

rigibility of the oracle's infallibility is a presupposed feature of the concrete reasoning process through which it is sustained and in the ways that the embeddedness of that supposition produces accounts which reflexively preserves its own incorrigibility, the oracle's infallibility presents itself as the given, stable feature, which from the point of view of the Azande it always was. (Pollner 1987, p. 57, emphasis added)

Pollner's distanced analysis of Azande reasoning points to empirical practices in a way that, for purposes of the analysis, neither confirms nor discredits the accuracy of Azande ideas. In parallel fashion Pollner analyzes rationality in a traffic court setting, revealing the same empirical set of practices. A foundational incorrigible in the traffic court is the unquestioned facticity of an internally consistent, noncontradictory and objective world which exists independently of human activity or perception and whose transcendent quality can be addressed, investigated, and discovered through rational inquiry (Pollner 1987, pp. 27–30). These presuppositions are beyond invalidation, "for they legislate in advance what mundane inquiry can find in the first place" (p. 29). In traffic court, objects of inquiry are often events presumed to have taken place as events-in-the-world whose specific identities can be revealed through skilled investigation as to what-they-are, each being a "what really happened" in reality. The effort of the judge is to discover the "what really happened" of a case in ways that accord with sound methods of rational investigation. It is the presumed nature of the presupposed solution that it will be an event that is consistent with every other event in the universe, indeed every other known and knowable aspect of reality, every potentially discoverable detail, and it will be an event that is itself internally consistent and noncontradictory and whose necessary implications also are connected to reality in these very same ways, that is, according to the presuppositions of rationality. This much, says Pollner (p. 29), is legislated in advance.

But the dominant method of documenting "what really happened," most often the gathering of verbal accounts of the event from eyewitnesses or other designated authorities, does not automatically or unequivocally guarantee the smooth discovery of a "what really happened" that meets the above specifications. Various investigative procedures might document different events or a single event with contradictory features, nullifying its possibility as an event-in-the-world from the point of view of rationality. A defendant and a police officer, for example, might tell different stories concerning the speed of a vehicle. These stories together, each manifesting a bona fide method of courtroom inquiry, would therefore document a contradictory event, that of a car traveling at two speeds at the same time (Pollner 1987, pp. 35–36), thereby discrediting the foundations of rationality or discrediting the taking of testimony as a legitimate way to address reality. That neither of these conclusions is reached in court is suggestive of the artfulness of rationality maintenance.

Simply put, rational actors will not *allow* their subjective orientation to deteriorate or undermine its own foundations. They are adept at managing whatever evidence is presented on behalf of an event to count as evidence of a noncontradictory event "nevertheless." These skills depend upon a limitless ability to decide and redecide—that is, to reconstitute—whatever is known, or was known all along, about the world in order to bring it into conformity with the "whatever" of here-and-now courtroom drama. At the same time, these same operations are performed on the here-and-now "whatever" in order to turn it into content that accords with everything else that is known about the world. Certain loosely conceived and readily adaptable formulas are ready-made for these tasks: someone is lying (tied to general theories of human behavior, interests, motives, circumstance, and so on), someone's vision was obscured (tied to the general theme of human error and fallibility, e.g. faulty memory), the speedometer was not working (tied to general themes of instrumental error), and so on. All of these are resources for the judge in ascertaining a master version of the event that counts as the rationally discovered *real* event, or at least the official version pending further evidence, which documents, clarifies, expands on, and fills out the presuppositions of rationality (Pollner 1987, pp. 61–67). Rational actors will not allow any other outcome.

Viewed from the outside, this self-preserving work of rationality makes it look like a dogma, a bias, a circular set of prejudicial assumptions that believers will not follow to their self-undermining implications. Indeed, the underlying foundations of rationality are not themselves provable, nor does anyone ever try to prove them; instead they are used. Yet viewed from within, from the point of view of courtroom members, this self-preservation is irrevocably compelling.

Pollner shows us the striking similarity between courtroom practices and Azande practices in preserving otherwise radically differing subjective modes. The practices are, in fact, identical. Within either mode the practices are self-evidently proper, so much so that to question them or the foundational assumptions they document is to invite befuddlement rather than further argumentation on behalf of these assumptions. Seriously questioning them is indicative of a level of incompetence not subject to therapy within the system under question. And for either mode, the practices, when viewed from the outside, are circular and self-preserving (see also Pollner 1974a, 1975).

Thus Pollner was able to analyze both religious and rational ideas without regard to their respective accuracies, and he was able to detail the self-preserving quality of these subjective modes as a separate topic, that consisting of a family of social practices. It is most important to note that these practices themselves are *not rational*, and they are *not religious* or inhabited by charisma; they are free of ideational content. Moreover, and this cannot be overstressed, *they are the same practices* in any ideational mode.

Pollner's work, especially against the backdrop of Garfinkel's studies, provides a theory to account for the compellingness of ideas without regard to ideational content. Consistent with Weber's qualifications, subjectivity is not a feature of individual psychology—it is an operation, a family of practices, methods of idea maintenance that are both empirical for science and irresistible features of the social environment for everyday actors. In Durkheimian terms, these ongoing activities are ritual practices, and they are social facts; it is this activity that provides for the compellingness of ideas. Ideas are *not* compelling because of their structure, nature, or integrity or because "their content" intrinsically has to make sense to anyone. Charismatic ideas, for example, are not compelling because they are charismatic; neither are rational ideas compelling because they are rational; the same goes for traditional ideas. Rather, the compellingness of ideas consists in their being *seen and experienced* as making sense in terms of their own content, as being true, or in specific subjective modes rational, traditional, or according to God's plan. That compellingness, as well as whatever it consists of substantively, derives from what specifically *is occurring* in anyone's social environment: the family of artful practices, which in strict Durkheimian terms are external to and constraining upon any individual's common-sense knowledge and participation in these very practices. These practices are, again, invariant to ideational content.

The nonideational foundations of ideas are nicely reminiscent of Weber's contention that all ideas have the "same psychological roots," no matter what their content. Weber focused most of his work on case histories in answer to questions about why certain ideational contents and not others evolved in various civilizations' histories, places, and periods. But this should not deflect us from the central dynamics that are embedded in all of these ideational contexts: the compellingness of ideas by virtue of their being *subscribed to* (in Weber's terms), that being *active subscription* (in modern terms) empirically available as artful practices.

8

BUREAUCRACY AND

RATIONALIZATION

As we saw in chapter 7, ideas are compelling to social actors because of social practices occurring in their environment, practices which they, by virtue of their membership, necessarily participate in. In doing this, actors actively produce their world and shared subjective orientations to it. In Durkheim's terms, the impression of a naturally given world, as well as the taken-for-granted accuracy of shared ideas about the world, is not an illusion but a direct experience of empirical social facts. In no case, however, are ideas compelling simply because of their substantive content.

In this chapter I take up the case of rationality in more detail. I begin with Weber's famous description of bureaucracy. As the dominant form of social organization in rational-legal society, it is important to clarify Weberian bureaucracy as subjective orientation rather than reified structure. Consistent with this, ethnomethodology finds the empirical integrity of bureaucracy accomplished by the same social practices discussed in earlier chapters. Only through such practices could the reality of bureaucracy and the beliefs engendered in bureaucratic settings be *compelling* for social actors.

I next move into ethnomethodological studies of Weber's most pessimistic forecast concerning the future of Western civilization, the societal evolutionary process he called *rationalization*. For Parsons, Weber is surely worrying needlessly, since "pure rationality" is analytically impossible; that is, rationality is always compelling by virtue of the charisma it contains. But "pure rationality" is analytically impossible only if we derive its compellingness from its own substantive prejudices. If instead its compellingness derives from social practices, if "pure rationality" is compelling not because it is rational but because of what people do to sustain it, then it is not only possible but is even exhibited in Parsons's own theoretical writings.

WEBER AND BUREAUCRACY

Weber's discussion of bureaucracy is one of the most widely cited in sociological literature. It not only arises in secondary analyses of Weber's overall work (Bendix 1962, pp. 423–30; Coser 1971, pp. 230–33; Freund 1968, pp. 234–35; Giddens 1971, pp. 157–60; Johnson 1981, pp. 225–28; Turner and Beeghley 1981, pp. 237–39; Wrong 1970, pp. 32–36), it also emerges in work devoted to the general topic of social organization (Abrahamson 1981, pp. 135–39; Bendix 1968; Blau 1968), including references made in the literature of applied social science and management (Bakke 1959, p. 30; Bower 1968, p. 122; Burns and Stalker 1961, pp. 105–6; Peters and Waterman 1982, p. 19). It has been subject to critique and revision in empirical studies that argue that real bureaucracies do not work the way Weber said they do (Barnard 1958; Bittner 1965; Dalton 1959; Roethlisberger and Dickson 1939; Selznick 1948). Some of these secondary discussions treat Weberian bureaucracy as a self-contained theoretical statement in its own right, separating it from Weber's general sociology (cf. Rogers 1969, p. 1; Seidman 1984). Others reproduce Weber's discussion in its original scholarly context in a wider effort to restate or clarify the overall work.

But many of these renderings of Weberian bureaucracy share the premise that bureaucracy is a structured thing. Little distinction, in fact, can be made between most renderings of Weberian bureaucracy and the views of bureaucrats or anyone living within a rational-legal order and orienting to it in that way. Such renderings are distinguished by their familiarity, their affinity with common-sense ideas about organization. More important, sociologists sometimes cast this familiarity as an affinity between Weber's sociology and functionalist conceptions of organizations as socially structured networks of normative behavior that oblige individuals to conform.

This gives aid and comfort to American functionalists in viewing Weber as one of their own, or at least his discussion of bureaucracy as an "implicit functionalist analysis" (Blau 1970, p. 142).

It is difficult to thwart the conventional wisdom on this matter, made more difficult by the fact that Weber himself forged his discussion of bureaucracy in this common-sense vernacular. Maybe this is why the discussion is so widely cited. In any case, we seem to have an intuitive grasp, through our everyday knowledge of bureaucracy, of what Weber is describing here. We are quite at home with this description; even though it is more articulate and highly detailed than we are used to, it seems nevertheless to be a refinement of what everybody already knows. And while the precision of Weber's writings may seem overstated, we at least think we know what he is writing about: something structural.

In functionalist circles this intuitive reading has been incorporated almost untransformed by the rest of Weber's sociology. The one general exception is where empirical studies turn up features of bureaucratic settings out of accord with Weber's description. One tack here is simply to remember that Weberian "bureaucracy" is an ideal type. As with other ideal types, Weber never intended his discussion as a description of something that could be found in the real world (Weber 1949, p. 90). It is a methodological device for designating organizational principles removed of traditional and charismatic orientations. The ideal-typical bureaucracy can serve as a comparative yardstick for concrete studies and as abstract beginning and ending points in studies of social change (Coser 1971, p. 223; Wrong 1970, p. 35). Yet even within these discussions, "bureaucracy" is still treated as an ideal type of a structured entity.

But as we have seen from Weber's comments on organization, his anti-reification stance, as well as all he has to say about social order, this ideal-type qualification to bureaucracy is not the only qualification; there is also the *ideational* qualification (cf. Hekman 1983). "Bureaucracy," then, becomes an ideal type of a subjective orientation to organizational legitimacy. In this context, Weber's famous list of bureaucratic features is a list of beliefs subscribed to by the membership, a subjective version of how bureaucracies work from the point of view of the ideal-typical bureaucratic actor. Weber is talking about ideas here, ideas about the legitimacy of such matters as policy, decision making, salaries, promotion, hiring and firing, professional jurisdictions, and competence—in short, anything that goes on in bureaucratic settings.

We see these concerns at work in Weber's preliminary remarks about bureaucracy as the typical expression of "rationally regulated association within a structure of domination" (Weber 1978, p. 954): "Legal authority rests on the acceptance of the validity of the following mutually inter-dependent *ideas*" (p. 217, emphasis added). Weber lists five ideas which set the framework for bureaucratic activity:

1. Norms can be "established by agreement or by imposition" on rational grounds with a "claim to obedience" which extends to members of the organization and sometimes to others "within the sphere of power in question."

2. Laws are systems of abstract rules intentionally established and are to be applied by administration to concrete cases in ways consistent with the rational mandate established for the organization.

3. Leadership is itself subject to these impersonal rules in the very way it exercises its authority.

4. Individuals' subordination to authority is limited to their capacity as "members" of the organization.

5. Obedience to authority is not to the person holding the authoritative position but to the impersonal order which has rationally delegated the authority to this person. (pp. 217–18, paraphrased)

Notice that once the ideational qualification is made, Weber proceeds to describe the ideas within their own frame of reference, which in part may explain why so many interpreters are inclined to read them as Weber's own ideas or his own vision of how legal authority works. In other words, their status as beliefs subjectively held by actors is easily lost in Weber's characterization of them. Indeed, as the discussion continues, the ideational qualification recedes further into the background. A lengthier and more detailed analysis of rational-legal authority is introduced with these words: "The following may thus be said to be the fundamental categories of rational-legal authority" (Weber 1978, p. 218). Weber proceeds to specify these categories in a vocabulary compatible with common sense and functionalist versions of collective action as a systemic structural entity with objective features (pp. 218–20). This vocabulary rings with "spheres of competence," jurisdictions, hierarchies, technical rules; in short, it is written in the very style which Weber has said earlier is the subjective style of rational legitimacy. The first discussion of bureaucracy (pp. 220–23) is likewise couched in an apparently structural vocabulary; in fact it is almost a prescriptive recipe for bureaucratic organization, an analysis that represents the bureaucrat's own version of what bureaucracies are and how they work.

Weber returns to a vocabulary of subjectivity in his remarks about the "spirit" of rational bureaucracy (Weber 1978, pp. 225–26), but there is no reason to suspect that he ever really turned away from his theoretical interest in ideas. These passages illustrate how smoothly Weber, in speaking of the spirit of an age, can pass unnoticed into a functionalist vocabulary as he expresses that spirit in its own terms, a move easy for us to misinterpret in reading the material. But it is inconceivable that he would have capriciously ignored his own warnings against reification in the case of bureaucracy above all other organizations. It is better to assume that he is describing the world from the point of view of the bureaucratic membership.

Skeptics should recall that Weber makes parallel terminological shifts in his discussions of other subjective orientations, for example, Calvinism.

> For the damned to complain of their lot would be much the same as for animals to bemoan the fact they were not born as men. For everything of the flesh is separated from God by an unbridgeable gulf and deserves of Him only eternal death, in so far as He has not decreed otherwise for the glorification of His Majesty. We know only that a part of humanity is saved, the rest damned. (Weber 1976, p. 103)

We would hardly regard such passages as Weber's own perspective, much less as his sociology. Nor should we allow ourselves to regard Weber's discussion of ideas popular in our age, ideas about bureaucratic organization, as Weber's own sociological views.

A lengthier discussion of bureaucracy (Weber 1978, pp. 956–1003) occurs much later in *Economy and Society*, the famous passage that was published as a separate essay in an earlier translation (Gerth and Mills 1946, pp. 196–244). This later discussion displays even less of the deliberate ideational qualification and more of the quasi-functionalist flavor, but this does not justify disembodying it from the rest of Weber's work, particularly the role of ideas in action and human history. It should be noted in this regard that Weber does not lay much emphasis on his ideal-type qualification in this passage either, though he occasionally references it (see e.g. Weber 1978, p. 1002). Both qualifications can be read as deeply underlying Weber's sociology and informing the substantive examples he examines in detail. And given Weber's denial of the existence of a "collective personality which 'acts' " (p. 14), some of his writing can even be taken as metaphor, for example his reference to obstacles that "bureaucratic organization has had to overcome" or the "march of bureaucracy" which "destroyed [nonrational] structures of domination" (p. 1002).

Still, it cannot be denied that Weber made little effort to avoid being misunderstood on this point. He could not have foreseen the rise to prominence of this passage as an essay in its own right, nor could he have conceived the issue of bureaucratic structure versus bureaucratic mentality as controversial to a degree approaching the analogous issue he faced with respect to capitalism. He may also have had some difficulty with the double status of rationality discussed above—that is, rationality both as a historical phenomenon and as a working premise of science (see chapter 6). Unremedied confusion in this area renders the impression that since both bureaucrats and sociologists are rational, then their versions of bureaucracy (or anything else) would have to be similar if not identical. This would explain Weber's occasional references to bureaucracy as truly efficient, truly superior to other organizational forms (Weber 1978, pp. 973–78), and, insofar as bureaucrats respect science, truly in accord with scientific principles. But notice that if sociologists were to hold to the general rational orientation of the bureaucrat, they would similarly have to "recognize" the inherent fallaciousness of charismatic reasoning.

A more intriguing possibility is that Weber's general theme of subjectivity came too late in his writing career for its full implications to have been systematically incorporated back into his earlier detailed analyses of religion, status groups, bureaucracy, and law. According to Roth (1978, pp. lxvii–civ), the great bulk of Weber's attention to "interpretive sociology," the ideational qualifications vis-à-vis social relationships and organization cited above, occur in part 1 of *Economy and Society*, written between 1918 and 1920, close to Weber's death and well after the older part 2. While the subjectivity theme enters significantly into the older work (e.g. Weber 1978, p. 1116), especially in the chapter entitled "Domination and Legitimacy" (pp. 941–55), it surfaces unevenly and sporadically compared with its more systematic treatment in part 1, where it receives a full measure of Weber's attention as a topic in its own right. The extent to which this renders interpretive sociology an afterthought in Weber's intellectual life is problematic. To the extent that it was, however, part 1 can be read not only as an afterthought but as a qualification to things said earlier. Indeed, Roth (1978, p. ci) views part 1 as a "reference text" that would have "facilitated the reading of Part Two had Weber lived to revise the old terminology in the light of the new." And it most certainly was not entirely afterthought; thus the order in which Weber turned to sociological themes should not deter us from viewing his overall work as a coherent whole.

Finally, none of this recovery of Weber's ideational qualification is a denial that there are observable behavioral consequences of bureaucratic mentality. Weber is clear that differences in subjective orientation produce "very real differences in the empirical structure of domination" (Weber 1978, p. 953). Indeed, as reviewed above, organization, like any social relationship, is a simultaneity of ideas and behavior—that is, a probability of *meaningful action*. But there is no justification in Weber's general theory for thinking that a scientific view of that action is the same view as the subjective ideas that go with it. Weber's notion of action "appropriate" to meaning does not insist that scientific description of action will simply reproduce the meaningful ideas that caused it or that the ideas, even when they are ideas about the action in question, are descriptively correct with respect to that action. This is thoroughly consistent with Weber's "distancing" principle discussed in chapter 6. Specifically, according to Weber, "appropriate" does not imply that either the subjective orientation or the action is correct by abstract standards (p. 27). We saw this, for example, in Weber's expressed distinction between legal and sociological reasoning.

Thus it is in every major sense Weberian to extend these insights to bureaucracy, which now becomes a reciprocity of subjective cause and behavioral effect. If we are not to denigrate charismatic orientations as "rank swindle" but to remain value-neutral with respect to them as sociological phenomena (Weber 1978, p. 1112), then neither ought we to embrace rational-legal orientations in a value-positive mode or treat them as modern and true. It would be idiosyncratic so to elevate the rational orientation simply because of its genuine familiarity. Again, we have seen Weber's distancing principle at work in his sociology of law. Extending this to bureaucracy, bureaucratic rules and policies do not specify what is or is not rational, any more than the law specifies what is legal. What distinguishes bureaucracy, from the sociologist's point of view, is the *belief* in rational structure, clarity, precision, and so on, all of which ties directly to bureaucratic reasoning and behavior, including the acceptance of a determination that a policy (say) applies to such and such a situation in such and such a precise way, together with the probability of appropriate action. This is not to deny the accuracy of these ideas but to remain indifferent to them.

Thus extending Weber's distancing principle to the rational-legal sphere yields the following: whether or not bureaucracies *really* display their Weberian features (Weber 1978, pp. 956–63, 217–23; see Bendix 1962, pp. 423–26; Giddens 1971, p. 158), that is, whether there are really clear jurisdictional areas with clear criteria, and whether bureaucratic members really limit their activities to their appropriate areas; whether activities of staff are really regular and standard, and whether these duties are really written down; whether hiring, firing, and promotion are really decided on the basis of clear rational criteria, qualifications, and special competence; whether there is really an existent office hierarchy which members adhere to in a process of appealing in a "precisely regulated manner"; whether management is really based on written documents; whether management really follows general rules which are clear, stable, and exhaustive; whether these rules are precisely recorded in written form and whether they can really be learned; whether there is really a clear disjuncture between personal and bureaucratic property; whether upward mobility is really provided for in the form of a career and whether such careers are determined strictly by seniority and rationally determined ability; whether technical knowledge is really used when available; whether or not *any* of these Weberian principles are "true" in a structural sense is *irrelevant for purposes of scientific analysis*. What matters is how the bureaucratic membership orients to a *belief* in such a machinelike entity, including how it works, as a source of bona fide legitimacy. What matters is how the membership regards authoritative commands as having come through "proper channels," a complex chain of commands with rational consideration to available and appropriate rules, policies, technical knowledge, standards of efficiency, data and formal documents, evidence, and so forth, even though the specifics of the presumed process is, from the membership's standpoint, understandably hidden from view. What matters, moreover, is the success with which leadership convinces followers that its commands and policies so accord with this impersonal system of rational standards and criteria (cf. Wrong 1970, pp. 34–35; Parkin 1982, p. 88). Where such efforts fail, leadership is open to charges from below of negligence, incompetence, or corruption.

Interestingly enough, the little attention Parsons gives to bureaucracy retains in its verbal style much of Weber's ideational qualification (Parsons 1968b, pp. 506–7). He does not go far enough with this for a determination of the significance he saw in this qualification. It is safe to assume he saw little other than that bureaucratic actors respect the system of rational rules that make up a bureaucracy, which remains, in both its normative and behavioral aspects, a reified structured object. This mode of analysis allows theorists to see Weber as presaging modern functionalist thought. Merton, in fact, expands Weber's theory taken in this vein, designating structural sources of dysfunctions within a bureaucracy (Merton 1968, pp. 249–60)—here too bureaucracy retains its status as a reified structured entity.

ETHNOMETHODOLOGY AND BUREAUCRACY

If for Weber bureaucracy is the dominant form of social organization within a rational-legal context, then from the point of view of the membership, bureaucratic behavior is structured behavior par excellence; accordingly it is the paragon of rule-governed behavior as well. Bureaucracy represents the most formal expression of belief in reified structural order and the rules that produce it. Formalized rules in this instance are bureaucratic policy; behavior flows from this in a strictly predictable fashion, at least to the extent that an organization is thoroughly bureaucratic. In accord with Weber's nonevaluative stance toward subjective orientations, it should be possible for sociologists to describe bureaucratic behavior without regard for the truth or falsity of notions of bureaucratic standardization. And here again ethnomethodological studies are most enlightening.

In chapter 3 I reviewed Zimmerman's (1970) study of a welfare bureaucracy, noting that skill in rule use, even where rules are formalized as policy or job descriptions, does not consist in "following" them. Indeed the lack of core meanings renders rules per se prescriptively sterile and nonspecific regarding behavioral outcome. Skill in their use includes the artful determination of what rules "mean and meant all along" in light of specific, heretofore unpredictable situational contingencies.

A more general and theoretical expression of these kinds of observations about bureaucracy is offered by Bittner (1965). Bittner recasts bureaucratic organization in ethnomethodological terms, defining his task as "the study of the methodical use of the concept of organization [which] seeks to describe the mechanisms of sustained and sanctioned relevance of the rational constructions to a variety of objects, events and occasions relative to which they are invoked" (p. 248, original in italics). From here Bittner moves to disassociate sociological interest from that of a bureaucratic orientation, which he calls "the author of the rational scheme, typically the managerial technician who deals with organization in the 'technical sense'" (p. 249). He then specifies the sociological task of addressing "how certain objects and events meet, or are made to meet, the specifications contained in the scheme" (p. 249), later suggesting that "problems referred to the scheme for solution acquire through this reference a distinctive meaning that they should not otherwise have" (p. 249, original in italics).

Thus Bittner focuses not on the rational integrity of bureaucracy per se but upon the artful manner in which the membership manages to produce and sustain the impression of such rationality. He does not require that an organization be rational in order to examine how it can appear rational "from within." Bittner's approach is not a denial of rationality any more than an affirmation of it but rather a shift in topic for sociology. Accordingly, he suggests investigations into the manner in which an organizational membership *assigns* events and behavior to rules for their warrantable identity as standardized bureaucratic behavior in conformity with bureaucratic standards or rules (see e.g. Cicourel 1968; Cicourel and Kitsuse 1963; Cicourel et al., 1974).

Bittner's recommendation to study bureaucracy empirically, with an ethnomethodological indifference as to the accuracy of the membership's own version of it, is a nice extension of Weberian indifference vis-à-vis traditional and charismatic ideas to the rational-legal realm. However, a curious aside concerning this article is Bittner's reference to Weber as a seminal representative of those he criticizes—representative, that is, of those who incorporate the rational-legal version of bureaucracy, the bureaucrat's version, into sociology as a science. Here, then, is an example of how functionalist readings of Weber, due in part to the publication of Weber's essay on bureaucracy as a piece separate from the theoretical spaces that surround it, have produced a discourse in which ethnomethodologists are seemingly obliged to announce their break not only from functionalism but from everything that went before it. Demonstrating that this obligation produces a distorted history of sociological thought is one of my purposes in the present work.

RATIONALIZATION

Notable in Weber's historicism is a lack of chronological sequence between the three societal types. There are no intrinsic reasons why one type would give way to another. This is determined within historically specific contexts, including material conditions and the substantive ideas available in a given time and place (see Giddens 1971, pp. 178–84). The details and multifaceted possibilities are elegantly brought out in Weber's case histories.

An important dimension of Weber's assessment of modern Western civilization has to do with the transition from either a charismatic mode or a traditional mode to a rational-legal mode. This is the process Weber called *rationalization* (Collins 1986, pp. 61–79; Loewith 1970; Wrong 1970, pp. 25–32). In accord with Weber's historicism, there is nothing automatic or inevitable about rationalization. In most cases rationalization is retarded by competing traditional ideas, disrupted by charismatic outbursts, or self-limited because of the kinds of substantive ideas being rationalized. But in Western society, Weber saw no precursors to decreased rationalization. Indeed, rationalization had already gone further here than anywhere else in human history, helping to produce capitalism, for example, which alone is unique by world history standards. At the organizational level, rationalization means the proliferation of bureaucracy. In Wrong's (1970, p. 26) terms, "Explicit, abstract, intellectually calculable rules and procedures are increasingly substituted for sentiment, tradition, and rule of thumb in all spheres of activity." As Weber looked to the future, he saw no end of the process in sight, despite its lack of inevitability (Coser 1971, pp. 233–34; Giddens 1971, pp. 182–83; Mommsen 1974, p. 80; Wrong 1970, pp. 28–29). Rationalization became in this way Weber's central process of Western civilization.

It is not the empirical accuracy of this Weberian prognosis that is my concern here. Indeed current Weberian scholarship suggests that Weber's pessimistic strains were more like warnings than predictions (see Mommsen 1987). Cavalli (1987) finds in current life much of the ideational content and charismatic interventions to reduce, modify, eliminate, or reverse rationalization in the West as elsewhere, and Roth (1987) counters the "iron cage" imagery by specifying multiple rationalizations in different spheres and by highlighting the valued choices required to decide the substantive content of rationalized ideas.

But my immediate interest in Weber's forecasts lies in the conceptual possibility of such a process in the first place. If, as Parsons says, charisma and tradition were necessary elements of rationalism, then Weber never would have fretted over the possibility of nonstop rationalization driving out the other elements. Yet his prognosis, accuracy aside, is rooted in the possibility of the rational orientation being uncontaminated by competing traditional or charismatic ideas. Indeed it is the simultaneous presence of these other ideas that stop, retard, limit, or reverse rationalization in other places and periods, that is, where capitalism failed to develop. The fact that Weber was worried about the absence of such checks on the process in the West suggests that for Weber, the rational orientation was analytically capable of operating on its own. Whether in fact it is operating that way is irrelevant to the analytic integrity of the type.

Parsons dismissed Weberian rationalism and rationalization, calling them "the central methodological difficulty of Weber's position [which] far more than any factual mistakes underlies whatever serious difficulties there may be in his empirical theories" (Parsons 1968b, p. 607). Beyond that, Parsons had little to say about Weber's pessimistic forecasts. Indeed he could not take the prognosis seriously, since he could not imagine the possibility of pure rationality, even in the abstract. He returns nonrational "values" to instrumentally rational action, for example, claiming that the difference between instrumentally rational and value-rational action is mainly one of the number of values adhered to (pp. 643–44). More generally, pure rationality is an impossibility for Parsons because it cannot provide the ends of action and therefore requires elements not contained in the type (pp. 607–10, 653–55). So he eventually finds charisma and tradition even within the rational ideal type as conceived methodologically (pp. 661–63, 674–76), suggesting, once again, that rationality is meaningless without bringing in other elements (pp. 607–10). I shall return to this topic in the next chapter; for now it is notable that Parsons did not consider the other options, for example the possibility that rationality (or ideas in general) is subject to ongoing ritual repair in the spirit of Durkheim.

ETHNOMETHODOLOGY AND RATIONALIZATION

So the dilemma is before us: if Weber's prediction is not an inevitability, it must be at least an analytic possibility for it even to make sense in his overall sociology. It must be conceptually possible for a historical process to progressively drive out traditional and charismatic ideas in favor of rational ones. Yet for Parsons, this was not a possibility insofar as rationality itself partook of charismatic and traditional elements. Charisma, in fact, is what makes rationality compelling. Pure rationality could not possibly sustain itself, says Parsons, as its only meaningful prescriptive power relates means to predefined ends, whose predefined status itself cannot be rationally decided. If rationality cannot be pure in this sense or, put differently, if "pure rationality" itself contains charisma, then rationalization as a driving force does not make sense.

Through ethnomethodological studies we have seen how rational ideas can be sustained on their own, not because of what it is about them (their rationality) that makes them believable but because of what is *done* that makes them believed. This activity—the ethnomethods—is free of ideational content and is invariant to the ideas it sustains. Pure rationality is analytically feasible in this sense, needing neither charismatic nor traditional ideas to make it happen. In that way the analytic integrity of the ideal type is sustained at the methodological level; moreover, rationalization, as a turning away from charismatic and traditional subjective orientations in favor of rational ones, is analytically possible.

I should emphasize that my arguments for the analytic possibility of pure rationality do not assert that rationality can ground itself rationally. Indeed no ideational mode can ground itself in terms of its own prejudices. Instead, the grounds are *nonideational.* They are not topical concerns within a membership's subjective orientation; they are social practices, and they are "uninteresting" to the membership (Garfinkel 1967, pp. 7–9). For Durkheim, they are ritual practices necessary for sustaining the integrity of the society, the collective conscience, in this instance a rational one. Note the additional convergence with Durkheim on this point: rationality in the absence of ritual practices cannot sustain itself; such would be anomie. This is not the same as to say that rationality without other ideational modes cannot sustain itself. What is required beyond ideational content, rational or otherwise, is nonideational social practices.

Indeed it is the inability of rationality to ground itself in conformity with its own rational prejudices that provides for the possibility of rationalization as endless historical process—that is, rationalization is a project without termination. There is no point at which the project thus far could not be found by rational actors to have fallen short of rationality's presuppositional idealizations. Thus what Parsons calls the inadequacies of pure rationality is precisely the locus of its possible renewal. Of course this does not have to happen; religion or tradition can fill in the irrationalities that rationality generates and recognizes. But only the possibility, not the inevitability, of rationalization is in question here. Thus our attention is drawn to two aspects of rationalization: (1) the sense in which rationality repairs its own recognized nonrationality, and (2) the sense in which the project of "pure rationality" is necessarily endless.

In order to access the character of rationalization, let me restate the manner in which rationality generates and sustains itself as compelling in routine social life. It is not sustained through its character as rational for those who subscribe to it but rather through a family of social practices. In everyday settings whose members subscribe to a belief in stable social structure as outcomes of following rules, this impression is maintained by " 'corpusing' and 'decorpusing' " (Zimmerman and Pollner 1970, p. 95) both structure and rules in terms of their "all along" identity and "all along" intent such that whatever takes place that could from some other vantage point be seen as damaging to this common-sense orientation can be seen as "nevertheless" more evidence on its behalf. In reality production, whatever turns up that could from another vantage point be seen as contradicting rationality's foundational prejudices or methods of inquiry is instead allowed to count as evidence on behalf of them. In bureaucratic settings, where ideas of standardization and prescriptive policies are most formally adhered to and enforced, events which might from another vantage point suggest the routinely nonstandard or the inadequacies of policy are nevertheless assigned to policy in such a way that documents the event as standard and the policy as prescriptive. These are ritual practices that provide for the compellingness of rationality in its course.[1]

The point here is that these practices are essential for rationality to appear rational to those within its jurisdiction; they are not voluntary or optional practices. As we saw in chapter 5, interfering with these practices can reveal the transparency of working assumptions and can lead to pain. These practices are what sustains the incorrigibility of such working assumptions. Thus practical bureaucratic life depends for its utility upon the subordination of bureaucratic idealizations to immediate here-and-now concerns making that action "nevertheless" in accord with these very idealizations. Rational activity could not proceed without these practices.

But notice that belief in formal rationality, while at every turn dependent upon and constrained by these practices, is not subject to these inevitabilities over the long haul. That is, with regard to long-term historical processes, as it contemplates its accomplishments in terms of its own foundational prejudices, rationality is free to puzzle at its failure to come up to its own idealizations and to provide endless proposals for remedy and repair. Over the long term it is free to "discover" some of ethnomethodology's observations about bureaucracy, for example, and to see these discoveries as policy problems to be overcome. Put differently, bureaucrats can engage in a kind of practical philosophy, chronically ready to see looseness as flaws in the organizational fabric, chronically prepared to acknowledge the possibility of improvement. Sociologically, such improvement could but yield further discrepancies which the membership would have to handle on a daily basis just as before; indeed such remedies would not move historically toward a more fully rational system but rather would produce increased resources with which the impression of rationality can be sustained. From the point of view of bureaucrats, however, these modifications move daily life inextricably toward a more fully integrated system.

To illustrate, recall Garfinkel's (1967, pp. 25–31) study of ordinary conversation. He asked students to write next to a conversational transcript what had been "really meant." In effect he was asking for literal rendition such that the conversation as spoken could be seen as in rational conformity to it; he was asking students to document the rational clarity of what they had said. When they complied, he asked them to clarify the clarity of what they had just written. That clarity too could be found to need further clarification, and so on. As we saw, absolute clarification was never reached; the import here, however, is that the task produced progressively *longer and longer versions of the conversation*, multiplying whatever remained to be clarified (p. 26). This could serve as a prototype model of rationalization as an endless process. It also serves as a contrast with real world rationalization in that (1) the conversation as spoken in the natural world did not itself generate the expanded transcripts, that is, students wrote the expanded transcripts only in response to Garfinkel's request; (2) such a requirement in practical life would first cripple then extinguish any possibility of a conversation going forward; and (3) the process stopped when it was allowed to stop, when Garfinkel allowed it to stop, when Garfinkel had "made" and students had "gotten" the point—that is, when the assignment was over.

Yet these observations also give us a glimpse into unyielding rationalization as the *multiplication of perceived features of bureaucracy in need of members' gloss.* From the vantage of bureaucrats, all of these newly created features are newly discovered discrepancies that can be repaired. In the abstract and over the long term, moreover, there is no stopping point, no practicality sufficient for calling the project complete. Unlike routine bureaucratic concerns that are settled in their course, allowing the membership to move onto other matters, the long-term repair project is at best provisionally finished, for example when a newly created policy is announced as "in place."

The consequence of rational action viewed this way is that in the name of clarification and efficiency, routine work becomes increasingly unclear and cumbersome (cf. Wrong 1970, p. 27). This is indexed empirically by the proliferation of documents, files, specialized job descriptions, criteria for success, paperwork, special jargon, tables, schedules, pre- and post-tests, reports, presentations, cost/benefit analyses, criteria for judging the appropriateness of other criteria, consultants, outside evaluations, and the rest of it—all of which leave the membership with the sometimes unspoken impression that nothing has changed but for the awkwardness of rational accountability. Nevertheless these newly created artifacts and vocabularies provide for the possibility of presenting general appearances of being ever increasingly rational, modern, up to date with the latest developments in management science—in general, sneaking up on bureaucratic regularity as ideally conceived.

A CASE STUDY OF RATIONALIZATION

An interesting case of rationalization is Competency Based Teacher Education (Hilbert 1981, 1982), a movement predominately of the 1970s that arose to answer some perennial questions: how can schoolteaching be removed of its traditional uncertainty and converted into a scientifically precise activity? How can the tried and tested principles of science be put to use in programs of teacher education to "guarantee graduates as 'safe' "? (Jones 1972, p. 106). In fact, what is teaching excellence, how can it be objectively identified and transmitted to student teachers, and on what basis is that transmission assured?

A working assumption of Competency Based Teacher Education (CBTE) is that these questions can be answered scientifically, that ambiguity can be removed from teaching once and for all through exhaustively breaking a complex behavior (teaching) into its unequivocal behavioral building blocks (the competencies), each with its unequivocal prescriptive rules of performance and "absolute criteria" (Dodl and Schalock 1973, p. 48) for recognition by any outside observer. Each competency is to be a *discrete behavioral routine* that can be unambiguously identified and transmitted by prescription to candidate teachers. Candidates in turn can simply follow the prescriptions, and evaluators can see simply for the looking, without need of interpretation, whether or not candidates are following these prescriptions (Elam 1971, p. 67; Hall and Jones 1976, pp. 10–11; Howsam and Houston 1972, pp. 7–8). And when the candidates so perform, the automatic result is the complex behavior of which the competencies are elements: competent teaching.

The important observation here is that CBTE enthusiasts publish their pronouncements as literal renditions of the social world. They anticipate a future in which the entire list of competencies will be written down (Ishler and Inglis 1973, p. 18; Cooper and Weber 1973, p. 15; Joyce 1974, p. 193), including lists of social contexts and their connections to appropriate competencies where demonstrated knowledge of these connections constitutes yet further competencies (Dodl and Schalock 1973, pp. 50–51; McDonald 1974, p. 24; Burke 1972, pp. 44–46). Even "personal teaching style" can be written into the universal formula which applies to all teachers in identical ways (Schalock and Garrison 1973, p. 42; Weber and Rathbone 1973, p. 62; Thomas and Kay 1974). An ideal CBTE-informed teacher education program would have the complete list in hand together with firm, unambiguous "absolute criteria" (Dodl and Schalock 1973, p. 48) for recognizing them as performed (Burns 1972, p. 17; Chase, Harris, and Ishler 1974, p. 26; Steffenson 1974, p. xiv; Kean and Dodl 1973, p. 36).

We could not have asked for a clearer expression of a rational subjective orientation and its related bureaucratic mentality with the promise of closing all discrepancies between behavior and policy. Notice that for rationality, repair projects are deliberately designed not for the express purpose of creating bureaucracy but rather for the sake of efficiency, standardization, and scientific objectivity. Thus CBTEists frequently draw comparisons between their enterprise and the sciences of medicine, nursing, and law (Andrews 1972, p. 150), or they simply state that CBTE is teacher education as a science in its own right (Houston and Burke 1973). Hall and Jones (1976, p. 364) compare it to the Newtonian scientific revolution, suggesting that CBTE has a comparable payoff that "defies description."

Modern sociologists will hardly be surprised at CBTE's inability to deliver as promised. Indeed, just as Garfinkel's subjects expanded their conversational transcripts in the name of clarity, so CBTE research has generated increasingly longer lists of what, exactly, competent teachers do. It was not uncommon during the 1970s to see several thousand competencies in a given CBTE program (Joyce 1974, p. 203), for example the list of over two thousand competencies at the University of Toledo (Ishler and Inglis 1973, p. 12). Noteworthy for present purposes is that all of these lists were considered far from complete by CBTEists; moreover CBTEists acknowledged that not one identified behavior, on any of their lists, measured up to CBTE standards. The practical solution was to define a "basic list" of competencies according to impressions and philosophies of program designers (Johnson and Shearron 1973; Jones 1972, p. 106; Hall and Jones 1976, pp. 26–58; McDonald 1974; Waterman 1974, pp. 1–2), under the assumption that "the rest" of the competencies can be learned on the job (McDonald 1974, p. 25; Burns 1972, p. 23; Chase, Harris, Ishler 1974, p. 19), and to caution program implementers regarding the unfinished character of such lists, reminding them of the need to "operationalize" objectionably vague competencies (Dodl et al. 1973). Yet these solutions were regarded as temporary, pending the full development of CBTE science. All shortcomings were treated as technical, contingent problems that could be overcome with time, research, and funding.

A significant document to come out of the CBTE movement is *The Florida Catalog of Teacher Competencies* (Dodl et al. 1973), designed to help teacher educators plan and implement their own CBTE programs. As written, the document is a paradigm of rationality, with its "Master List" of 1,301 stated competencies cross-classified according to eight indices for "retrieving" them for one purpose or another. Precision and context-free identity are built into the document, as the identity of, say, competency no. 638 remains constant whether one finds it in the master list or restated in a subindex of one sort or another. Each competency is considered to be a stable behavioral *thing* which can be precisely combined with other elements in the production of teaching competence, but which nevertheless never loses its identity as the thing-that-it-is, named in the master list.

A glance at the catalog tells us what we might have expected: each behavior carries its own ambiguity no less so, perhaps more so, than "competent teaching" does in the first place. Here are a few examples, chosen quite arbitrarily:

suppress immediate impulses to advance some long-range purpose (no. 224);

accept responsibilities for teaching subjects outside his own specialization as it is appropriate to a team-teaching plan (no. 1,083);

select activities on basis of individual abilities and interests (no. 656);

utilize new information (no. 555);

perform interpersonal relations (no. 552);

meet with parents (no. 844);

comprehend the realities of social stratification in our society and begin to evaluate its effects on her own behavior (no. 1,222);

adjust freely to varied environments and human situations (no. 169);

plan projects best suited to the individual needs of children (no. 747);

diagnose the cause of a pupil's incorrect work (no. 316);

give precise directions for carrying out any instructional activity (no. 140);

maintain consistency as to what is expected of pupils without losing flexibility or adaptability to changing circumstances (no. 410);

interpret standardized tests (no. 269);

emphasize responsible group living with standards of conduct comparatively determined (no. 1,247);

present data and ways to manipulate it (no. 1,178);

structure situations which encourage students to seek the teacher's counsel on non-academic matters as well as academic ones (no. 1,059).

Suffice it to say that any one of these could be a candidate for a CBTE-oriented breakdown and *could generate a competencies catalog all its own.*

In light of the essential inability of CBTE to make good its promise, two observations are noteworthy. First, nothing need prevent CBTEists from their continued efforts as long as they can convince relevant research foundations that they are making progress. There is no theoretical stopping point for this enterprise. Second, this inability did not inhibit the practicality of CBTE-inspired programs at points along the way toward their perceived goal. Programs were hailed regarding the types of records they could keep on students and the ways in which such records could facilitate employment decisions (see Chase, Harris, and Ishler 1974). One observation, then, is that CBTE programs, however implemented, nevertheless can produce files, documents, and dossiers useful for bureaucrats in maintaining the rational impersonality of their decisions. A student teacher who has mastered 975 out of 1,000 competencies according to some checklist is objectively superior to someone who has mastered only 972; that bureaucratic truth will seem evident within a rational-legal orientation regardless of the concrete circumstances within which either the checklist was constructed or items on it were checked (cf. Garfinkel 1967, p. 24), especially if each item has its own set of standardized documents such that the final checklist may be seen as a "summary." Extensive documentation produces its own impression of rational objectivity (Smith 1974), and CBTE may be viewed as generating the possibility of such documentation in specific settings. Yet it remains axiomatic that no program of teacher education will attain rational legitimacy by being literally rational, that is, by literally fulfilling the CBTE dream of rational role specification.

Indeed, more generally, rationality does not require fulfillment of its own specifications but only the active manipulation of appearances so as to produce the sustained impression of such a fulfillment. Over the long haul, rationalization is the production of resources useful in maintaining these impressions in local settings as well as the premise of perfectibility regarding whatever shortcomings may be noticed along the way. Thus rationalization is a historical process, no longer a mysterious evolutionary development in society as such but rather an empirical phenomenon visible in concrete workaday human affairs.

9

DURKHEIM-WEBER CONVERGENCE AND

FUNCTIONALIST RATIONALIZATION

The last eight chapters have presented arguments that ethnomethodology's empirical program has resurrected and confirmed many of the theoretical directions in classical thought that were dropped, overlooked, or dismissed in Parsons's introductions of these texts to American sociology. As we have noted, Garfinkel began his work as investigations into the profound issues passed to him by Parsons and ultimately traced to these classical texts, hence these connections are not merely coincidental. Indeed Parsons derived and passed to his student the seminal issues in classical theory that would invite investigation in more modern light, issues such as objective social structures, moral regulation, shared culture, rationality, and intersubjectivity, but he cast these issues in ways that served his own evolving action theory, deflecting them away from the kinds of empirical research that Garfinkel undertook more or less independently. It is little surprise, then, that Garfinkel's empirical studies vis-à-vis Parsons's profound issues would retrieve some of the key classical themes that Parsons dismissed.

But Parsons not only interpreted Durkheim and Weber; he also argued for an implied similarity between the two, all the more striking in light of their differing national and intellectual backgrounds and relative unawareness of each other's work. In this convergence thesis he was right, as I will argue in this chapter, though not in the ways or for the reasons he said. Indeed, just as the dismissed themes are recovered in ethnomethodology, so also is the nature of the convergence.[1]

This chapter will also revisit the ethnomethodological characterization of "traditional sociology" (specified here as American functionalism) as a folk science, a formalized version of common-sense theorizing that routinely occurs within the very society under investigation (specified here as Western rational society), rendering such a science an example of that society rather than an analysis of it. This revisit will be to suggest the exaggerated visibility of Western social reasoning in functionalist reasoning and thereby to begin an ethnography of functionalism as a concentrated look at rational social order. Such ethnography can reveal Parsons's theory as an empirical case of the very phenomena that Durkheim and Weber discussed and predicted.

SUMMATION OF THE DURKHEIM-WEBER CONVERGENCE RECOVERED BY ETHNOMETHODOLOGY

Chapters 2–8 discussed connections between ethnomethodology's empirical research and the theoretical formulations of Durkheim and Weber. Here I review some of these connections, specifically those which draw attention to correspondences between the two classical theorists. The imagery here is that of ethnomethodology providing terms for understanding the two theorists in ways that simultaneously draw them together. Thus each of the following points ought also be viewed as a case for the advantages of ethnomethodological research, insight, and theory.

1. Garfinkel's *reflexivity* recovers the sui generis quality of Durkheim's social order, and it does so in ways consistent with progressive readings of Weber's use of ideal types (e.g. Hekman 1983). That is, the targets of Weber's methodological typifications are simultaneously cause and effect, for example social organization as subjective orientation and behavioral consequence. This simultaneity of subjectivity and objectivity—which is to say, their inseparability—is consistent with Durkheim's sui generis order, which is thoroughly factual and thoroughly moral. While neither Durkheim's nor Weber's theoretical principles are identical to reflexivity, they are highly compatible with the notion that objective social order is inseparable from descriptions of that order by members of that order, that description of social order is part of that very order, particularly when we

recall how such descriptive work is regulated and enforced by members of that same order.

2. Ethnomethodology pursues the Weberian policy of nonreification of social structure, but it does not thereby collapse into what otherwise might appear to be the only other possibility: a theory of individual autonomy or any other kind of reductionism which Weber would have equally disapproved of. Indeed, it retains, without reification, all of the exteriority and constraint a Durkheimian could ever ask for. Following Durkheim's explicit policy of empiricism, ethnomethodology asks what is *observably* external to and constraining upon human behavior. Finding social practices, research then focuses on how these practices are external to those who engage in them, how members artfully regulate each other, in a strictly sui generis (Garfinkel's term: "incarnate") way. In that manner, members are collectively constrained, but they are constrained by their own activity rather than by the disembodied products of that activity.

3. Durkheim's society/reality equivalence, tied to ethnomethodological appreciation of conformity/discovery, provides insight into the dynamics whereby "society" for the Weberian actor possesses such an undeniable, incorrigible, opaque, objective status. Termed "reification" when engaged in by sociologists themselves, members' social practices produce a world of social structure, order, organization, and the concomitant array of institutional realities which, while not existent for science, are incorrigible features of the Weberian actor's social environment. They cannot be ignored or disavowed for the same reasons that any aspects of objective reality cannot be disavowed. Their exterior and constraining status is real, in that sense, in that the empirical social practices that sustain them are exterior and constraining.

4. Likewise, Weberian ideas become compelling for actors on their own terms, not as scientifically available objects whose truth-value or other characteristics make them believable, but rather as ritual practices necessarily engaged in by the membership which produce the compellingness of ideas simultaneously with the incorrigibility of their reified belief-objects. In Durkheim's terms, "psychic entities" are social facts, not to be distinguished from objective reality as social facts.

5. Members' practices are ritual practices, particularly in limiting cases where they save the objective compellingness of imminently collapsing beliefs and objective truth. Thus Durkheim's anomie theory, especially his discussions of anomie-prevention practices, helps account for how beliefs

and objectivity remain compelling, even where directly threatened by countervailing tendencies. It is notable in this regard that where ritual anomie-prevention practices fail, the result is simultaneously the disintegration of society and reality, which, as we have seen, includes a reduction of experience and subjective commitment. In other words, the compellingness of Weberian ideas about social order and the corresponding incorrigibility of objective social structures wear thin precisely as Durkheimian anomie-prevention practices fail.

6. The policy of ethnomethodological indifference to the practical projects of the membership both advances Weberian indifference to the truth content of ideas about society and provides a sophisticated Durkheimian distinction between viewing the world from within a moral community versus viewing it sociologically from without. The external status of organized reality, transformed by this research policy to the external status of empirical social facts, becomes attributable to empirical social practices for sociology. This indifference to social structure and reality as viewed and renewed by the membership is also referred to as a topic shift in ethnomethodology.

7. Intersubjectivity also emerges as an accomplishment of social practices in ethnomethodology, indeed the same practices that sustain an objective world and the compellingness of ideas. This is understandable in light of common-sense conceptions of shared understanding as overlapping subjective content, as shared by virtue of simultaneous orientation to a shared objective world. Again, there is no reason for sociologists to reify, or take for granted from within a Durkheimian moral universe, either the objects of consciousness or intersubjectivity itself.

8. For Parsons the search for features of ideational content that make it compelling led to charisma and consequently the breakdown in Weber's ideal type distinctions even for methodological purposes; hence rationality could not work alone. In our renewed vision, rationality can work alone, as can charismatic and traditional orientations, whether or not any of this ever actually happens. Indeed, all three work through identical processes: the ritual society/reality maintenance that Durkheim speaks of and that reemerges in ethnomethodology as members' methods. These are nonideational practices of creating and reproducing Weberian charismatic, traditional, and rational social orders—that is, saving them as belief-objects even as beliefs in them are simultaneously sustained.

9. Durkheim's "sacred" is recovered in ethnomethodology, not as We-

ber's "charisma" as a real element for science, but as members' transcendent reality whether it is charismatic, rational, or traditional, whether we are talking about metaphysical, religious, scientific, or bureaucratic reality, all of this being equivalent to society for Durkheim and emerging in ethnomethodology as social practices. Indeed Durkheim saw the necessity of social practices and ritual repair for the maintenance of society/reality, that is, for the prevention of anomie.

10. Moreover, the "sacred" emerges in rational society as the reified rational social order, including the bureaucracy that rational actors know "ought" to be but never is in actual local settings, idealized proper procedure in comparison with which actual goings on look shoddy—this is the common-sense belief that "somewhere" in the society real rationally administered bureaucracy is (or could be) proceeding as it should. Wherever members orient to reality unavailable to them concretely but sustainable anyway through artful practices, there is the Durkheimian sacred object, the belief-object of the Weberian actor. In this way, then, rational actors can sustain the rationality of here-and-now projects through orientation to the presumed order where somewhere, or in some general sense, bureaucratic procedure lives up to rational expectations.

FUNCTIONALISM AS FOLK SCIENCE

It is an irony of Parsons's theorizing that while it asserts the analytic impossibility of pure rationality, it now emerges as an example of that very phenomenon. Both the manner in which it conceives social order and the way it goes about explaining order radically approaches the Weberian rational-legal ideal type. This is not to say that Parsons thought social actors were themselves necessarily rational or that norms were or that actors oriented toward norms in rational ways. Indeed Parsons had to account for the various kinds of societies and social action that were decidedly nonrational; as we have seen, Parsons sees rationality itself as containing elements of charisma. But what is nonrational about social actors nevertheless becomes rational for functionalists themselves viewing social systems as consequences of prevailing social norms. In other words, the rationally working functionalist model of culture produces order, even where it includes "institutionalized mistakes" (Heritage 1984, pp. 27–30).

Specifically, the bedrock of Parsons's reasoning—the view of action in terms of its necessary properties discussed in chapter 1—is closely similar to the subjective version of action described by Weber as rational. More generally, the presumption of an "out there" society made up of regularities, patterns, repeating behaviors—in a word, social structures—is almost identical to the ideal-typical rational-legal actor's common-sense orientation to social organization. Indeed, functionalists discuss organizations within that factually existent society in ways indistinguishable from the way in which rational actors talk about them. The existence of social structure is taken for granted as part of reality, an aspect of it in addition to the array of "natural" nonsocial phenomena, things that are incorrigibly present. For rational actors, this assumption becomes most formalized in bureaucratic settings, so that its heightened expression and extension to society per se renders the functionalist version of society analogous to huge, megabureaucracy.

Not coincidentally, functionalist explanation for this mammoth structured entity runs parallel to bureaucratic explanation. Here shared culture becomes analogous to bureaucratic policy, a set of shared prescriptive recipes—norms and values—that actors follow and abide by because of socialization and internalization. Policy produces stable organization as long as the policy is rationally coherent and organizational members can be persuaded to abide by it. Once again, the rationality I am referring to here is a feature of the subjective orientations of functionalist observers, not necessarily the actor or the normative scheme into which actors are socialized.

To clarify, Parsons and his followers have created, in the abstract, a theoretical society of bureaucratic efficiency, but it is important to remember that this efficiency is only for purposes of functionalist explanation. Parsons is by no means asserting the rationality of societies, particularly not in the terms of those societies. Indeed, the whole notion of values, as governing the ends of action as opposed to norms, as governing the means, is sometimes postulated as a cultural given for which no rational justification can be offered. Given values, norms can be rational, irrational, or nonrational. Yet for the analyst, these values, once they are ascertained, can be put to use for rational sociological explanation. Even irrational norms are rational explanations of standard behavior by functionalists once they are ascertained. Thus the rationality I am identifying is a rationality of and within the orientation of functionalist theory itself, not something functionalism substantively posits as a feature of society. This is part and parcel of functionalism's turning away from the subjectivity of the concrete actor in favor of subjectivity as an analytic category within functionalist theory itself (Heritage 1984, p. 21).

Parsons's commitment to bureaucratic theorizing is neither peculiar nor capricious. Just as, in his terms (1968b, p. 51), utilitarians inherited a "common-sense" version of actors sufficiently saturated in individualism as to preclude concepts of collective action, so likewise did Parsons inherit a common-sense version of collective action sufficiently rational-legal as to preclude empirical investigations of society. Within the terms of that common-sense reasoning, Parsons's reading of Durkheim is almost inevitable: the collective conscience is a set of rules. Combined with the long-term rationalization project of the rational orientation, the functionalist agenda is equally inevitable: find the collective conscience, clarify its formal properties, discover its precision necessary to produce collective behavioral stability, and, in substantive studies, specify its prescriptive content.

Thus functionalism is a descriptive and explanatory theory thoroughly embedded in the rational-legal society that Weber writes of and prognosticates about. Because of the foundational prejudices of this subjective orientation, substantive research premised on functionalist theory consists, in advance of moving into any research setting whatsoever (including non-Western societies), the incorrigible assumption that whatever else is going on, there *will be* standard social structures observable or discoverable for the trained sociological investigator. Also known in advance is that there *will be* discoverable norms and values which members of the setting have already internalized that produce the observed structures. The model is one of actors being buffeted around by cultural forces, however complex, much as a computer's output is ultimately traceable to its input. Where there is deviation from this model, one needs to look more deeply into the norms that qualify other norms or that override them on occasion. Where there is an apparent "free will" factor, one can find the structured prerequisites or parameters of this free will or even discover it is not free at all. However the behavior may look, however complex and multifaceted, to whatever extent it fails to conform with standardized cultural expectancies, sociologists looking hard enough will find the sufficient degree of prescriptive complexity to account for exactly that amount of behavioral complexity. This is the "cultural dope" model of the actor that Garfinkel criticizes (Garfinkel 1967, pp. 66–75; see also chapter 2).

In this manner, then, the bureaucratic model of society and normative prescription has been pressed by functionalists into the service of sociological explanation for every kind of society imaginable. In Weberian terms, not just rational society but also traditional and charismatic societies can be analyzed in terms of norms and values that cause their corresponding social regularity. The bureaucratic model thus becomes a vision not only of bureaucracy but of society-in-general as conceived theoretically.

For functionalists, the bureaucratic model takes priority over empirical evidence suggesting that societies are not organized that way. Such evidence is perhaps most striking in examinations of bureaucracies themselves, where studies repeatedly show that not even bureaucracies conform to the bureaucratic model. A traditional way to manage such evidence is to claim that since formal policy cannot account for behavior actually occurring, some other "policy" (e.g. informal rules) is contributing to the observed regularity (Barnard 1938; Dalton 1959; Roethlisberger and Dickson 1939; Selznick 1948). Therefore the bureaucratic model is sustained at a descriptive level in ways that may even be irrelevant to the bureaucrat, who is anxious to bring informal rules under formal control. Yet these informal rules function analytically the same way the bureaucrat envisions the workings of formally designated policy.

Through precisely the same maneuvers, functionalists can sustain the bureaucratic model in any type of society at all, and they can even do so in advance of empirically examining any particular society in question. Because of their general foundational commitments, functionalists can invoke norms and values that function to produce order-in-general, thereby sustaining the bureaucratic model in ways that are utterly irrelevant to concrete actors, some of whom in fact have had no exposure whatever to Western rationality and its precepts. In functionalist terms, these norms and values are the content of actors' subjectivity, despite their irrelevance or unavailability to concrete actors. Once again, this illustrates how functionalists displace the subjectivity of concrete actors with an "actors' subjectivity" of their own device, a formal concept that has a distinctive place in functionalist explanation (Heritage 1984, pp. 21, 30).

So Western rational society produced not only bureaucracy but a distinctive style of bureaucratic theorizing highly formalized in functionalist sociology. This returns us to ethnomethodology's characterization of "traditional sociology" as an example of the society that it presumably set out to study. Having "gone native" in this sense, traditional sociologists missed the phenomenon they had originally sought, the production of social order. They could not see the phenomenon while participating in it; in order to see the phenomenon, sociologists would have to suspend belief both in the integrity of objective social structures and in the assumption that behavior is rule-governed (Zimmerman and Wieder 1970). The qualification I add to these arguments is to specify "traditional sociology" as American functionalism and "the society" (i.e. the society that functionalism "went native" in) as Western rational-legal social order, including the reasoning style members of that order engage in when describing and explaining human behavior generally. Not all pre-ethnomethodological sociology is inherently subject to the same limitations as functionalism, and not all societal memberships subscribe to theories of rule-governed behavior. But situated as we are within rational-legal society, this is the order that will be the most difficult of all to transcend in an effort to move beyond, in Durkheim's sense, moral community or, in Garfinkel's sense, membership, in order to examine society from the outside.

THE RATIONALIZATION OF THE COLLECTIVE CONSCIENCE: TWO INEVITABILITIES

If we are to move outside Durkheimian moral community, and if functionalist sociology is part of that very community, we will have to move outside of functionalist sociology; indeed to do so, since functionalism appears to be an exaggerated version of rational society, should produce an unusually clear vision of the manner in which rational-legal society operates. This is not to say that functionalists share societal members' practical projects at the substantive level. Bureaucrats, for example, tend to work prescriptively and without any commitment to abstract general theory when formulating policy; functionalists operate more descriptively, investigating the culture that (for them) prescribes, remaining indifferent to the here-and-now substantive projects that rational actors engage in routinely. Moreover, functionalists' commitments are to academic sociology and theory development. However at a much deeper level, the manner in which they go about positing the nature of their phenomena and their manner of explanation mirror the formal features of bureaucratic work. They are, once again, creating a folk culture of bureaucratic efficiency with special attention to rules.

Since Parsons originally found justification for the idea of external animating control in Durkheim's collective conscience, and since he argued for the prescriptive content of the collective conscience, we may conceive the functionalist agenda as the *rationalization of the collective conscience*. The conversion of the collective conscience to norms and values, together with its distinctness from that which it prescribes as stable collective behavior, constitutes the rational-legal orientation. In light of Durkheim's society/morality equivalence, the rationalization of morality is congruent with the rationalization of factual behavior. We can now capture within functionalism precisely what a classically informed ethnomethodological theory would predict. This amounts to viewing functionalist theory ethnographically as a miniature rational society-in-brief, Western society in a bottle, a transparent example of the society it purportedly reports on.

For heuristic purposes, then, we can imagine functionalist theorizing as a lived world analogous to the lived world of rational-legal actors. We can expect to find within this world the same phenomena that ethnomethodologists have been recommending as topics of study: social practices necessary for sustaining this world. At its root this mode of analysis is not at all without precedent. Ethnomethodologists have repeatedly commented on social research that assumes the stability of social phenomena as "out there" in the world and the practices that necessarily sustain such research. Consider, for example, Garfinkel's discussion of the "documentary method of interpretation" as practiced by these researchers.

> It [the documentary method] is recognizable . . . in deciding such sociologically analyzed occurrence of events as Goffman's strategies for the management of impressions, Erickson's identity crises, Riesman's types of conformity, Parsons' value systems, Malinowski's magical practices, Bale's interaction counts, Merton's types of deviance, Lazarsfeld's latent structure of attitudes, and the U.S. Census' occupational categories. (Garfinkel 1967, pp. 78–79; see also "Examples in Sociological Inquiry," pp. 94–96; "The Rational Properties of Scientific and Common Sense Activities," pp. 262–83; and Zimmerman and Pollner's [1970] discussion of members' methods as practiced by demographers, ethnographers, and survey takers.)

However, a classically informed ethnomethodological theory allows more specificity with regard to how functionalists have been theorizing. We can now view, for example, the transformation of the collective conscience to rules as rationalization, and we can also see the inevitable social practices as Durkheimian ritual repair work. In fact we should find, in this heuristically imagined functionalist lived world, any of the classically postulated phenomena clarified in ethnomethodological studies.

For present purposes, two classical themes will be discussed, one from each of the classical theorists and related to the other theorist in line with the convergence summarized above. Each of these examples has a distinctive predictive flavor coming out of classical thought, but given our place in history, both examples can only now have a more or less retrospective flavor when applied to American functionalism. For present purposes I refer to them simply as theoretical inevitabilities. They are (1) the ongoing, unfinished, and necessarily unfulfillable character of pure rationalization, and (2) the necessary recruitment of deviance as anomie prevention.

LIMITLESS FORMAL RATIONALIZATION OF SOCIETY SUI GENERIS: MERTON'S ROLE THEORY

According to Weber, rationalization could proceed indefinitely unless there were something about the content of the ideas being rationalized, traditional pressures in other directions, or charismatic interventions that could retard the process. He worried that there were no such redirecting forces at work in the West. As indicated in earlier chapters, however, the present concern is with the integrity of pure rationality and the analytic possibility of rationalization, not whether Weber was factually correct in his pessimistic forecasts. In chapter 8 I reviewed ethnomethodological reasons why pure rationalization would necessarily be an endless process. Rationality, I argued, can sustain itself through ritual practices, by subordinating itself to here-and-now practicality constituted as "nevertheless" in conformity with rationality's presuppositions; yet, wedded to the possibility of literal policy and precise consequence, rationality can inevitably discover these glosses in historical process and reproduce them as "flaws." Flaws, in turn, become the bases of reformed policy, which becomes progressively complex, increasing the versatility of the routine gloss and the possibility for newly discovered flaws. In short, rationalization is the endless multiplication of problems to be rationalized.

Two case studies illustrated this process in chapter 8. One was Garfinkel's (1967, pp. 25–31) request to conversation participants to bring their utterances into rational conformity with "what was really meant," and the other was Competency Based Teacher Education (Hilbert 1981, 1982). American functionalist sociology is yet another case. Just as CBTE can be either reviewed as the science it claims to be and thereby come under heavy criticism or be viewed not as bad science but as a historical event taking place within organized education, so also can functionalism be critiqued as sociology within sociological circles or viewed as a natural expression of Western civilization. The latter approach in both cases reveals CBTE and functionalism to be nearly identical in presuppositions and styles of explanation. Both presume the possibility of standard, stable behavioral structure, both find this stability originating in a prescriptive mechanism that gives rise to it, and both thereby depend on a literal correspondence between the elements of behavior and prescription. The main difference is that CBTEists work prescriptively, trying to control and produce the desired stability, while functionalism works descriptively, trying to discover the mechanisms that prescribe and produce the stability already observed. CBTEists, in fact, use the latter approach in their assumption that where competent teaching is happening already, there too is the program sought after, the recipe that can be discovered, expressed, and integrated into teacher education for those novices who would not otherwise do such a good job.

Of the two, CBTE is a more simple-headed case of rationalization, even within its own idiom. CBTEists simply "list" the prescribed behaviors in random order, expecting someday to finish the list and later to specify the interconnectedness of the rules. That the list would yield longer lists is the crux of the inevitability. In fact, had Parsons stopped theorizing with *The Structure of Social Action*, this might be exactly the agenda for functionalism: find and list the norms and values in the collective conscience, and we will understand why the factual society we see before us is there. Instead, Parsons later elaborated and developed his theory (including Parsons 1951; Parsons et al. 1951; Parsons, Bales, and Shils 1953) at a level of abstraction far greater than simply listing rules. His theorizing takes us into discussions specifying types of rules (e.g. the pattern variables), types of interrelations between rules, categories of situations in which different kinds of rules apply, rules for deciding between alternate sets of rules, the allocation of rules to different categories of societal members ("roles"), movement beyond a strict "rules" format further specifying distinctions between values (ends) and norms (means), the relationship between prescription and knowledge, the location of values within a cultural subsystem and norms within a social subsystem, mechanisms for connecting these two subsystems to each other as well as to personality and biological subsystems, subsystems within each of these subsystems with their own elements and organizational integrity, the internal organization of systems in terms of "levels" and the leveling of systems in relation to each other in listable ways, mechanisms for sustaining internal coherence within and between systems and subsystems, typologies of systems needs and internal integration within action systems, subsystems of society as a complex social action system and various mechanisms regulating these subsystems, and so on (see Lackey 1987). All of this serves Parsons's interest in developing a *general* theory of action and a grand theory of society. This, then, is a general project far beyond the CBTE attempt to specify a single role or otherwise to list concrete rules for concrete behavior. Parsons's scheme is supposed to apply to any society and ultimately to any social circumstance. However, insofar as this theory elaboration is descriptive elaboration of prescriptive policy, the underlying logic of Parsonian functionalism and of CBTE science is essentially the same, whatever the level of abstractness or generalizability.

The implication is that functionalist theorizing would have to generate increasingly complex versions of itself in order to sustain itself, through continually repairing the theory as it has progressed thus far—for example, discovering loopholes, missing links, and newly required mechanisms to ensure that previously postulated mechanisms would work. Within the functionalist idiom, all this work is in pursuit of a grand theory displaying the elusive but desirable scientific quality of "logical closure." Viewed ethnographically, however, functionalism will never achieve closure for reasons that are unavoidable. Instead it can only repair its progress thus far, producing endless versions of the society as increasingly complex. Within the functionalist idiom, moreover, this endlessly increasing complexity, the complexity required in the specification of normative order, mirrors the progressively revealed complexity of society itself as a factual phenomenon, providing the impression that the evolving complexity of scientific explanation is in service to ongoing discoveries about the natural complexity of natural social order. That functionalist theorizing generates the complexity of natural factual order as it simultaneously explains that order with evolving theory lies at the heart of my ethnographic observation.

Thus functionalism orients to "society," that is, to no society in particular but rather to society-in-general as a theoretical object, in much the same way bureaucrats orient to social organization as their practical object.

That is, functionalists orient to their theoretical object as bona fide members of a rational-legal order. In keeping with Durkheim's society/morality equivalence, we would expect a congruence between rationalization of the belief-object, the society, and rationalization of the explanatory mechanism, normative order; the rationalization of the factual and the moral is one selfsame set of practices. Following Garfinkel's *reflexivity*, we would expect that the work of functionalists is the work of describing and explaining an increasingly complex order where that work is also the methods whereby the order is generated as both factually and morally present (cf. Wieder 1974a). In other words, the rationalization of social order is part of that very order. This means, for example, that functionalist rationalization even of traditional or charismatic societies (or any non-Western society) as theoretical objects within functionalist theorizing is a feature of the rational-legal order which functionalism both participates in and exemplifies.

As a case in point, consider Merton's theory of "role-sets" and "status-sets" (see Hilbert 1990b). An elementary Parsonian model of cultural prescription would predict behavioral uniformity throughout a society, but this does not happen. Thus enters "role" in Parsons's terminology, and later in Merton's theory, to explain how a single recipe could produce so many different kinds of behaviors: different bundles of rules attach themselves to different types of people ("statuses") so that they can behave differently as well; the terms of this norm allocation are contained in the overall prescriptive formula. This would predict uniform behavior only by members of specific categories, even as those categories differ from each other. However, even this prediction is at obvious variance with the details of observed social life; in order to sustain the functionalist model, more repair work is necessary.

The repair came in the work of Robert K. Merton, whose role-set and status-set provide for a proliferation of behavioral diversity all nevertheless emanating from the same prescriptive entity. Borrowing from Linton (1936) the original terms "role" and "status," Merton goes on to say that for any given status, for any given social position within a social system carrying its specified rights and duties, there is not, as Linton implies, just one bundle of prescribed behaviors, one role, but rather a variety of roles and their concomitant role relationships. This differs from "multiple roles" in that the latter designates roles associated with different statuses. A role-set, then, is a bundle of roles that goes with a single status (Merton 1957, pp. 110–11). Moreover, following Linton, Merton reminds us that the same person can occupy multiple statuses, each with its respective role-set. These statuses simultaneously occupied by one individual Merton terms a status-set (1968, pp. 422–24).

A familiar example of role-set, one which Merton focuses on, is one that goes with the status "scientist" (Merton 1973, pp. 519–22). Roles attached to that social position include at least four: research, teaching, administrative, and gatekeeper. Each of these roles involves role relationships with a distinct set of others; together they constitute a role-set. Additionally, any given scientist may occupy other statuses, such as homemaker, each with its role-set, in this case mother, wife, PTA member, and so forth. Together these positions constitute a status-set.

Yet Merton's solutions to his observed complexity of factual order yields a new kind of theoretical puzzle: in the theory stated thus far, nothing would prevent the complexity of normative order from making multiple and simultaneous contradictory prescriptions. Thus the elementary Mertonian role theory might not produce order at all but rather chaos and disorder. Role relationships exerting pressure on a status incumbent could inhibit or stifle his or her ability to perform in other role relationships. Or the role-sets of differing statuses could come into conflict, inhibiting the incumbent from fulfilling any of them effectively. That this does not happen, or seldom does to a degree sufficient to the breakdown of society, is Merton's observation and puzzle. More repair is necessary.

The next layer of repair comes in the form of "social mechanisms." In the case of role-sets, Merton identifies normative mechanisms which counteract potential instability, or, in his words, "social mechanisms which produce a greater degree of order than would obtain, if these mechanisms were not called into play" (Merton 1957, p. 113). The mechanisms include these observations: (1) various members of a role-set may be less concerned than others with the status associated with the role-set and will therefore exert differential pressure upon the incumbent to conform; (2) some of these members are plainly more powerful than others and may exert corresponding degrees of pressure upon the incumbent; (3) the incumbent may fulfill contradictory role relationships by insulating each from the visibility of the others; (4) where such contradictory pressures are fully visible to all, members of the role-set may appropriate and solve the problems as their own, thereby reducing stress upon the incumbent; (5) incumbents find solidarity with others in similar circumstances, which is itself a structural response to the troubles of role-sets; and (6) incumbents can simply terminate roles not compatible with the role-set and not resolvable in other ways (pp. 113–17; 1968, 425–33).

Similarly in the case of status-sets, potential conflicts between statuses with their respective role-sets are avoided in ways such as the following: (1) public perception of status conflict reduces the pressure brought to bear on the incumbent by role-set members within some of the statuses; (2) common value orientations regarding the relative importance of the conflicting status obligations cause certain role-set members to modify their demands; (3) structurally generated "empathy" because of others' having experienced similar status conflicts likewise reduces their pressure upon the incumbent to conform; (4) certain adaptations themselves become standardized and therefore learned and conformed to; and (5) statuses self-select, that is, are not joined in sets at random but lead to one another through structured chains ("status-sequences")—socialization into one status inculcates values amenable to certain new statuses and not others, and so on (Merton 1968, pp. 434–38). Merton acknowledges that even these mechanisms fail to reduce contradictions and conflicts to nil or produce perfect social order, as he observes that social systems may operate at less than full efficiency most of the time (p. 434; 1957, p. 116). However, without these mechanisms, the present level of observed social order would not obtain.

Within the functionalist idiom (and despite Merton's concessions to societal inefficiency), statuses, roles, and their structured interrelatedness sustained by operating social mechanisms are what *theoretically* could produce an observed order. We should remind ourselves that all this is an elaboration of the nonempirical prescriptive entity that Parsons posited as normative order. The use of such devices by theorists to unravel an increasingly complex system of norms and values indexes their place in functionalist theory. What these moves toward specification imply for functionalists is the potential for analytic precision. As we move toward progressively qualified systems, unraveling, say, role-sets as we go, we eventually unravel roles as networks of prescriptions for concrete action that would, through the processes of socialization and internalization, produce the concrete action prescribed and therefore observed. Actors at this theoretical level "need not improvise new adjustments" (Merton 1968, p. 436).

From the vantage of classically informed ethnomethodological theory, such specification and elaboration is the rationalization of moral regulation. Once wedded to the common-sense orientation of rational actors, functionalists necessarily engage in rationalization in order to sustain what they presuppose about social order and its regulation. Indeed Merton's mechanisms will not work without still further repair. One device is to list "structural prerequisites" for the mechanisms to operate (Coser 1990). Rationalization is a theoretically endless process of ritual repair.

In chapter 2 I reviewed ethnomethodological argumentation and evidence regarding the empirical status of rules. We saw how rules are unnecessary for action except when they are required, how they cannot be required unless they are required by a concrete somebody, and that they need not be required by anybody. Generally they are required by common-sense actors on comparatively rare occasions for practical purposes, for example as devices to clear up trouble. We also saw that where functionalists claim the *constant* necessity of rules, this can be a correct claim only in relation to the empirical source of the requirement: functionalists require it themselves. Functionalism is thus an exaggerated version of a rational-legal orientation—while rational actors generally believe that "somehow" rules stand behind most behavior, they actually require rules only a bare minimum of the time. These are the moments of ritual repair and reconstitution of society and common-sense reasoning as transcendent to actual occasions.

And yet we are also now better prepared to catch a glimpse of the sui generis order within functionalism as functionalism posits the omnipresence of normative structure. The requirement that actors are constantly following rules is itself an inevitable requirement within the idiom, an orientation that sees social order as something to be explained in the first place. What for mundane actors would be situated "trouble" (a problem of order) is an ongoing, chronic problem for functionalists ("the" problem of order). Functionalists have elevated the workaday problem of order to a constant theoretical concern, thereby requiring the constant use of rules to clear up the ongoing problem, that is, to establish the order, to recognize it as a factual matter.

Moreover, as the recognized phenomenon eludes literal specification, decaying into its inevitable and unyielding complexity, such complexity, as recognized and reconstituted from a problematic status to an ordered one, will of necessity generate a corresponding network of norms and values in the very course of its recognition. The rules used to explain that order are the same rules already used to identify it; thus the taking for granted of a patterned factual order continues to yield to functionalism what Merton himself might call, ironically, a self-fulfilling prophesy (Merton 1968, pp. 475–90). The factual and the normative orders are simultaneously generated by functionalist reasoning. In the functionalist vision of members constantly requiring rules, functionalists are watching their own reflections.

Thus functionalists are not simply explaining organized society but are organizing it. An easily accessible example of this can be found in one of Merton's mechanisms relative to status-sets (Merton 1968, pp. 434–38). Why is it, he asks, that the same person occupying different social positions does not face chronic confusion or other social disorientation? Among his answers is a self-selection mechanism within status-sets (status-set mechanism 5, above) or, in the case of his example, nonselection: committed Christian Scientists are not usually also medical doctors (pp. 436–37). If they were, the argument goes, there would be tension between the status commitments of the two positions. That this does not happen is due to the values associated with the statuses. Socialization into one status precludes socialization into the other. Or, more generally, people reject otherwise achievable statuses because of the value-orientations internalized during socialization into other statuses. That keeps status-sets more fully integrated than they would be without this mechanism operating.

Observe that Merton's appeal to his readers to see Christian Science and medicine in potential conflict is predicated on the very same distinction in values that he then uses to explain the resulting lack of conflict. If we can see the potential conflict, we have already explained how people avoid it. There would be no perceived hypothetical conflict without the disparate values which Merton says prevents the conflict from manifesting. Rather than say, therefore, that without this mechanism there would be more status conflict (e.g. there would be more Christian Scientist physicians, with all the trouble that implies), it might be more to the point to say that without this mechanism, Christian Scientist physicians would constitute an integrated status-set. Contrarily, what makes this possibility troublesome in Merton's hypothetical is precisely what in Merton's explanation prevents people from entering into such trouble. Why do they not face contradictions? Because that would be a contradiction.

Thus Merton is organizing the society, including its chaotic alternative, in the very process of explaining why people conform to it, including their avoidance of status conflict. He is doing what rational actors do in the routine ordering of their lives, in their decisions about consistency and inconsistency, and the rest. He shares tacit rational knowledge of order versus disorder and in that sense is participating in society from within rather than from a disinterested empirical standpoint. He sees the social world as rational actors do, the difference consisting in the fact that he presses these folk explanations into the service of science; as we have seen, however, this renders his science a folk science from within rational-legal society, a formalized version of common-sense reasoning from within that society (Zimmerman and Pollner 1970).

The case just cited is an especially clear case of sui generis order. Indeed one would expect this transparency where Merton himself strives to clarify the underlying logic of his position. He calls the Christian Science physician example an "extreme case" that will "illuminate the general theoretical point," shortly stating, "To say this is self-evident is of course precisely the point" (Merton 1968, p. 437). The self-evident status of Merton's arguments is precisely my point as well. That Merton would reproduce the common sense of his society is the crux of my observation.

With varying degrees of clarity, we can find these same underlying commitments throughout Merton's discussions of status-sets and role-sets. A general observation is that wherever Merton reveals potential trouble within the functionalist idiom, that same trouble is solved within that idiom as an outcome of some presumed structural entities which rational actors themselves also orient to and take for granted. Merton's solutions mirror their solutions; he solves trouble the same way; his theory is a formal version of their theory. That these solutions are specifically *structural* in Merton's theory and thereby are operative *continuously*—that is, independently of the volition or perception of individual actors—is but an extension of the functionalist commitment to see order as continually problematic and actors thereby in constant need of solutions, rules, mechanisms, and so on. Yet once again these constantly operating mechanisms are Merton's requirements, not necessarily requirements of the people observed or of their behavior. The fact that when rational actors encounter routine trouble they generate precisely the solutions they require and that these solutions are a lot like Merton's solutions should not mislead sociologists into thinking that these solutions are required by people all the time or independently of the trouble. For routine actors, social order is probably problematic less often than not.

To cite a few more examples, a Mertonian mechanism that reduces status conflict is prior agreement regarding which status obligations are more important than others (Merton 1968, p. 436). Yet a world in which all conflicting statuses are considered equal, resulting either in social gridlock or chaos, is a fantasized world for which the functionalist world is the cure. Here again is the presumption of chronic trouble requiring chronic structural solutions. This is a requirement of functionalist theory. Or in the case of role-sets, conflict is reduced by the fact that relevant others exert differential pressure on the incumbent to perform, because of their differing degrees of power or practical concern (Merton 1957, pp. 113–14; 1968, pp. 425–28). The fact that rational actors solve trouble this way when they encounter it does not mean for sociology that the solution is in effect whether or not trouble is encountered, nor does it mean that actors-in-general (e.g. nonrational actors) ever solve problems this way. Much less does it mean that these solutions are worked out in advance, avail themselves to actors in any precise way, or could conceivably do the analytic work that functionalists seek. Likewise, the fact that certain differing role obligations fulfilled in the open for all to see would result in some predictable conflict (Merton 1957, pp. 114–16; 1968, pp. 428–30) does not mean that their not being fulfilled that way is an ongoing solution to latent conflict. That people sometimes strategically conceal their behavior from troublesome others does not mean that they are constantly doing it or that the terms of the strategy are structured for them prior to their attending to the trouble. And none of this says anything whatsoever about how members of nonrational societies go about solving routine trouble or sustaining their sense of stability.

Nevertheless, functionalists are able to sustain the reality of their premises within its own terms through this ongoing ritual repair, rationalizing their reified object as they move along. They generate that which they wish to explain and explain it the same way. They observe the rule-governed society and say that the reason it is there is that there are rules. They prove this by demonstrating that for every variation in factual structure, there is a corresponding variation in normative structure. The reflexivity inherent in this activity indicates that there would *have* to be such a correspondence in order to even recognize the behavioral structure. The correspondence is more like a necessary congruence. Thus explaining norm-based order with norms is like explaining the shape of an inkblot by the corresponding shape of the white surrounding that comes up to its edge (cf. Wittgenstein

1953, p. 85). This is explanation of the order from within the order and is thereby part of the order; it is a paragon of sui generis order.

THE INEVITABILITY OF FORMAL DEVIANCE
RECOGNITION: MERTON'S ANOMIE THEORY

Just as the formal terms of Competency Based Teacher Education can be relaxed for the practical purposes of specific teacher training programs, so are the formal requirements of functionalist theory relaxed for its utility in substantive research. Lackey (1987), for example, lists and summarizes many substantive studies that make use of Parsonian concepts, for example the pattern variables (pp. 32–36), Bales's interaction categories (1987, p. 43), and Stinchcombe's (1975) application of four systems-maintenance problems to traffic patterns (Lackey 1987, pp. 45–46). However, as functionalism proceeds as a theoretical endeavor in its own right, it requires ongoing repair to sustain belief in its theoretical object: rule-governed society. Members of bureaucracies also know of the need to relax standards for practical purposes; they know of the routine practical gloss and recognize it as a distinction from how things "ought" to be and how they are imagined to be from the outside. As I discussed earlier, this distinction is often made as one between the sloppy way things are done "around here" versus the proper way they could be taking place somewhere out there in the society.

Thus just as bureaucrats orient to a belief in a possible but heretofore unrealized maximally efficient organization, despite the fact that no one has ever having witnessed one, so too do functionalists orient to the potentially discoverable rule-governed society whose specification would provide coherence for science, despite the fact that no single instance of such specification has ever been realized. Indeed, bureaucrats, CBTEists, and functionalist sociologists all maintain and sustain their belief objects through the social practices identified by ethnomethodologists, including the documentary method of interpretation: allowing the "whatever" of what is observed to count as evidence of the very belief-objects presumed and thereby used to generate the observation. In that way the integrity of a transcendent nonempirical order is maintained in all three cases.

As we saw in chapter 4, the reality which transcends anybody's experience but which is collectively subscribed to and respected is the sacred reality which Durkheim investigated in his late work and which he settled on as equivalent to empirical social facts available to sociology. These social facts became highly visible in Garfinkel's work as members' methods, discussed in the present work as social practices or ritual repair practices. But Durkheim also knew that no matter how rigorously transcendent reality was sought by the membership, it would never be witnessed as precisely what members presumed it to be. Expressed in the language of his earlier work, no matter how rigorously the collective conscience was enforced or how diligently people tried to live up to it, it would always transcend anybody's behavior; no one would be it, express it, manifest it, or conform to it precisely (see chapter 3). Its unavailability to direct experience could thereby reduce it as an object of respect but for the recruitment of deviance from the fringe and the ritual constitution of crime through juxtaposition with the collective conscience as ideal. These are the anomie-prevention rituals that save the integrity of transcendent moral reality. This, Durkheim says, is why crime is inevitable and necessary and why trial and punishment is positive and reinforcing for society.

Within the heuristically imagined functionalist lived world, then, something would have to count as formal deviance categories. Rationalization and other ritual repair could not yield the postulated stable order, but no more could the routine gloss necessary to sustain such belief allow for the possibility that just *anything* found would in principle count as conformity with that order. This is to say that the very concept of conformity as rationally conceived includes the certain-things-and-not-others postulate. We have encountered this principle before in the consideration of why members will not count just any use of a word as in conformity with its definition, why they will not allow just any application of a rule to count as in line with its intent, why not just any behavior is allowed to pass as accountable behavior, why "not any account will do" (see chapter 3). Should such circumstances prevail, the word or rule degenerates into meaninglessness, and a society into worse circumstance: general anomie. Thus Durkheim sees the recruitment, trial, and punishment of crime within a society as essential to the very experience of order within that society, rendering such activity ritual anomie-prevention practices.

For exactly this reason functionalist theorists would need to provide for deviance as a theoretical object to save the artfulness of the essential gloss and the concept of conformity-with-norms (i.e. not just anything is conformity), and moreover to make such provisions in ways that reinforce the integrity of the functionalist model even as it produces theoretical instances of its own violation. Without such provisions, functionalist theory, *within its own terms and for functionalists themselves*, would necessarily wither and degenerate into anomic incoherence. If functionalists, when faced with the ongoing discrepancy between empirical observation and the literal functionalist model, simply asserted that *everything* is conformity "anyway," then the impression of the possibility of the model operating in the background, as potentially discoverable for science, could not be indefinitely sustained; it would dry up, so to speak.

In chapter 5 I discussed major differences between Durkheim and Merton on the question of anomie and deviance. Now we are better prepared to understand these differences, with special attention to Merton as a practical theorist (see Hilbert 1989). Durkheim recognized that crime was a matter of societal recruitment and was appropriately silent on the question of what specific action was or was not crime. Merton, quite the other way, entered his theoretical discourse with thorough background knowledge concerning what is and is not deviance. His categories of behavior were, in fact, the same categories used, presumed, and glossed by the formal deviance-recruitment agents of our own rational-legal order: law violation, drug use, mental illness, and so on. He could not allow such cases of gross nonconformity nevertheless to count as conformity without degenerating into an "anything goes" version of conformity to normative order.

Of special interest is how Merton uses prevailing deviance as evidence of the same normative order it presumably violates. That is, he turns what, within a functionalist idiom, otherwise might count against the existence of shared normative order (and functionalist processes such as socialization and internalization) into evidence of that very order, much as members use "nonsense" to document a world in every way sensible (Hilbert 1977; see chapter 5). In fact, the very terms of the normative order, when specified in this manner, appear to produce the observed deviance—*prescribe* it in this sense—though the resultant behavior nevertheless violates these very prescriptions. Just as a computer may "bomb" when fed contradictory programs, just as its failure to perform either operation can nevertheless be explained by its having been fed both programs at once, so too can anomalies within normative order result in deviance. For these reasons, functionalists term such anomalies dysfunctional.

Specifically, Merton extends Parsonian action theory and general sociology, finding the elements of action, ends (goals) and means (norms), within their Parsonian domains, cultural and social subsystems respectively. His famous offering is his typology of individual adaptations to social order conceived in these very terms (Merton 1968, pp. 186–211). In the hypothetically stable society, adherence to social norms yields culturally valued goals, making the most likely individual adaptation *conformity* with the social order (p. 195). But when the ends (goals) and means (norms) are structurally severed for portions of the population, conformity is impossible; hence Merton (pp. 193–211) lists four types of *deviant* adaptations to the social order in terms of acceptance or rejection of cultural goals and institutionalized norms. *Innovation*, where the individual accepts ends and rejects normative means, involves the illegitimate access to goals, that is, crime and delinquency, which includes crime of the lower-class sort, white-collar crime, and organized crime and rackets (pp. 195–203). *Ritualism*, the rejection of goals with the acceptance of normative means, provides the outward appearances of conformity, but it is a ritual conformity, a goal-less conformity, a dry and joyless conformity, typified by lower-middle-class Americans said to be "in a rut" (pp. 203–7). This Merton says is a "departure from the cultural model in which men are obliged to strive actively . . . to move onward and upward in the social hierarchy," thus putting to rest as a "terminological quibble" (p. 204) any arguments over whether ritualism is truly deviant behavior. Clinard (1964, p. 17) characterizes this compulsive behavior as neurotic. Where both means and ends are rejected, *retreatism* (Merton 1968, pp. 207–9) indicates all manner of social dropouts, including "psychotics, autists, pariahs, outcasts, vagrants, vagabonds, tramps, chronic drunkards and drug addicts" (p. 207). An adaptation where prevailing norms and goals are rejected but alternative norms and goals are embraced is *rebellion* (pp. 209–11), more or less characterized by an allegiance to an alternative society which individuals seek by their action to bring into existence at the expense of the prevailing order, which they reject. Hence they organize for political action or otherwise attempt to do away with the current order.

Thus for Merton, a logical consequence of the breakdown in the means-ends relationship for certain social sectors is that the available logical outcomes in terms of the acceptance or rejection of means and ends neatly embrace the categories of conventionally recognized deviance. Merton (1968, p. 194) summarizes this fit between logical possibilities and deviance categories in table format. Again, the elegance of this approach within a functionalist idiom is that it saves the integrity of the model at the very point where it is most threatened: its own violations. These violations now become accountable to the model as contained under the model's

jurisdiction. The model can now anticipate and assimilate its own exceptions, much as the Azande were able to anticipate and assimilate exceptions to the truth-finding power of the poison oracle (Pollner 1987).

In this way Merton assimilates common-sense ideas about deviance
within his own society to a formal theory of society per se. That is, not just
rational society but any society would produce deviance according to the
logical outcomes of means-ends separations—which is to say, society as
the theoretical belief-object of functionalist thought. To recapitulate, Merton begins with common-sense categories of deviance, formalizes them in
his theory of the means-ends split, and takes that assimilation to functionalist theory beyond its origins in his own society to account for deviance
within society theoretically conceived. Thus a general theory of social
order is derived from common-sense ideas contained within one kind of
order—rational-legal order.

It is superfluous to recall that Merton identified the dysfunctional
means-ends split with Durkheim's term: anomie. We have seen in chapter
5 how these two usages of anomie operate in separate theoretical domains
anyway. What is left is to emphasize how Merton's anomie theory is an
empirical example of Durkheimian anomie-prevention practices. Consider
Spector and Kitsuse's (1977) work regarding functionalist social problems
theory and its alternatives. Their recommended alternative, freighted
heavily with ethnomethodological insight, is to treat neither the objective
social order (the functionalist system) nor the things that can go wrong in it
(functionalist social problems) as objectively given, "out there" phenomena. The recommendation is to suspend belief both in structured social
order (see Zimmerman and Wieder 1970; Zimmerman and Pollner 1970)
and in problems within the order to reveal the observable processes whereby people discover, recognize, take for granted, describe, define, diagnose,
and analyze—in a word, constitute social problems and related issues as
well as debate and provide for remedies and cures. This research agenda
returns sociology to the empirical origins of social problems in concrete
human activity. As did Durkheim, it remains noncommittal and indifferent
to questions about what specific conditions are social problems or what
kind of behavior constitutes deviance, these remaining irrevocably context-
specific, empirical questions. Their answers are products and accomplishments of what Spector and Kitsuse call claims-making activities.

Analyses of claims-making activities reveal that social problems and
deviance-recognition are invariably practical projects, not scientific or the-

oretical ones, and that empirical progression within these activities often runs roughly opposite to what practical considerations assert. For example, problems are constructed around practical goals that count as solutions, indicating that solutions precede problems (cf. Hewitt and Hall 1973), or values are mobilized on behalf of claims rather than giving rise to them in a manner similar to Mills's (1940) famous consideration of motives (Spector and Kitsuse 1977, pp. 92–93; see also Hazelrigg 1986; Schneider 1985; and Woolgar and Pawluch 1985a, 1985b). Returning to Durkheim, claims-making activities become Durkheimian rituals for problems recognition, activities which simultaneously reify moral order; they are devices for saving the appearances of objective social order in the absence of other corroborative evidence. Just as the meaning of the law is maintained by the recruitment of its violators, just as professional competence is maintained by the recognition of incompetence (Bittner 1967) or meaningfulness by the recognition of nonsense (Hilbert 1977), so does social order stand in relation to its constituted exceptions.[2]

It is no accident, therefore, that Parsonian functionalists, who took social order for granted as objective, structured, and prescribed, soon turned to objective deviance and social disorder as fundamental problems for sociology. They needed such devices to save the appearances of the very social order they presupposed, and they needed these devices for the very reasons Durkheim might have predicted. Such devices, as well as the theorizing about them, are part of the ritual practices through which collective morality is kept alive. Within the functionalist lived world, these are the ritual repair practices that allow functionalists to sustain the reality of what they presuppose. Merton's theorizing is an empirical example of these ritual claims-making practices.

To summarize, Merton's theory as an expression of functionalism is theory from *within* a moral community, namely a rational Western orientation in the sense Weber delineated, a social universe that respects rules and believes in both their necessity and their potential adequacy, a culture that produced bureaucracy and attempts to mimic human behavior with programmed computers. Merton shares a common-sense belief in stable society and the potential adequacy of the norms that produce it, as well as in the problems and difficulties that can occur with respect to those rules. It is no surprise that those difficulties result in precisely the same kind of behavior-as-deviance that rational actors recognize as deviance. Merton joins them in their judgments, their versions of truth and falsity, here offering a refined analysis of why reality is the way that it is. By sharing the Parsonian reliance on rules and the ongoing repair work the commitment requires, Merton continues to rationalize Durkheim's collective conscience in the sense of Weber. By designating the things that can go wrong with this normative structure, much as a bureaucrat designates organizational inefficiency as standard procedure gone wrong or inadequacies in established policy, Merton has explained deviance from within the lived world of functionalist theory.

10

CLASSICALLY INFORMED

ETHNOMETHODOLOGY IN CONTEMPORARY

THEORETICAL CONTEXT

Throughout, I have attempted to establish continuities between classical theory and ethnomethodology that recover key themes that Parsons dropped in his derivation of voluntaristic action theory from Durkheim and Weber. Chapter 9 summarizes my argument with special attention to a new convergence between Durkheim and Weber, ethnomethodologically conceived, and to how functionalist theorizing is an example of the very phenomena classically informed ethnomethodological theory points to. In this final chapter I want to move beyond the thesis itself to show its relevance to other contemporary debates in sociological theory.

Though no systematic effort will be made to cover all of the current issues, one of the more prominent ways of finding ethnomethodology's place in contemporary theory is to group it with a number of "micro" sociologies that stand in relation to various other "macro" sociologies; thus I begin with the *micro-macro debate*. I will be arguing that ethnomethodology is not microsociology as generally conceived and that attempts to see it that way obfuscate the profundity of its phenomena as well as its ability to transcend the terms of the debate. Closely related to this discussion is *conversation analysis*, for here is where ethnomethodology's seductive similarity to microsociology is most deceiving. Thus I will look at conversation analysis as an extension of ethnomethodology and the way in which it too transcends micro- and macrosociology. I will also review Collins's notion of "interaction ritual chains" for the service a refined version of that concept provides to conversation analysis and ethnomethodological theory generally. This will prove helpful in a final section which addresses connections between ethnomethodology and Karl Marx, the classical theorist conspicuously absent from this text. These final considerations could fill an entire book on their own; consequently what I have to say about them will be necessarily sketchy and frankly speculative. I think, however, that they are worthy of attention precisely because of a misleading tendency to view both Durkheim-Weber convergences and ethnomethodology as somehow in opposition with Marxist or conflict perspectives.

THE QUESTION OF MICRO-MACRO LINKAGES

Ties between ethnomethodology and classical theory could not be made if ethnomethodology were itself microsociology or macrosociology, for it would at the very least require the joining of Durkheim and Weber together in one of those two camps. The discussions in this book have avoided the micro-macro vocabulary and, in passing, discard versions of Durkheim as paradigmatically "macro" and Weber as "individualistic"; just as forcefully we can see past possible counterclaims that Durkheim was a microtheorist or the more likely understanding that Weber was an implicit functionalist macrotheorist. Both were empirical. Durkheim's comments on rules referred to empirical legal codes or other routinely invoked rules, and his discussion of morality in general focused in his late work upon empirical ritual practices. Weber, finding ideas expressed in empirical documents, qualified what otherwise might be seen as macrosociology with a theory of organization that joined subject and object and rejected reification of macroentities. In short, Weber's focus on subjectivity balanced the problem of reification, while Durkheim's organicism balanced the equally objectionable strain toward reductionism. Both contained possibilities for *transcending* what would later become the micro-macro debate (see Hilbert 1990a), but this should be distinguished from saying that they provide the "link" in the debate, though such claims are interesting in themselves (cf. Alexander and Giesen 1987, pp. 7–8, 15–19; Alexander 1987a, p. 294).

Though the micro-macro debate did not originate in late twentieth-century sociology (see Alexander and Giesen 1987), here is where it has been most consciously and explicitly developed. Despite the widely diffuse and varied approaches to this problem, participants in the debate tend to agree, for the most part, that (1) there are macrostructures, (2) there are microstructures, and (3) these two domains are related to each other in some as yet unspecified ways. The mandate to theorize these relations is sometimes expressed in a scientific vocabulary that calls for "linkage" (pp. 31–37), much as the natural sciences might seek to connect, for example, biological metabolism with the laws of chemistry. The premise, in other words, is that microsociologists and macrosociologists have each turned up some structural properties within their respective domains but that exclusive focus within each domain has overlooked, left out, ignored, glossed, illegitimately subsumed, misappropriated, or even denigrated the compellingness of the phenomena in the other domain.

Within the terms of the above premise, theorists of the micro-macro link have tried multiple approaches. These include (1) prioritizing one phenomenal domain and accounting for the other in terms of its principles (Boudon 1987; Collins 1981b; Fine 1991); (2) seeking an "interpenetration" between the two domains (Giddens 1984; Lidz 1981); (3) making the macro domain the source of (loose) constraint upon microprocesses, where these microprocesses alter and change these very macroconstraints in a back-and-forth "feedback" relationship between the two domains (Alexander 1987a; Alexander and Colomy 1990; Colomy and Rhoades 1988); and (4) seeking a holistic picture of the entire society in terms of its "leveling" from one domain to the other and specifying how these levels interface with each other and articulate in various ordered ways (Duster 1981; Luhmann 1981; Wiley 1988). This quick sketch by no means covers all of the approaches to micro-macro, nor does it do justice to the subtle differences within these categories (for overviews, see Ritzer 1988, pp. 366–84; Knorr-Cetina 1981; Alexander and Giesen 1987). But it is safe to say that theorists devoted to linkage assume the structural integrity of the domains they seek to link, whether conceived as independent, causally related, mutually interdependent, or merging into each other through interpenetrating, intervening levels.

One solution to the micro-macro problem, interesting because of some minor similarities with ethnomethodology, is the "neofunctionalism" proposed by Alexander and his colleagues (see Alexander 1987a; Alexander and Colomy 1990; Colomy and Rhoades 1988). They conceive microprocesses as interpretive action within a macrostructural context that both constrains and is a product of these processes. That is, macrostructure constrains concrete action, though not in a completely determinate way. Rather, it constrains through its necessary actualization by interpreting actors; their interpretive action simultaneously transforms structure, thereby altering the macroenvironment of future action. This can have a limited appeal for ethnomethodologists because of the apparent similarity between these interpretive acts and Garfinkel's "documentary method of interpretation." Interpretation includes both "typification and invention" (Alexander 1987a, p. 300) and in its more calculating modes, "strategization" (p. 302). This, then, is a "link" between the micro and macro social orders.

While this approach holds much promise for substantive sociology and for some theoretical and political social issues such as conflict and social change, it is puzzling why neofunctionalists still see the necessity of structural reification to do the work of environmental constraint. Whatever the macroentities constructed by interpretive acts are, the neofunctionalist argument gains no power through invoking their power to constrain interpretive acts. Put differently, no analytic scheme to date can account for a *structure's* ability to constrain at all, whether in a determinate fashion or by setting some kind of parameters within which various action can take place. Such parameters require specification, even lose specification, to explain why not just any action is accountably within them. In other words, the problems with theories of prescription discussed in chapter 2 will not go away just by making the prescriptions "loose" and adding the necessity of interpretation, for we are still left with the same basic question: why are some interpretations allowable and not others? Lacking any determinate standards for measuring the success of interpreting nondeterminate constraint, we are left with the basic Hobbesian problem unsolved. Thus any theory which invokes the possibility of structural constraint, however indeterminate, not only reifies structure but animates it with a certain policing power. Neofunctionalism attests to how deeply felt is this power of structure to regulate in Western thought and how reluctant even the most insightful analysts are to abandon such presuppositions.

If, however, social constraint is part of human action, then structure need not be built into sociological theory at all. What makes neofunctionalism frustrating is that its more substantive advances, which are considerable, might just as easily be made without incorporating structure into its arguments. The remediation suggested by ethnomethodology is finding constraint in the here-and-now empirical activities of human beings acting on each other, members who themselves orient to a macrostructural order and who reify and reproduce it in the course of their interpretive work, imposing its reality on each other as they go (Hilbert 1990a); the belief-objects of this work need have no ontological status, let alone a constraining capacity, in the sociologist's lexicon. While this improves the accuracy of sociological investigation, nothing is lost in terms of consequences for real-life actors. In fact, it would seem that neofunctionalist research would suffer little and could proceed almost intact without this concession to structural reasoning (cf. Zimmerman and Pollner 1970, p. 98).

One reason why theorists are reluctant to give up structure is the impression that to do so is to give overemphasis to the micro side of social life at the expense of the equally compelling macro side. We have already seen how macroentities are compelling through participation in ritual practices and how sociologists benefit from removing themselves from this process. Indeed, if we do not suspend this activity, then any further attention to here-and-now empirical activity will always leave the gnawing impression that something formidable has been "left out" of the analysis, something big, something transsituational and structural. To make these macroentities loose and subject to microinterpretation seems, seductively, to be the ideal compromise. But *suspending* this membership work, while it "reduces" the compellingness of structure to empirical phenomena, is not a reduction specifically to microprocesses without a nonreflective characterization of ethnomethodology as a form of microsociology.

As we have seen, ethnomethodology sees social constraint with an "artful" as opposed to a "programmed" metaphor and in so doing leaves the question of prescription, even loose prescription, entirely behind, and with it all commitment to structure as explanatory or ontologically present. When it comes to micro-macro, ethnomethodologists at the very least can close ranks with theorists seeking to transcend the terms of the whole debate (e.g. Giddens 1984). This would be necessarily so, given ethnomethodology's commitment to social practices as a topic in its own right and its indifference to the ontological status of the accomplishments of these practices; any of the varied belief-objects of members' practical theorizing, sustained by that very theorizing, are excluded as phenomena to be investigated or assumed one way or the other by ethnomethodology.

In line with this nonreification stance, ethnomethodology is best known for its indifference to large-scale social structure such as "society" and other institutions and organizations, what many sociologists today regard as macrostructure. What is not quite so obvious is that ethnomethodology's research program no less indicates a policy of indifference, nonreification, and suspension of belief relative to so-called microstructure as well. Indeed, since the whole idea of structure and patterned behavior is a members' idea anyway, and since it cannot be sustained without the use of members' categories in the production of patterns, then matters of "how large" a structure is, whether it is micro or macro, how structures link together, or how microstructure is related to macrostructure, will have to be settled by members as practical matters through these same artful practices. The "size" of structure is irrelevant to its incapacity to regulate— indeed, to its very existence for empirical sociology.

While ethnomethodologists have not been quick to dissociate themselves from microsociology and indeed often seem to join the micro-macro debate as advocates on the micro side (see Schegloff 1987), such a commitment, including the predisposition to be drawn into the debate in the first place, is not derivable from Garfinkel's seminal investigations. Here we find concerted focus not on "interaction" as normally conceived as between "individuals," not on subjective meanings as content arising from interaction, not on microcategories of behavioral events or structural linkages between people conceived in categorical terms such as status (however micro), but upon *ethnomethods*; in fact we see little emphasis upon "people" or "individual" or "persons" as theoretic entities at all but rather upon *membership*.

Put differently, people are what they are by virtue of their membership, that is, they are members, and membership in turn is empirically identifiable solely by membership activity—members' methods. Members are not then bio-organisms or psychological or social units of analysis. They are not the "actors" of symbolic interactionism. They are not the "individuals" of exchange theorists or rational choice theorists, no matter how thoroughly the latter revamp their understanding of "individuals" and "human nature" to locate them within a collective environment which influences them as they create it (see Wippler and Lindenberg 1987). Members are, strictly and solely, membership activities—the artful practices whereby they produce what are *for them* large-scale organization structure and small-scale interactional or personal structure.

To stress this one more time: members' methods exhaust the social in human life, such that members are whatever their membership consists of;

members are their methods of producing and reproducing membership. Members' methods are social at the outset. They are not "owned" by anyone, and no one can perform them independently of social life. In the spirit of Durkheim, they transcend anyone's "individuality"; in fact, individuality can be accomplished only through participation in these methods. Therefore the topic of ethnomethodology will not allow a study of individuals "coming together to interact," even to do members' methods. Such a model presupposes membership on the part of the analyst in its vision of who could be interacting in the first place. Rather, ethnomethodology's investigation into ethnomethods as a topic in their own right requires a disciplined disinterest, a suspension of belief, in the stuff with which interactional studies are normally concerned: persons, individuals, identity, subjective content, behavioral outcomes, and so forth. Paramount among these disinterests is a disinterest in structure. With the notion of membership, sociologists do not need structure to account for social constraint. Ethnomethods are social practices whereby members orient to a presupposed social-structural order, reifying and reproducing it in the course of their activity and *imposing its reality on each other as they go.*

Nevertheless, and in juxtaposition with sociology's long-standing concern with macrosocial processes, there has been a tendency to group ethnomethodology with less-dominant sociologies of "everyday life" that emphasize microstructures and processes (e.g. Lyman and Scott 1970; Knorr-Cetina 1981, p. 1; Collins 1981b, p. 984; Alexander and Giesen 1987, pp. 27–28; see also Denzin 1970 and Zimmerman and Wieder's [1970] reply). To enter a discourse that orients to the existence of social structure but recognizes only microstructure would indeed be puzzling, since the compellingness of structure at all levels is sustained through the same social practices. The model induced thereby is that of ethnomethodologists recognizing the facticity of microstructure while stubbornly resisting or denying the compellingness of macrostructure. That is, within the terms of the discourse, such a position seems narrow-minded and dogmatic (cf. Alexander 1987a, p. 295). Worse, ethnomethodology is sometimes seen as denying structure altogether in favor of the disembodied "individual" as the source of all meaning, order construction, and subjective content (see Coser 1975 and Zimmerman's [1976] reply). Yet ethnomethodological indifference to structure at any level, neither to deny nor to affirm its objective status but rather to describe the methods of its production, makes it clear that ethnomethodology should not be considered a variant of the several "microsociologies." Rather, given this methodological stance, ethnomethodology in a very unique and intellectually satisfying way transcends all questions of micro or macro or their interrelatedness, and it does so while retaining classical themes usually thought to be in one domain or the other: Durkheimian exteriority and Weberian subjective belief.

As research policy, this indifference is most familiar vis-à-vis macrostructure in such works as Cicourel 1964, 1968, Cicourel and Kitsuse 1963, and Cicourel et al. 1974. In these kinds of studies the reality of macrostructure, bureaucratic integrity, organizational matrix, social class structure, procedural regularity, and due process are demonstrably accomplishments of members' artful practices. In Cicourel's research these practices turn out to be variants of Garfinkel's "documentary method of interpretation," notably skills relative to the classification of events and people for further processing, the creation of folders, the maintenance of files and documents, and the construction of summary statements relative to myriad indexical events (see Cicourel 1981 for an overview). While members may view such constructions as objectively "out there" and invoke them in explanations, sociologists cannot so orient themselves without "going native" and reification.

But again, this is no less true with regard to microstructure. Indeed Garfinkel (1967, p. 95) asserts that the ethnomethods that produce survey research results are the same methods that "laypeople" use to produce what acquaintances mean by utterances, for example referring to something "Harry" says with "Isn't that just like Harry?" Much of Garfinkel's pioneering work illustrates ways that "microstability" is used, produced, and glossed no less so than any larger macrostability. This includes matters that structural theorists might regard as individualistic or interpersonal, such as cognition and intersubjectivity (pp. 24–31, 38–44, 79–94) and small-group decision making (pp. 11–24, 104–15). It also includes such matters as interpersonal identity (pp. 58–65), the stability of family routine (pp. 44–49), and gender roles (pp. 116–85). More widely, ethnomethodologists have written about cognition and perception (Cicourel 1973; Coulter 1979, 1989; Hilbert 1977, 1984; Pollner 1987), relationships and person-identity (Jefferson, Sacks, and Schegloff 1987; Maynard forthcoming; Maynard and Zimmerman 1984), professional competence (Bittner 1967; Lynch 1982, 1985; Sudnow 1965), social roles (Halkowski 1990; Hilbert 1981, 1990b; Zimmerman and West 1975), and what might be regarded as social organization at a "submacro" level (Bittner 1965; Sudnow 1967; Wieder 1974a; Zimmerman 1970, 1974). In all of these studies, the stability referenced is bracketed and disallowed by the analysts in order to examine the social practices whereby it is made to appear real or incorrigibly present by and for the membership. Thus, once again, ethnomethodologists do not allow microstructures into their phenomenal domain any more than they allow macrostructures such as bureaucracy or "society as a whole." To assert the reality of microstructure would be reification no less than with regard to macrostructure.

One source of the mistaken impression that ethnomethodology is microsociology is no doubt a misconstruing of ethnomethodology's commitment to *empirical* phenomena. This means that social facts must be immediately available to scientific inspection, not surmised, presumed, or theorized into existence as a matter of logical necessity. More recently, Garfinkel has referred to the *local* as the proper phenomenal domain for ethnomethodology, again limiting scientists' observations to what takes place presently before them. Moreover, the here and now of observed data ought not be allowed to stand in proxy for "unseen" phenomena or patterns independently theorized as necessities, certainly not patterns that invoke structural imagery with its pieces linked together and stretching off into hypothetical space. The approach calls for a more problematic relation between multiple observations than simply glossing them into categories that in turn fit into a theory. This in itself presents enormous challenges to ethnomethodologists and may in part account for an enlightened reluctance on their part to theorize their work. In any case, this emphasis upon the local and the empirical ought not to be confused with microstructure as it is normally conceived.

This is not to say that ethnomethodology is atheoretical or that it approaches human behavior from the point of view of a neobehaviorist empiricism. Ethnomethodological empiricism does not remove the analyst as an interpreter of data, nor do ethnomethodologists claim privileged exemption from the social practices they investigate. If, for example, astronomers cannot engage in "unmediated observation" (see Garfinkel, Lynch, and Livingston 1981 and chapter 4 above), the same is true for ethnomethodologists.

However, there is a certain brand of "mediation" that ethnomethodologists steer away from, one that is not particularly characteristic of the traditional sciences but is commonplace in the social sciences, particularly American functionalism. This is what Garfinkel calls "formal, constructive analysis" (1988, p. 106; see also chapter 1 above). Here is the assumption that real society cannot be observed in the "concreteness of things" but only as a product of formal logical theorizing and formally administered research methodologies. Hence we see all of the traditional recommendations for coding social events and operationalizing concepts for purposes of counting and so on (see chapter 3). In this way the presumption of nonempirical entities can become the sociologist's instructions for deciding what surely somehow must be empirically the case; the theoretically constructed society replaces the "concreteness of things" as the society sociologists study. Garfinkel's return to the "concreteness of things" is a form of empiricism similar to that of the classical natural sciences, but this emphasis should not be confused with a preoccupation with microstructure.

CONVERSATION ANALYSIS

Feeding the impression of ethnomethodology as microsociology has been a turn of many ethnomethodologists toward an evolving area known as *conversation analysis*. Proliferating into a huge literature from a relatively small body of seminal work (Harvey Sacks's unpublished lectures; see also Sacks, Schegloff, and Jefferson 1974; Schegloff 1968; Schegloff and Sacks 1973; for recent overviews, see Boden 1990; Heritage 1984, pp. 233–92; Maynard and Clayman 1991, pp. 396–403), this development at once exacerbates the misunderstanding and provides promising new directions for transcending these difficulties. It exacerbates the problem by its focus on tiny pieces of conversation as taped and transcribed in minute detail. For example, care in transcribing the actual *sounds* of conversation, including nonverbal sounds, stutters, laughs, false starts, repetitions, precise pronunciation (of both words and nonverbal sounds), silences, interruptions, and so on (see Zimmerman 1988), together with an evolving transcription notation and time measurements detailed to small fractions of a second (see Jefferson 1984), make these transcripts difficult for all but the practiced to read fluently. To the unpracticed, in other words, such detail seems disembodied from whatever else is relevant to naturally recognizable conversation. At best, and not at all remedied by conversation analysts' occasional references to their phenomena as structural, this detail begins to look like the microstructure of microsociology. Hence ethnomethodologists' concern with such detail begs a fit with traditional micro-macro issues and appears to document a "one-sided" emphasis on microissues, that is, ethnomethodology as "radically micro" (Alexander and Giesen 1987, p. 36; Collins 1981b, p. 984) or "individualistic" (Münch and Smelser 1987, p. 364). Alexander (1987a, pp. 292–99) appropriates this misunderstanding in his criticism of Garfinkel and Schutz, along with other "microtheorists," for claiming to have discovered new empirical phenomena, when all they really have is microstructure, something even classical theorists knew about.

However a closer look at the conversation analytic literature reveals that conversation analysts are not concerned with their data because they are "micro" but because they are undeniably, empirically there. That is, they can be recorded, transcribed, inspected and reinspected, and shown to other analysts (see Heritage 1984, p. 238; Sacks 1984). They are, as Garfinkel puts it, "inspectably the case" (1988, p. 108). They do not, in other words, draw upon common-sense folklore or logically derived formal theories either for confirmation or disconfirmation. They do not draw upon such theories for their recognition or scientific significance (cf. Zimmerman 1988, p. 415).

One indication of the empirical status of conversation analysts' phenomena is their counterintuitive nature, happening independently of anyone's will, volition, or theorizing. They are "discovered" by analysts in the tradition of classical science in that they could not have been presupposed or imagined by conversational participants or by members generally. They could not have been imagined by sociologists either and are therefore surprises (cf. Heritage 1984, pp. 234–38; Garfinkel 1988, p. 108; Zimmerman 1988). In that regard, they transcend the terms of culture, or any culture in particular, not drawing upon prevailing folk theories of behavior either to confirm or disconfirm those theories. They are witnessed by scientists working under the disciplined stance of ethnomethodological indifference to members' formulations and practical projects. They are distinctively social phenomena, deeply coordinated activities between conversants, but they could not be deliberately or consciously performed, involving, for example, units of time sufficiently tiny to escape anyone's conscious ability to notice or monitor. Transcending both culture and personal volition in this way, they approach the status of species-specific social behavior (see Boden 1983 for a cross-cultural comparison of these conversational practices).

Another reason for dismissing conceptions of ethnomethodology as "radically micro" is that empirical phenomena are of interest at whatever "level" they are found; that is, ethnomethodologists hold no theoretical priority for "micro" other than its superficial similarity to "local." But conversation analysts also have deep interest in the *distribution* of these events across myriad settings and types of interaction as varied as conversation between courtroom judges and attorneys (Maynard 1984), doctors and patients (West 1984), and caller and complaint taker on a telephone helpline (Whalen, Zimmerman, and Whalen 1988; see also Wilson 1991; Zimmerman 1988; cf. Schegloff 1987, pp. 209–14). The interest in distributional phenomena might be misleadingly read as macrosociology, just as concern for the local can be read as microsociology; either reading is in error. But the mere fact that ethnomethodology could, by this turn, be misconstrued as macrosociology should help put the more common misconception to rest.

The interest in distributional phenomena, in fact, should help to clarify the distinction between the phenomena of conversation analysis and those of more conventional, structural studies. The former are witnessed, recorded, and counted independent of members' structural categories, yet they *repeat* across space and time. Their mere repetition is cause for comment, since they are not "coded" events (cf. Heritage 1984, pp. 234–36). That is, they are not categorized or glossed into existence by analysts' preoccupation with theoretical categories, professional methodological criteria for recognizing theoretically required events, or other simplification techniques. They are known by their empirical features rather than by some underlying principle they are supposed to represent (see Zimmerman 1988).

In keeping with my earlier comments on ethnomethodological empiricism, I am not claiming that conversational regularities are "there" in the transcripts independently of the complex work on the parts of analysts, which includes an evolving set of transcription techniques and conventions (see Jefferson 1984). However, I suggest that these techniques are more analogous to the observation technologies of the natural sciences, such as staining a tissue sample or focusing a sophisticated microscope, than they are to coding, operationalizing, or any of the myriad methodologies that serve a priori theorizing. Taken this way, the repetitions and distributions of conversational phenomena are more closely akin to the regularities of natural science than they are to microsociology or macrosociology. The inner dynamic of the turn-taking model (see Sacks, Schegloff, and Jefferson 1974) or "an adjacency pair with an insertion sequence" (Wilson 1991; see Schegloff 1972; Heritage 1984, pp. 245–53) is visibly before analysts in transcripts, and when such phenomena are found occurring in differing social contexts, their repetition is equally visible in the transcripts. Contrast this with "repeating" events in microsociology, for example several instances of democratic problem resolution within a family, itemized instances of following a role prescription, or differential "counts" of instrumental versus expressive leadership events in small groups in the sense of Bales (1950).

Beyond these methodological concerns, there are theoretical reasons for viewing conversation analysis as leaving the question of micro-macro altogether, specifically in the way it returns and readdresses members' own sense of structure. As we have seen, ethnomethodology, while remaining indifferent to such structure, is anything but indifferent to the methods of its production; indeed these *methods* indicate the topic-domain of ethnomethodology. It becomes apparent in the work of conversation analysts that the phenomena they find, easily misconstrued as microstructure, *are* those methods, at least some of them. They are, that is, methods of producing, maintaining, sustaining, and reproducing social structure by and for the membership, whether oriented to large-scale institutional (macro) structure or to smaller, more intimate (micro) structure.

Ethnomethodologists and conversation analysts are aware of and have addressed the question of the interface between their phenomena and members' common-sense domain, but this is completely different than questions about micro-macro relationships. One persistent question is the extent to which it is proper for analysts to invoke members' structural concepts as relevant to conversational regularities, either as causes or consequences. For example, Schegloff (1987, p. 214) cites "the reported asymmetry of interruption between the sexes—men interrupting women far more frequently than the opposite" (West and Zimmerman 1977, 1983; Zimmerman and West 1975; West 1979). At issue is whether common-sense gender categories and differential social status and power attached to them is relevant to the observed regularities. Schegloff is pessimistic regarding such ventures, holding that they prematurely foreclose upon "full technical exploration of the aspects of interaction being accounted for and the micro-level mechanisms that are involved in their production" (1987, p. 215).

To those unfamiliar with ethnomethodology, and in part because of Schegloff's use of terms like "micro-level mechanism" (but see his cautious disclaimer to microsociology and his doubts about the micro-macro discourse [1987, pp. 209, 228]), this looks like nothing better than a call for yet deeper microsociology rather than the topic change envisioned by Garfinkel. Yet it is the production of interruption asymmetries occurring within conversations, as actively produced from within those very conversations, that interest conversation analysts rather than structural constraints, either of a micro or macro kind, that necessitate these asymmetries. So it is important to conversation analysts that they account for their observations solely from the empirical data at hand; this, rather than a commitment to micro, is why they seek to understand their phenomena as self-ordering, self-producing—that is, conversational regularities as emerging from within conversations themselves (cf. Heritage 1984, pp. 280–90). No doubt Schegloff's willingness to be swept into a micro-macro discourse for purposes of an edited volume on that topic contributed to the editors' characterization of ethnomethodology as microsociology and individualistic (Alexander and Giesen 1987, pp. 27–28; Münch and Smelser 1987, pp. 364–65).

Wilson (1991) specifically addresses the relation between sequential conversational practices and members' social structure. He distinguishes these practices from structure as "universally available [context-free] devices employed by members in [the] work of construction [of their own social-structural matters]," not themselves socially constructed in the way usually understood by social constructionists (p. 26). He raises much the same questions as Schegloff (1987) and settles on similar answers, but he moves on to accentuate a question that will not go away: vis-à-vis these conversational practices, particularly where conversants jointly produce regularities but where they can be distinguished according to their contributions, what determines which conversant is which? For example, having identified internal regularities in requests for information or for help, what determines which participant does the asking? Likewise where one conversant exercises more control in the allocation of turns, what determines which conversant this is (Wilson 1991, p. 37)? Wilson eschews any references to structural concepts like institutional authority, such as a judge might have in a courtroom, as proper sociological explanation, since they neglect the empirical details displayed in the transcripts. The dynamics of power differences, he says, can be understood from within the conversational practices themselves. Yet the "which is which" problem remains. That is, "one can account for the distribution of subsequent [conversational] events as a product of sequential mechanisms, but only if the distribution of antecedent events is already given. The problem, then, is to account for the antecedent distribution" (p. 38).

Wilson solves the problem by returning to social structure as explanatory but only when it can be empirically demonstrated that conversants themselves orient to such structure and thereby initiate the terms of their conversation (Wilson 1991, pp. 38–39). He declares that even the most plausible structural explanations, such as differential power by gender in the studies cited above, are purely speculative in the absence of such demonstrations. It should be kept in mind that even where the terms of such demonstrations are successfully met, structures are useful to analysts strictly in addressing the "which is which" problem and are by no means implicated in the conversational regularities themselves; structure does not, then, order behavior. Indeed, structures are not presumed by analysts to exist at all and are relevant, even to the "which is which" problem, only as accomplishments oriented to by the membership. Thus Wilson's solution harkens back to early ethnomethodology and to Weberian subjective orientation and should not be construed as a solution to the micro-macro problem.

Coming from a slightly different angle, Schegloff (1987, pp. 219–28) makes points similar to Wilson's, further specifying that whatever might be otherwise misconstrued as the macrocontexts of conversation should show up empirically as characterized within the very conversation in question: "Relevant contexts should be procedurally related to the talk said to be contingently related to them. That is, there should be some tie between the context-as-characterized and its bearing on 'the doing of talk' or 'doing the interaction'" (p. 219). That is, without reifying structure, analysts can nevertheless see its relevance for actors in its here-and-now actualization in real-time activity. The structure which allegedly constrains activity is oriented to and reproduced in that activity, the empirical source of that constraint being one more feature of that very activity. Through conversation, conversants make the constraint that organizes what for them is a structural constraint external to the conversation. Here, then, is the Durkheimian sui generis order, that is, order-of-its-own-kind, not requiring anything external to the order as its cause. With regard, for example, to the general observation that physicians tend to ask questions and patients tend to provide answers, Schegloff recommends:

Rather than treating this as the observation that persons independently formulated as physicians disproportionately engage in a particular form of conduct, one might ask whether these persons can be
"doing being doctor" by conducting themselves in a particular way.
One is then directed to close examination of the conduct in order to
specify in what respects it might constitute "doing, and displaying
doing, doctor." One might note that constructing turns as questions
is one part of "doing being doctor," and one might be drawn into
further specifying aspects of the talk (e.g., the type of question, the
manner of the asking, the manner of doing recipiency of the response, etc.) as parts of this process—*if*, that is, there are such
specifiable aspects. If there are, then attacking the problem in this
fashion allows a claim of the participants' orientation to the "doctor/
patient"-ness of the interaction, rather than the more positivistic
correlation of a type of activity with an independently given (but not
demonstrably party-relevant) characterization of the parties.

The point, then, is not merely to impose a formal (or formalistic)
constraint on the use of certain forms of description, but to be led by
such a constraint to a new direction of analysis, with the promise of
additional, and possibly distinctive, findings. (Schegloff 1987,
p. 220)

Thus it is apparent that conversation analysis is an extension of Garfinkel's investigation of members' methods into the domain of empirical
talk. This focus on method remains indifferent to the facticity of structure
at any level and is not itself a preoccupation with microstructure. Conversational regularities do not "add up" to macrostructure, nor are they influenced by it, but they are the methods whereby structure is presumed,
maintained, and reproduced as embodied art forms by and for the membership. Similarly, theoretical concerns with the relationship between conversational practices and members' concepts should not be confused with
attempting to forge a micro-macro link.

A RADICAL THESIS

These theoretical developments suggest an intriguing possibility compatible with considerations taken up in earlier chapters, namely, that (1) the
empirical phenomena that conversation analysts witness but which mem-

bers cannot possibly know about and (2) the structural phenomena that members orient to and take for granted but which nevertheless are nonempirical and unavailable for social science are (3) *the same phenomena.* Since, as we have seen, it is members' methods that are exterior to and constraining upon anyone's participation in those same methods, then these methods would have to be, following the radical claim of Garfinkel, Lynch, and Livingston (1981), the empirical correlates of what participants know as objective reality and truth known in common. This is a radical thesis yet satisfying in that it provides an articulation between species-specific social behavior, known in early ethnomethodology as invariant procedures, and culture, which since the dawn of sociology and anthropology has been recognized as anything but invariant. It provides for a cultural "overlay" on social practices that provide for their experience, that is, terms and ways for people to experience their own activity. For example, the same practices which in Western society would be experienced as the external force of structural constraint might elsewhere be experienced as routine supernatural control.

This thesis is also intriguingly Durkheimian vis-à-vis his method of transforming reality as experienced within a community to social facts from without for science. Here we would have conversation as experienced from within manifesting the realities of structural constraints, role playing, or status differences, for example, while those same realities would be coterminous with empirical practices as observed by analysts outside the conversation. Thus would the diversity and relativity of culture emerge as congruent with invariant practices.

Whatever difficulties and anomalies there are with this thesis, and there are undoubtedly many, the thesis does raise a family of fascinating questions. One derives from the fact that social structure is only part of members' perceived reality-Gestalt. But we have seen, for example in Garfinkel, Lynch, and Livingston's (1981) pulsar study, how members' conformity to structure and discovery about reality are congruent; hence some headway is foreseeable in conversational studies toward completing Durkheim's conversion of objective reality (and such matters as scientific or metaphysical truth) to social facts. Once again, cultural content in terms of whatever members take to be "the real world" provides an overlay for experiencing concrete social practices which are exterior and constraining upon participation in these very practices, features of these practices attributed by members to objective reality.

Extending the Durkheimian thesis in this manner raises additional questions, some having to do with the relationship between members' reality and members' topic. In the case of social structure, for example, conversants need not be talking about any power differential between them to experience its force and reproduce it in kind. Might this also be true for other aspects of reality that could be topicalized yet need not be? One might experience being-in-the-library, for example, even while discussing entirely different matters, and that experience is accompanied by an indefinite array of other background knowledge: books, authors, publishing, buying and selling, academia, capitalist enterprise, printing and paper, trees and conservation, trucks and mechanics, environmental activism, nature in general, including stars, political action, unwelcome incarceration, and on and on, here recovering the indefinite "outer horizons" (Gurwitsch 1964) of phenomenological experience and any ties that it may have to conversational practices here and now, *whatever* the topic.

Or, quite the other way, there could be distinctive reification practices relative to conversational *topic* to be distinguished from the Pollnerian global reality that is quite possibly reproduced in every instance of a conversation's going forward. Along those lines, for instance, social-structural matters do come up as conversational topics. This sort of research would require a renewed effort to study the *content* of talk in its semantic aspects, something thus far, and with good reason, bracketed out of analysis by conversation analysts. Perhaps a beginning could be found in research to date on conversational topic, that is, how a topic is constituted as what-the-conversation-is-about and how topics change within conversation (see Maynard 1980).

INTERACTION RITUAL CHAINS

One of the most promising conceptual tools for ethnomethodological theory to have come from outside of ethnomethodological circles is Collins's *interaction ritual chains* (Collins 1981a, 1981b, 1987). Collins developed this notion in service to a micro-macro link, specifically grounding nonempirical structure like "state," "economy," and "social class" to concrete empirical events (1981b, p. 988). In other words, Collins is proposing a microsociology to account for macrostructure, converting the traditional concerns of sociology to microevents through a method of "microtranslation" (1981a, 1981b). It is not the proposed "link" that is of interest here but rather Collins's determined commitment to empiricism and the phenomena he thereby proposes as empirical.

First, the commitment to empiricism will allow as data only those events that can be seen, heard, recorded, or otherwise witnessed by scientists. Instead of the structural categories of sociology, Collins (1981b, p. 988) says, "There are only collections of individual people acting in particular kinds of microsituations." He adopts Cicourel's observation, and in fact cites Cicourel and Garfinkel, in noting that the macrotopics and discoveries of sociology are never actually *seen* by their discoverers but exist in and through the activities of their discoverers, working solely and completely within microsituations in which they make micro-observations, compiling summaries "by a series of coding and translating procedures until a text is produced which is taken as representing a macroreality, standing above all the microsituations that produced it" (p. 988).

Second, the phenomena Collins proposes, interaction ritual chains, are "aggregates" of microevents, but not in the way ordinarily conceived by social science. They are not categories of these events or typified versions of these events, but rather *simply these events* as they accrue through space and time. The fact that someone in one microsetting leaves that setting and walks to another microsetting is indicative of the kind of phenomena Collins is suggesting. The fact that a business meeting adjourns and its members drive home by various routes, that they do this or that on the way home for example, and that they arrive at various times in their respective home environments are all suggestive of interaction chains. In all this activity, and throughout life, no one ever leaves a microscene for a macroscene; there are no macroscenes. The business meeting is an empirical event, as is walking to the car; so are traffic patterns, interaction in the grocery store, and interaction at home. Indeed, for Collins, a person's entire life, from birth to death, is a stream of microactivity and could theoretically be recorded and diagrammed in physical space-time as a body moving from place to place, from one ritual scene to the next, and so on. In Collins's (1981b, p. 998) words, "a lifetime is, strictly speaking, a chain of interaction situations."

There is some conceptual ambiguity over Collins's sense of what happens at sites along interaction chains vis-à-vis members' methods of producing macrostructure (Hilbert 1990a). At times it would appear that Collins is referring to the microevents that members classify, typify, count, and so on; this serves a micro-macro link in which macrostructure is composed of microstructure. The microevents would be something like the "raw data" that members organize in the production of macrostructure.

At other times, though, Collins seems to be referencing the act of classification, typification, and counting as itself the phenomenon of interest along these chains. This is a better reading for ethnomethodological theory. The former reading requires the nonproblematic identity of microevents independent of their being aggregated, sorted, and collected into structure, while the latter reading holds fast to Garfinkel's observation that it is in the classification, sorting, and so on that the identities of the classified microevents are constituted. Here microevents are accomplishments of the same members' methods that produce macroevents. Macrostructures are idealizations or typifications that are documented, filled out, and continually reproduced and modified by their microexamples, these examples being exactly what they are by affiliation with the very macropatterns they are used to document (cf. Wieder 1974a and chapter 3 above). The macropatterns exist solely and completely through that membership activity, and the microevents exist solely and completely as instances of those macropatterns. Only the work of producing this unified object, only the membership activity itself, is empirical.

The latter reading, then, serves our interest in an evolving ethnomethodological theory, and it probably also best captures the subtlety of Collins's own vision. Where he augments the empirical status of his "micro" situations with theoretical commentary about these empirical sites, we see that he is not really directed to microstructures or microstructural matters. Here in fact is the *ritual* in interaction chains, and by that he means Durkheimian ritual (1981b, pp. 998–99). Each site is an occasion for re-celebrating the "myth" or "Durkheimian sacred object," that is, reconstituting it as true and real, coterminous with reestablishing group membership. Moreover, and especially noteworthy for our purposes here, Collins indicates that each could be a *conversation*, making interaction ritual chains closely similar to "chains of conversation" (1981a, p. 104; 1981b, p. 998). Within that terminology, the sacred (transcendent) object of conversation is its literal content, and the conversants constitute a conversational cult (1981b, pp. 998–99; cf. Wallace and Hartley 1988, pp. 96–100).

On first consideration, even with the caveat offered here, interaction ritual chains do not seem to be much improvement over structural concepts. The imagery they evoke, that of linked chains spreading out everywhere into space and time, seem just as hypothetical as the imagery of functionalist normative structure and immeasurably more scattered, chaotic, and methodologically unmanageable. At least the traditional structures imply patterns, while interaction chains would be impossible to pin down in their totality and do not, in fact, specifically recommend any patterns whatsoever. Furthermore, we cannot exactly see them, so do we not then have to reify them to allow them into our theory?

In response to these misgivings, note first that the nonobservability of interaction ritual chains in their totality is a contingent sort, subject to the technical limitations of practical methodologies. Imagine the technical awkwardness of recording even one biography on videotape as a chain of concrete events; what we would have would be an empirical case history, an indexical biography listed as a series of exchanges connected in space-time solely by the motion of a body from one place to another. While it may be impossible to witness interaction ritual chains in this kind of totality, they are nevertheless observable in principle, that is, they are *theoretically empirical*. Interaction ritual chains are empirical events "connected" in real time and real space, and these connections are themselves empirical. Indeed they completely fill up societal space-time. This is in direct contrast to the way in which traditional structures are unobservable, for traditional structures are not even empirical in theory; they are analytically indefensible as existent entities and unworkable, especially with regard to the work theorists expect them to do, most often prescription or the objective display of "patterns." Traditional structures are empirical *solely* as accomplishments of summarizing, coding, operationalizing, and glossing structural concepts which theorists require to sustain their theory and to produce their phenomena; structure is available in no other way. In short, the reification necessary to sustain structure is not necessary for interaction ritual chains, which are empirically available in terms of their here-and-now features wherever in the society an analyst chooses to look.

Second, no patterns are necessarily implied in the positing of interaction ritual chains. They fill up societal space-time and are empirically connected, but they are available solely by their empirical features and concrete connections. The connections are not necessarily ordered or patterned, though this remains a matter of empirical investigation. More important, they *need* not be ordered; the theory does not require that of them, nor does it require that they themselves, the interaction ritual chains, do any kind of work. Thus there is no presumption of order or constraining power attached to the notion of interaction ritual chains.

In short, interaction ritual chains are empirical in roughly the same way that Parsons would have his "factual order" be empirical, and they are theoretically observable in just that way. Yet they are not structural in the way Parsons's social order is supposedly structural. Indeed, their character as nonordered, which is not to say disordered, is in part what makes their "totality" not only technically impossible to witness but also unmanageable as data. Put differently, analysts make necessary choices regarding where within this "totality" to direct their attention, but wherever they look, they will find interaction ritual chains or their pieces. Any regularities among interaction chains await empirical discovery; most certainly, though, they are not the "social order" that members take for granted and that Parsons postulates as factual phenomena for sociology. Indeed members need have no awareness whatsoever of interaction ritual chains, any more than they have awareness of detailed conversational regularities.

Collins's concept, with its chainlike imagery, is metaphoric to be sure, but it provides a vocabulary for accessing what conversation analysts have been calling the *distribution* of conversational regularities in space and time. And it helps in addressing such questions as Wilson's "which is which" problem discussed above. In stating the problem, for example, Wilson (1991, p. 38) says that the distribution of events within a conversation can be understood as products of mechanisms internal to the conversation "only if the distribution of antecedent events is already given. . . . The problem, then, is to account for the antecedent distribution." He says that antecedent events may be "produced in a similar way," but this would only push the problem back a step: "Eventually . . . we reach the beginning of the interaction and so must face the issue directly." From there, Wilson moves into his qualified structural solution as discussed above, that is, structure as relevant only insofar as it is oriented to by conversants and only in setting up the initial distribution of events. But with Collins's interaction ritual chains, we can see that there is no reason for invoking an event like "the beginning of the interaction"; there is no beginning-of-interaction, as all of these events are connected in space-time. These connections, like "mechanisms" internal to conversations, are biographical, temporal, and sequential. Without altering or correcting Wilson's solution to the "which is which" problem, therefore, we can now account for how it is possible for conversants to enter a scene with already-constituted ideas about institutional relevance. They are accomplishments and reified entities derived from concrete antecedent events with empirical connections to the events in question in real time and real space.

Collins's concept is also helpful in responding to one of Giddens's better-known criticisms of ethnomethodology, which is that it addresses only matters that members talk about and ignores the possibility of "unintended consequences" (Giddens 1984). This criticism is related to a more general misunderstanding of ethnomethodology as strictly phenomenological—that is, phenomenological in a crude sense, one that examines only subjectivity or "reality from the point of view of the subject," the content of people's minds (Coser 1975). I trust that this notion has been dispelled in earlier chapters. Ethnomethodology does not deny unintended consequences in asserting that *structure* is an accomplishment of language use and cannot exist in any other way. But interaction ritual chains designate a conversational quasi *ecology* of events, albeit nonstructural. For example, one conversation may be between an employee and employer wherein the latter fires the former; this may have a direct though unintended bearing on the details of conversation later that night between the former employee and other family members. Again, while it may be methodologically fruitless and theoretically pointless to try to map out this constantly moving ecology, it nevertheless serves an evolving ethnomethodological theory to know about it.

As indicated above, Collins developed his concept to forge a micro-macro link. In his imagery, the conversational events along chains are the microphenomena of interest to ethnomethodology, while the interaction chains themselves are macrostructures. In that sense, macrostructure is composed of microevents. While this imagery seems compelling, it is helpful again to recall why the details of empirical events should not be confused with microstructure. Rather, these details are the methods of generating, reifying, and reproducing both microstructure and macrostructure. Now on a macroside, we can see why interaction ritual chains are not macrostructure. Rather, they are the distribution of activities wherein microstructure and macrostructure are reproduced.

Put differently, Collins sees members' macrostructural concepts as a gloss for empirical macrophenomena, these being interaction ritual chains (Collins 1981b, pp. 996–98). He sees these chains as the "pure macro-variables" (1981a, p. 101). But what members produce in the way of structure need be related in no way whatsoever with these ritual chains. Indeed members need have no knowledge concerning either the detail of empirical events or their empirical connectedness. Moreover, as indicated above, the "events" that both members and functionalists summarize, classify, count, and so on in the production of social structure are not the empirical events of ethnomethodology; the summarizing, classifying, counting, and so on are themselves the empirical events for ethnomethodology. Members do not, in other words, count and classify instances of members' methods, including conversational regularities. Where they engage these methods to use aggregate microevents in the production of macrostructure, the microevents are themselves accomplishments of these same methods. Indeed, it was part of Garfinkel's (1967, pp. 7–9) initial observation that members find their methods of structure production, and by implication the concrete distribution of these methods, specifically "uninteresting" as topical concerns.

Thus a refinement of Collins's vision can be summarized: macrostructural concepts are not the gloss for interaction ritual chains, but the gloss as human activity is located at "sites" along these chains; interaction ritual chains are not reified or glossed but are the empirical distribution of the gloss, that is, the gloss as human activity wherein both microstructure and macrostructure are presumed, reproduced, managed, and enforced. Likewise the empirical gloss is not the microstructure that "adds up" to macrostructure but the activity that simultaneously produces both. "Linkage" from event to event is biographical, temporal, and sequential and ought not to be confused with a "micro-macro link" (Hilbert 1990a).

ETHNOMETHODOLOGY AND CONFLICT THEORY

Ethnomethodology was one of two broadly conceived attacks on American functionalism; it faulted the theory for being analytically unworkable and empirically false. The other line of attack, broadly conceived as Marxist studies, conflict or critical theory, faulted functionalism for its positing of social harmony and concord as a paragon of social health or an accurate rendering of the way society operates (Gouldner 1970; Horowitz 1962/67; Mills 1959; see Bernard 1983). From this angle, functionalism has a hidden agenda. It is a politically conservative theory that camouflages perpetual class conflict and material interests in the name of disinterested science. It is, in the Marxian sense, ideology (see Huaco 1966, 1986).[1]

In my pursuit of ethnomethodology's classical roots, it will be noted that no mention was made of Marx. This omission was deliberate but does not preclude finding connections between Marx's writings and ethnomethodology or the utility of a general conflict perspective for ethnomethodology or, in fact, the other way around. The omission first derives from the fact that Parsons himself omitted Marx, and from that omission, combined with Parsons's readings of Durkheim and Weber, sprang American functionalism. It was my intention in the present work to show how Parsons passed Durkheimian and Weberian themes, which he himself suppressed, to Garfinkel, who turned them into empirical phenomena. This is to say that no Marxist themes were so passed, so any connections between ethnomethodology and Marx will have to be made on another basis. They are not, in any case, historical connections.

A second reason for this omission is that connections between ethnomethodology and Marxist studies have been tried, not without a degree of success (see Mehan and Wood 1975, pp. 218–24). Such projects were the focus of a flurry of departmental activity in the early 1970s at the University of California at Santa Barbara, for example, and while none of this was ever formalized or systematically specified, the project might well be taken up again in a more rigorous manner. Moreover, some of the visionaries in this endeavor and others have been working with a more or less ethnomethodologically informed conflict theory for quite some time (Bogen and Lynch 1989; Maynard 1984, 1985a, 1985b; Molotch and Boden 1985; Molotch and Lester 1974; Spector and Kitsuse 1977), so while the details may still need spelling out, attempting links between ethnomethodology and Marxian approaches is a more conventional effort than the ones I have undertaken in this book.

Besides connecting Marx directly to ethnomethodology, another general line of attack would be to connect Marx with Durkheim-Weber or otherwise to show that there is a politically radical side to the latter that was lost in Parsons's theory (see Alexander 1988b; Collins 1988; Giddens 1971) and that the "conservativism" they are saddled with is due in part to their artificial severing from Marx, partly derived from Parsons's own conservativism and omission of Marx from his analysis. This kind of synthesis would necessarily follow from established ties between Durkheim-Weber and ethnomethodology on the one hand and ethnomethodology and Marx on the other. Thus one of the advantages of ethnomethodological readings of Durkheim and Weber is that in modernizing and empiricizing Parsons's forebears, it provides for their reintegration not only with each other but with general conflict theory. Since this was not a goal of the present work, leads in this direction come in the form of unsought insight.

I will not undertake systematic attempts to integrate conflict theory and ethnomethodology here, but consideration might be given to the possibility of liberating conflict theory from the reification of social class. If conflict and power allocations can be understood as internal to conversations or other kinds of members' methods and if occasions of these artful practices are "linked" in empirical space-time, then it could conceivably turn out that most of the political dynamics that Marx spoke of happen as he said they do but that the analyst would not require Marxian macronotions such as social class. Moreover, such detailed investigations could reveal aspects of conflict hitherto unknown in its empirical specifics to conflict theorists. "Class exploitation" might include advertising technology, for example television commercials that sell not only products but political leaders and common-sense ideas about society and its structure, that is, cultural resources for the artful reproduction of these ideas and structures —in a word, ideology (Dayan and Katz 1988; see Fishman 1980; Schiller 1989). That audiences to such displays, who can be conceived as disadvantaged participants in one-sided "conversations," would carry cultural resources accomplished within these time frames into other conversational settings and everyday discourse is almost axiomatic.

On the other end, television productions are products assembled, packaged, and sold in real time by concrete people in myriad concrete settings (e.g. strategy meetings and editing sessions). In other words, most of the big power games in society may be played out in a few-on-many style, where the determining few can be tied to their memberships, their bosses and managers, and they to theirs and so on—in *real time*, it must be emphasized, as opposed to structurally. The question as to where these chains lead is empirical: how many people are making what kinds of decisions for whom, and what are their practical methodologies and "sell" strategies? Thus could class conflict "reduce" to empirical instances of impression management, reification of structure and ideas, social manipulation, conversation, data gathering, memo passing, career building, story telling, news production and editing, poll taking, fashion selling, and so on. In that sense, power relations and class conflict are played to long-term outcomes that nobody knows, strictly, in advance.

Such a theoretical approach could be undertaken with concepts akin to

Collins's interaction ritual chains. Where sites along empirical chains become occasions for reification and advancement of causes, one can envision the theoretical possibility, though perhaps not the technical or methodological possibility, of unlocking the exact, orderly, processual, empirical history of an exact set of encounters that produced "the Vietnam War" as a reified macrohistorical event. This would include enormously complex chains of conversations connected in space-time and their cumulating effects and snowballing impressions from room to room, phone call to phone call, meeting to meeting, strategy session to spokesperson, spokesperson to camera, interview to notes, article to news editorial room, audience to public discourse, and the like (cf. Alexander 1988a; Dayan and Katz 1988). It is doubtful that anyone would ever have a methodological technology—not to mention the time or patience—for conducting such a study, but it is not doubtful in the same way that completing the list of CBTE teaching competencies or realizing "closure" in functionalist theory is doubtful. It is not *theoretically impossible*.

Whatever the efficacy of thinking along these lines, at least we have a theoretically empirical phenomenon, whether or not we ever gain access to it. For example, in a study of a teacher's classroom management styles, we know that whatever is witnessed in the classroom can be "linked" in space-time to teacher strategy meetings or other kinds of backstage talk, including informal talk in the lunchroom. Whatever the specifics, we know there is such backstage talk, that is, we would not need to observe backstage talk to know that it takes place and is observable in theory. Similarly, consumers on the receiving end of a media display are in the direct presence of cumulating backstage activity that carefully orchestrated the display, whether it is a commercial for aspirin, for George Bush, or for some corporation's public image and vision of America. Again, we do not need the detail to know about it. To repeat, interaction ritual chains *completely fill up* societal space-time.

There is nothing in this approach that could predict which impression-management displays will be successful. There is nothing "predetermined" in ritual chains, nothing structural, but much in human life turns on which displays of reified structure are successfully marketed as "reality"—that is, which structural ideas enter the domain of public discourse as common-sense presuppositions for routine reproduction. Surely a belief in social classes and notions like class interests and class consciousness has had something to do with revolutionary strategies and insurrections occurring time and time again throughout history. Along those lines, it is notable that comments heard in the 1988 presidential elections having to do with social class came in the form of discourse *not* of class conflict but of conflict over whether or not there *is* class conflict; indeed, sustaining and reproducing a discourse of natural class harmony seems to be a rhetorical leadership strategy in the United States (see DeMott 1990). Another recent example is a leading corporation's advertising claim that their line of product research is in fulfillment of what John F. Kennedy "meant" when he said, ". . . ask what you can do for your country."

Wherever these theoretical leads might go, there remains a disquieting impression that both ethnomethodologists and conflict theorists would object to such integration, and for parallel reasons. Conflict theorists rarely see themselves as removed from the terms of conflict to a degree approaching ethnomethodological indifference. Likewise ethnomethodologists may find the advantages of their research attitude subverted by any linkages to theory as embroiled in substantive political issues as Marxist studies. This is perhaps an irreconcilable gulf between the two disciplines, but if ethnomethodology maintains its indifference to structure—whether it exists or not, whether it is patterned or chaotic, whether it is micro or macro—it can continue in this vein to an indifference as to whether societal members are in harmony or in conflict, leaving that question to the detail of specific empirical investigations. Notably, recent conversational studies have revealed detailed methods whereby members organize and carry out conflict (Maynard 1984, 1985a, 1985b; Molotch and Boden 1985). And on the conflict theory side, it should be remembered that ethnomethodological studies leave the social world intact. While ethnomethodology could provide an improved empiricism and theoretical detail for conflict theory, it would leave the substance of those studies, for example Piven and Cloward's (1971) examination of public welfare in the United States, largely untouched.

Perhaps the aspect of conflict theory most difficult to reconcile with ethnomethodology is the notion of material interests, the economic mode of production, or the distribution of wealth, for that almost forces us to bring back the material world as a theoretical object. The material world is absolutely crucial in Marx's theory. It may be, therefore, that an ethnomethodologically informed conflict theory leaves the domain of ethnomethodology entirely, clipping and taking along any insight it can gather from these studies. One could ponder what kind of empirical sociology would derive if we were to allow these two, and only these two, phenomena: (1) the distribution of material resources (who has what), and (2) members' methods (predominately conversation). Material distribution would include various "institutional" arrangements, such as ownership, say, of CBS, which provides for a massively lopsided power allocation in "conversation" between owners and audiences. However, ownership is also an empirical matter owing to documents, which in turn are produced and managed and can theoretically be traced to their origins in concrete members' methods (see Smith 1974). Pushing these frontiers back this way could, however, lose the interest of conflict theorists oriented toward more substantive understanding, and it would certainly lose the interest of ethnomethodologists, who prefer to get their data wherever they can find them.

Nevertheless, Collins helps move theory in these directions with his use of interaction ritual chains in his own conflict theory, suggesting, for example, that through routine conversations members reproduce structural matters that uphold property and authority arrangements (Collins 1981b, pp. 996–97). This can be done nonreflectingly or with deliberate design. In either case membership is sustained, characterizable, especially in the latter case, as membership "coalitions" (pp. 997–98). Here in these concrete instances of coalition activities is where social classes, power groups, and status groups are sustained and managed. Here also is where the legitimacy of the "state" is reproduced (1981a, p. 86), where property changes hands (when it does), and where the legitimacy of ownership is reified (1987, p. 203). It is no small matter for Collins that in the ongoing reproduction of organized society, some of its members have weapons and can summon their concrete use through concrete channels in concrete ways that simultaneously legitimize their use as morally correct, legal, and easily understood from the common-sense vantage point. Success in such exercise of power depends in no small way upon the strategic "selling" of cultural resources to the membership at large where it enters routine public discourse (see Schiller 1989). Though Collins does not say so directly, the use of cultural resources by the disadvantaged to reproduce their own oppression harkens back to Marx's "alienation," or the processes wherein people are induced to work actively against their own interests; here members' methods are turned against them.

My purpose in this section is not to argue conclusively for a connection between ethnomethodology and Marx, much less to say how such a connection would be made or what it must look like. I offer suggestions, but these are necessarily tentative and speculative. I do want to argue forcefully, however, that the political conservatism of Parsons's theory is not due to his focus on Durkheim and Weber at the expense of Marx but is due rather to Parsons's own conservative theorizing, indeed his bureaucratic theorizing, and his subsequent readings of the two masters in service to that theory. That is, a modern empirical sociology derived from Durkheim and Weber, even without Marx, need not be conservative and can quite easily find its way over to conflict-oriented perspectives. There is nothing in Durkheim that will not allow that members manipulate the collective conscience, or compete for control of its content, in the production of Weberian legitimate order. Certainly conflict theory is amenable to ethnomethodology in ways it is not amenable to American functionalism. Ethnomethodology and conflict theory can at the very least serve one another as respective sources of insight, an affinity that could conceivably produce an integrated approach. While such integration may do sufficient revision to either perspective as to lose the interest of both, nevertheless the possibility is notable in its own terms.

CONCLUDING REMARKS

My purpose in this chapter was to suggest ways of locating ethnomethodology within contemporary theoretical issues. That is, not only is ethnomethodology continuous with respect to classical sociological themes, the central thesis of this book, but it also speaks to current debates in sociology. There are other ways such a concluding chapter could have been written, and no specific recommendation is made here to the exclusion of other possibilities. Nevertheless paths are open to reintegrating ethnomethodology's radical thesis, itself an extension of radical themes in classical thought, back into the substance of the sociological mainstream (though, it could be argued, not the mainstream itself). As we have seen, sometimes the effect is to transcend the terms of a contemporary debate, as in the micro-macro issue, providing sort of a therapy for sociologists; in its therapeutic role, ethnomethodology discharges the compellingness of current discourse, freeing intellectual energies to pursue more fruitful lines of theoretical development. In other cases, ethnomethodology is immediately served by modified understandings from current discourse, as in the case of Collins's work. In still other cases, as with conflict theory, integration is more elusive and may damage either parent discipline in the eyes of its proponents; yet the prospects of integration are interesting on their own terms, and the possibilities of mutual aid are always present.

It should not be forgotten that ethnomethodology remains a coherent body of empirical work in its own right, with a program of research and theoretical perspective. Too much integration, or integration too soon, may distress ethnomethodologists who worry that premature dialogue risks a subtle undermining of ethnomethodology's radical vision. Such efforts could in fact lead to premature generalizations about ethnomethodology's theoretical implications or the significance of its findings. Here, then, is the impetus to postpone theorizing and dialogue with other sociologies.

These reservations and misgivings are well founded; thus the offerings in this chapter are not intended as "new directions for ethnomethodology" or "suggestions for further research," at least not in the way this often comes up in closing chapters. They are certainly not a call for an abandonment of "pure" ethnomethodology. It is nevertheless helpful to see how ethnomethodological research and commentary can become relevant to the ongoing interests of other kinds of sociology, especially when such relevance is helpful to them. It would not, however, be helpful to anyone to modify ethnomethodology's radical stance in order to serve reintegration. Indeed, the claim of this book has been that many of the radical themes of classical sociology were lost to trendy bureaucratic reasoning, themes later picked up by Garfinkel. It would be tragic in the extreme to see these radical themes lost once again.

There are indeed some misgivings within ethnomethodological circles concerning developments even within those circles. Though conversation analysis derives directly from the theoretical advances of Garfinkel, its methodological precision makes it possible for someone to be highly trained in its technology with little or no appreciation of the sociological theory that gave rise to it. And since this precision is in part what has contributed to ethnomethodology's newfound respectability in the sociological mainstream, Pollner (1991) worries that the vision of "radical reflexivity" integral to Garfinkel's work may be dying, even for ethnomethodologists. The concern here lies with the publicly accepted efficacy of ethnomethodological research lying with the technical sophistication of its method, which allows it to gain stature by affiliation with more traditional standards of credibility, rather than with its theory, which at the outset was inseparable from reflexivity radically conceived. As originally conceived, radical reflexivity enabled ethnomethodologists to see even their own work as radically situated, a special vision that is lost with grounding in mere technical precision. If ethnomethodology should lose that vision, Pollner reasons, then it will have lost its theoretical angle on social life generally, becoming just a "better way" of doing traditional sociology. These concerns are in no small way related to any kind of claim that conversation analysis, because of its rigor, is "true" ethnomethodology at the expense of other types (see Maynard and Clayman 1991). They are also connected to any concessions to the notion that technical methodology has enabled ethnomethodologists to identify "microstructure" (Hilbert 1990b).

In any case, whatever its future, ethnomethodology is no longer the curious aside to sociology it once was. Boden (1990) itemizes numerous contributions of ethnomethodology and conversation analysis and forecasts a rich and diverse future of ethnomethodological endeavors, both "basic" research and research oriented to more substantive domains, to make the deceptively simple point that "ethnomethodology is here to stay." Conversation analysis especially continues to turn up huge amounts of empirical surprises whose significance is assured but yet still unknown; data are being generated faster than they can be covered by cumulating theory. One is reminded of Tycho Brahe and his lifetime of work cataloging the motions of stars and planets with his jointed sticks—amassing unprecedented detail before anyone could even imagine the advantages of such precision, that is, before anyone had ever heard of Kepler or Newton, whose theoretical advances depended in no small part on Tycho's patience and attention to detail. Whatever future developments in ethnomethodology reveal about social life, they are certain to be counterintuitive, revolutionary in their potential for understanding humanity, and empirically grounded.

NOTES

1. Parsons (1968b, pp. xv–xx) viewed his functionalism as a refinement of voluntaristic theory, although some of his interpreters have viewed the transition as more problematic (Alexander 1978; Menzies 1977).

2. Parsons also derives his theory to a lesser degree from Alfred Marshall and Vilfredo Pareto, but he is more known for the textual analyses of Durkheim and Weber. In any case, only the latter two figure in my analysis.

3. Alexander (1987b, pp. 34–46) reminds us of the interconnections between substantive challenges to functionalist theory and efforts to separate Parsons from Durkheim and Weber, that is, to "de-Parsonize" the classics (Pope 1973; Cohen, Hazelrigg, and Pope 1975). Where Durkheim remains un-de-Parsonized, he is often rejected, along with functionalism, by some of these challenges (Collins 1988, p. 107).

4. My drawing historical connections in this way should be distinguished from discovering the "true" meaning of classical texts or delineating what their authors, after all, "meant" (see Coser 1981; Fine and Kleinman 1986; Jones 1977; cf. Alexander 1987b) or constructing "syntheses" between otherwise disparate theories (e.g. between Durkheim and symbolic interactionism, as proposed by Stone and Farberman 1970). I am not arguing that Durkheim was an ethnomethodologist, for example, or that Garfinkel was a secret Weberian. Certainly Durkheim and Weber had more to say about society than the points I am raising in this book, and the same goes for ethnomethodology. Nevertheless, ethnomethodology builds upon some crucial classical themes that were otherwise eliminated or forgotten in the evolution of sociological theory. These themes are the same themes that Parsons suppressed, and they come up again in ethnomethodology precisely through addressing Parsonian ideas based on that suppression. Undoubtedly ethnomethodology has developed these classical ideas in directions that Durkheim and Weber could not have imagined, but connections between classical sociology and ethnomethodology on an almost one-to-one basis are grounded in historical process, despite what Durkheim, Weber, or Garfinkel would have to say about these connections. Whether any of these ideas are scientifically *accurate* or not and whether ethnomethodology ought properly to be viewed as empirical verification of classical ideas are different questions entirely, questions that turn on the degree of Durkheim's and Weber's genius as well as the quality of Garfinkel's empiricism. How-

ever, I find both classical theory and ethnomethodology deeply sophisticated and regard continuities between them as a source of wonder and as a basis for solving many of the paradoxes in modern sociological theory (see chapters 9–10; Ritzer 1990).

5. Parsons does not invent his theoretical bedrock out of thin air. These principles were rather fundamental to classical utilitarian economic theory. But they are by no means integral to Durkheim and Weber, from which Parsons derives only the upper edifices of his voluntarist theory.

6. Warner (1978, pp. 1322–24) questions Parsons's appreciation of Hobbes on this point, saying that Hobbes did not conceive of the "war of all against all" in terms of randomness of ends but as a lack of restraint on means toward ends. In my discussion, the accuracy of the derivation from Hobbes is of little significance compared with the "Hobbesian problem" as Parsons himself sees it, i.e. the *Parsonian* problem of order, and the solutions Parsons later offers, which he derives from Durkheim and Weber. Accuracy concerning these later derivations is quite central to my arguments.

CHAPTER 2

1. The equivalence of society and morality is part and parcel of why Durkheim viewed "dynamic density" as causing the transformation of mechanical solidarity to organic solidarity. Parsons rejects this equivalence, which leads him to suggest that here Durkheim was briefly and temporarily thrown off course in his theoretical direction, since the historical connections between "dynamic density" and "material density" render the former little more than population pressure, not social as such but biological pressure (Parsons 1968b, pp. 320–24). But dynamic density is also *moral* density for Durkheim (1933, pp. 256–63); thus the transformation at hand is indeed amenable to investigation at the social level (cf. Pope 1973, pp. 401–2). Yet Parsons says Durkheim at this point had relatively little understanding of organic solidarity, a blind spot from which Durkheim recovered in *Suicide*.

2. This becomes less so as we move into Durkheim's (1947) late sociology, where moral regulation becomes deeply entwined with ritual (cf. Lukes 1972, pp. 163–67).

3. Quoting extensively from Durkheim's *Education and Sociology*, Lukes (1972, pp. 112–15) identifies "rules" as one of three elements of morality in Durkheim's work, the other two being "attachment to social groups" and "autonomy." Of these three, the second is most conducive to my arguments, particularly when it comes to a society/morality equivalence sui generis, the equivalence that Parsons worked expressly to reject. In Durkheim's words, "Moral goals are those the object of which is *a society*"; "we are moral beings only to the extent that we are social beings" (quoted in Lukes 1972, pp. 112–14; see also pp. 412–21). This seems to be the quintessential morality for Durkheim, for the extent to which morality assumes a "rules" format could simply be an index of social evolution from a mechanical to an

organic mode—even in the latter case, though, morality need not be entirely expressible in a "rules" format and would require a Durkheimian "something else" to sustain them (cf. p. 421). If what is essential in a pure mechanical morality is ritual practices, such practices undoubtedly underlie general rules in organic solidarity much as they underlie rational contracts. Incidentally, the third element Lukes identifies, autonomy, comes closest to Parsons's rendition of voluntarism or internalization—individuals act morally as a matter of "free acceptance" (Durkheim, quoted in Lukes 1972, p. 115).

4. For Parsons, subjective respect is essential for normative order to be moral. I will take up the question of subjectivity in chapter 4; for now I am addressing only the "mechanics" of morality as Parsons understands it: prescriptive normative order, the logic of Parsonian morality once the necessary subjective respect is provided. In deriving normative order from Durkheim, Parsons says Durkheim's emphasis was "on the existence of a body of rules which have not been the object of any agreement among the contracting parties themselves but are socially 'given.'" (Parsons 1968b, p. 312). Parsons refers here to a page in *The Division of Labor* where "rule" is the idiom, but this is not to say that Durkheim formalized the concept or expected it to do the work of deductive behavioral prescription.

5. Once again I am postponing consideration of the Parsonian "subjective respect" requirement for the broader discussion of reality and experience in chapter 4.

6. Parsons himself regarded his normative order as empirical. Note e.g. his reference to Durkheim's "empirical emphasis on the existence of a body of regulatory norms" (Parsons 1968b, p. 318).

7. Alexander (1984, pp. 152–69) writes of Parsons's "methodological ambivalence" concerning the relative merits of empiricism and analytic theorizing. He notes, for example, that Parsons spent "more than 700 pages arguing [his nonatomistic theory's] analytic rather than empirical validity," all the while claiming that the theory is "simply empirical" (p. 154). In *The Structure of Social Action*, Parsons considers convergence between Durkheim and Weber itself to be empirical, thus allowing him to "claim empirical proof for what is essentially a purely theoretical argument. He can achieve verification without actually referring to any empirical facts" (p. 155). Alexander goes on to show how this tension between empiricism and analytic theorizing inhabits Parsons's later work, where emphasis is upon deriving empirical specifics from theoretical generalities; this tension is never resolved. Alexander sees Parsons's efforts to empiricize his theory, including his broad analogies with relationships between theory and phenomena in other sciences, as obscuring the importance of Parsons's general theorizing taken on its own terms, though he still regards the latter as "empirically oriented" (p. 9). By contrast, I am arguing that an a priori theory need not be taken as scientific in the first place, no matter how elegantly formulated or logically compelling it seems and no matter how easily it lends itself to operationalizations or other methodological transformations (see Garfinkel 1988).

CHAPTER 3

1. The "have" example is adapted from a classroom demonstration in Eugene Troxell's 1969 course in Ordinary Language Analysis.

2. In accounting for this "error," Parsons asks: "How, then, did Durkheim come to *identify* society and moral obligation?" (1968b, p. 392). Parsons grounds the error in Durkheim's failure to distinguish his interest in scientific ethics, normatively conceived, from the empirical study of morality, descriptively conceived (pp. 394–95). Given Durkheim's confusion on this point, moral reality seems to be available to the scientist just as it is available to common-sense actors; along with heredity and environment, morality is a third objective cause contributing to human behavior, and it must be society—a mistake Parsons attributes to Durkheim's overcommitment to positivism (pp. 392–93). Parsons's alternative is to hold that morality is not available for science the way it is for actors, which is to say that the moral validity of norms is not up for scientific study but that morality is nevertheless available for science in another way—as objectively present systems of norms and values. Thus "causal efficacy," not "moral validity," becomes the sociologist's preoccupation (p. 393). In this manner, then, Parsons provides a rationale for suppressing Durkheim's society/morality equivalence and producing a theory based on the ability of prescriptive morality to cause objective society. Parsons needs to reject the society/morality equivalence in order to locate morality as analytically external to social order as its cause. Taken alone, however, this analytic separation would render morality footloose and fancy-free (i.e. unregulated). So morality is tied to and contained within a normative order whose concrete content is no one's personal idea but one to which all people voluntarily surrender their subjective respect. This order is thereby capable of regulating. For Parsons, Durkheim's failure to note this implication of a normative system of rules and values leaves Durkheim's version of morality, and ultimately society, which is equivalent to it, hanging in the air. This critique runs parallel to Parsons's rejection of Durkheim's society/reality equivalence as idealism (see chapter 4). It is interesting that someone as routinely disparaging of metaphysical claims as Parsons would attach subjective moral commitment to a body of rules that no scientist has ever seen.

CHAPTER 4

1. Notice that if subjective respect were all that it takes for rules to regulate behavior, then there would have been no inherent need for functionalists to work so diligently in the development of their theory. For example, Hobbes's "social contract" might work by itself, if we added the element of moral respect and awe. Or in Durkheim's terms, there is no apparent reason why rational contracts would require underlying morality if they were sufficiently respected at face value. A more profound question, however, is whether *any* set of rules could prescribe behavior, no matter how deeply they were respected (see chapter 2).

2. Warner (1978, pp. 1336–37) sees Parsons's interpretation not as a mistake but

as a one-sided overstatement; he says also that critics' emphasis on subjectivity as an effect rather than a cause is an overstatement in the other direction. Neither position is correct, says Warner, since no one has demonstrated that "what is an effect for one purpose cannot be a cause for another" (p. 1336). But if Durkheim is correct on the equivalence of society and reality and later between society and ideas, then there are no empirical distinctions to be made across these equivalences; there are not "two things" (even interpenetrating things), such that one may be said to be causing (or affected by) the other. They are all wholly and at the same time one sui generis phenomenon, simultaneously regulated and regulating.

3. These Durkheimian principles undermine Parsons's recurrent distinctions between the ways the empirical and the nonempirical worlds are experienced by societal members (Parsons 1968b, p. 422), as well as similar distinctions between the ways nonsocial and social environments exercise constraint. Such distinctions figure prominently in Parsons's formulating of the problem of social order in the first place: the factual order differs from normative order in that it consists of patterns of behavior objectively given to the scientist, where normative order is social by contrast. Another use of the distinction is contained in Parsons's critiques of radical positivism that has individuals responding to the "givens" of a natural environment, givens that are insufficient for Parsons but whose existential status for sociology he never questions (see chapter 1). These distinctions also contribute to Parsons's impression that Durkheim's theory was a progression of promising beginnings, false directions, objectionable implications, fresh syntheses, new beginnings (see Parsons 1968b, p. 304), and ultimately an unfinished implication (Parsons's voluntaristic theory)—this as opposed to a comprehensive and internally coherent innovation at the outset (Giddens 1971). For example, Parsons suggests that Durkheim was periodically sidetracked with biological and other nonsocial concerns, such as his equivalence of "moral density" and "dynamic density," which Parsons by contrast equates with population pressure and "nonsocial" aspects of the environment (Parsons 1968b, pp. 320–24). These distinctions are also apparent in Parsons's reasons why normative order, which is analytically capable of regulating behavior, cannot assume a regulative role in sociology without actors' subjective respect: without subjectivity, normative order (still *analytically* capable of regulating) assimilates to the environment to which individuals must adapt, this general formula having been rejected earlier in the critique of radical positivism.

4. Parsons might well view Durkheim's focus on ideas as idealism, given his own framework, one that ties subjectivity to cause. If society equals reality and ideas are not therefore derivable from an external and objective universe, then this would make ideas preeminent, a priori "eternal objects" (Parsons 1968b, pp. 444–45). Ideas that cause behavior would themselves be neither caused nor regulated. They would be free-floating, unattached to anything, coming from no place; and if they *were* equivalent to society, then society also would be free-floating and uncaused. Hence Durkheim's free-floating ideas render his late sociology idealism. The only alternative for Durkheim, says Parsons, would have been radical positivism, which would not allow subjectivity at all (see chapter 1), but Durkheim's empirical rigor

ironically led him to the subjective dimension of society at almost every turn (Parsons 1968b, p. 446); he thereby made the mistake of thinking that subjectivity and society were the same thing. This constraint-free society is just as objectionable as the radically deterministic model of positivism (1968b, p. 446); nothing would stand outside of ideas as obstacles to their realization; there would be no boundaries in whose terms actors could make subjective decisions. In that sense, then, Parsons says the element of subjective will and effort would have no more place in idealism than in radical positivism; there would be no social action. Parsons rescues Durkheim from this dilemma by grounding ideas as subjective respect for an objectively present normative order. Notice that this is directly analogous to Parsons's rejection of society/morality, for where morality causes behavior, it needs objective grounding to avoid being footloose and fancy-free. Parsons grounds morality in a system of norms and values which members respect. Parsons says that in general it was Durkheim's main failing that he did not recognize this system.

5. Parsons exemplifies Bloor's observation that Durkheim's hints about the implications of his work for a sociology of science "have fallen on deaf ears" (Bloor 1976, p. 2).

6. Parsons also periodically distinguishes between the point of view of sociologists and the point of view of members, but he makes this distinction almost wholly in service to the distinction between "empirical, objective, nonsocial" reality (which scientists know about) and "mythological, common-sense, social" reality (which societal members know about but which scientists know is false), i.e. a distinction between reality and society. The latter may be available to social scientists, but only as it consists of scientifically available norms and values; taken on its own terms, it is still subject to error. Thus for Parsons, social scientists join with natural scientists in investigating "global reality," some of which happens to be social. Parsonian findings would conceivably integrate with those of natural science in some way, connecting social with nonsocial reality. In that way, sociologists would continue in the tradition of distinguishing real reality from false reality. This requires that sociologists take for granted the same empirical realm that the natural sciences by necessity take for granted, investigate, and discover. We would have to take that for granted as a presocial environment. However, since the empirical investigation of social phenomena sets sociology off from the other sciences, calling any of these phenomena "presocial" loses them as topical concerns entirely. This is true whether the alleged presocial phenomena are the regularities in behavior that Parsons begins with as factual or the natural world that biologists, physicists, and astronomers presuppose. Notably, Parsons barely touches Durkheim's remarks about the social character of the natural sciences.

CHAPTER 5

1. This conception of ritual repair indicates its omnipresence throughout society, even in the routines of everyday life. This is consistent with Durkheim's sense of renewal as an ongoing, moment-to-moment social reality as opposed to some-

thing engaged in only occasionally. As Alexander (1982b, p. 246) states it, religious ritual for Durkheim becomes "the model for all social practice and association."

CHAPTER 7

1. Because Weber's types are part of his methodology, I will not argue that they are formalized versions of members' types or that sociologists cannot use ideal types without "going native" as discussed earlier. While members do generate their own types and use them in the production of social order, for members these are types *of society* that exist in the world, i.e. society as conceived by common-sense reasoning. They are not qualified by members as types of subjective beliefs about society; indeed they are not qualified by members as methodological tools at all. They are simply types of real entities. Conceived methodologically, however, Weber's ideal types present no more of a problem for ethnomethodologists than their own use of terms like "school," "welfare bureaucracy," "halfway house," and so on in establishing the settings of investigation. What is needed is empirical and theoretical specification concerning what ideal types are types *of* (see Hekman 1983), not a general rejection of methodological vocabulary.

2. Parsons's argument for element analysis presumes the possibility of revealing a finite number of selfsame elements whose features transcend context and/or association with each other. Also they would have to be incapable of being broken further into more primitive elements; otherwise they would display the same weaknesses of Weber's ideal types. If Parsons is right about this, then Weber is wrong on the necessity of subjective value decisions on the part of scientists regarding what aspects of the social world they intend to study. If typifications are all reducible to elements, then presumably these elements would be the same for any competent scientist, no matter which initial set of concepts (assuming it is comprehensive enough) is broken down to obtain these elements. Thus any social scientist would make the same discoveries.

3. It is interesting that Parsons limits this distinction to specific case studies, e.g. the Indian caste system versus Brahmanic philosophy, and does not carry it into more generic types, e.g. bureaucratic organization versus bureaucratic mentality.

4. It is puzzling that Parsons on the one hand ties legitimacy to moral obligation, which in his discussion of Durkheim meant subjective respect for norms, and on the other hand ties it to the normative system itself, making it a cause of subjective respect and a condition of action in his own scheme (1968b, p. 652). It is not of major consequence to unravel this, since the connection to Durkheim is really a connection to the Parsonian version of Durkheim as implying Parsons's own theory. As already noted, neither Durkheim nor Weber states that ideas can be rendered as formal rules. Yet Parsons repeats the convergence later in the text, which solidifies the position.

> Legitimacy is for Weber a quality of an order, that is, of a *system of norms* governing conduct, or at least to which action may (or must) be oriented. This quality is imputed to the order by those acting in relation to it. Doing so

involves taking a given type of attitude toward the norms involved which may be characterized as one of disinterested acceptance. To put the matter somewhat differently, for one who holds an order to be legitimate, living up to its rules becomes, to this extent, a matter of moral obligation.

Thus Weber has arrived at the same point Durkheim reached when he interpreted constraint as moral authority. Moreover, Weber has approached the question from the same point of view, that of an individual thought of as acting in relation to a *system of rules* that constitute conditions of his action. There has emerged from the work of both men the same distinction of attitude elements toward the rules of such an order, the interested and the disinterested. In both cases a legitimate order is contrasted with a situation of the uncontrolled play of interests. Both have concentrated their special attention on the latter element. Such a parallel is not likely to be purely fortuitous. (p. 661, emphasis added)

Thus legitimacy, for Parsons, is the same thing as subjective respect for normative order, and it is also a feature of that very order. The fact that he says it is "imputed" to normative order by people does not prevent him from discussing it as a real and puzzling phenomenon for science. Indeed for Weber, what could only be "factual" order in Parsonian theory is itself imputed by people as factual, and legitimacy is lodged there as a feature of its very presumption as order. Parsons, quite the other way, finds legitimacy only in the normative order, which for him is objectively present every bit as much as the factual order it causes. Factual order is not imputed, normative order is not imputed; if anything is imputed, it is the legitimacy attached to normative order. Yet legitimacy is also a *real element* of that order. It is a "quality of an order"; Parsons unaccountably assigns this attribution to Weber (p. 661). Moreover he terms the legitimate order itself as "legitimacy norms, in relation to action," in keeping with his action theory (p. 658).

5. Earlier, in reviewing the four types of social action, Parsons is impressed with Weber's use of the term "sanctity" with regard to traditional action, e.g. in reference to the sanctity of tradition. This suggests the *normative* element in traditional action, says Parsons (1968b, pp. 646–47). Parenthetically, Parsons accounts for the normative element in value-rational action by virtue of the values adhered to and in instrumentally rational action by distinguishing it from value-rational only in the number of values oriented to. He says instrumentally rational action involves the weighing of values (ends), where value-rational action involves only one paramount value (pp. 643–44). He thus returns "values" to purely instrumental-rational action, saving the elements of his action scheme in that case. But traditional action would have no source of legitimacy without the element that "sanctity" suggests; otherwise it would be mere habit. Parsons expressly postpones this discussion to a later consideration of charisma in relation to legitimacy (p. 647), noting that "charisma makes no appearance at all in the four types of action" (p. 649). He hints that it could have something to do with affectual action, a fruitful line that he never follows up. Instead he calls affectual action a "residual category" of nontraditional and

nonrational action, one that has no positive place in Weber's sociology (p. 648). Returning to the question later, Parsons eventually argues that *charisma* is the principle suggested by the sanctity in traditionalism. He arrives at this through a circuitous argument that connects charisma first to morality and then to legitimacy, along the way. On an analytic plane, Parsons notes simply that charisma, in Weber's discussions of it as applied to a person, evokes respect among the person's following; to disobey charismatic authority is to be "delinquent in duty" (p. 662). Charismatic authority is therefore a *moral* authority, a "specific attitude of respect . . . clearly the ritual attitude of Durkheim" (p. 662). Having already linked Durkheimian morality to legitimacy (above), Parsons arrives at what surely must be a controversial claim: "In other words, charisma is directly linked with legitimacy, is indeed the name in Weber's system for the source of legitimacy in general" (p. 663). Since charisma is moral, it now becomes formally equivalent to the sacred in Durkheim's theory as the origin of respect for norms in general, i.e. the origin of legitimacy (p. 669; cf. Nisbet 1966, pp. 251–57; Shils 1965).

6. Historical accuracy aside, there is no reason for asserting the contemporary presence of elements from a previous era without empirical warrant. In Durkheim's theory, for example, the "sacred" is an essential feature of any society; it is the society in essence. Its historical origin in religious practices does not signify that the sacredness in organic solidarity is the same "substantive thing" as the sacredness of mechanical solidarity, that it has its source there, or that it is currently or subconsciously "religious." Rather, the sacredness of organic solidarity is sustained in its own terms through social practices presently engaged in and observable by sociologists. *The "source" of contemporary sacredness is necessarily in contemporary practices.* In that light, the Durkheimian sacred principle can be expected to be operative within a Weberian rational-legal order as well as within a traditional or charismatic order. But it need not be the case that sacredness indicates a real element whose identity transcends place or period. By analogy, we would not argue that since the computer revolution rides upon industrial and technological innovations of earlier eras, therefore clocks (say) and computers are "the same thing." In that way it cannot be, for Durkheim, that modern society is sacred because of real elements it picked up in an earlier religious era. No more need it derive from charisma as a real element in Weber's sociology. Still less is there any reason for confusing the Durkheimian sacred principle, featured in any society, with Weber's charismatic type, which is an ideal type of a subjective orientation.

7. Even for Parsons an equivalence between charisma and the Durkheimian sacred was not by itself sufficient for establishing convergence, which is why he went on to connect charisma and "sanctity," as Weber used the term with respect to traditionalism. He did this in order to account for Weber's lack of focused attention to ritual, which was indisputably integral to Durkheim's sociology. Parsons acknowledges this absence (Parsons 1968b, pp. 673–77) but says that Weber nevertheless was not unconcerned with ritual and that his general theory thereby approaches that of Durkheim. He finds Weber's interest in ritual in his sociology of religion, particularly in his discussions of magic. Following out Weber's case histo-

ries, Parsons finds the "failure to root out ritual, especially magic" as the failure to "break through traditionalism" toward a rational mode (p. 674); indeed hostility toward ritual characterized the Puritan ethic and in part set the conditions for rationalism (p. 673). Thus ritual, for Parsons, is tied to traditionalism. From here he moves on to argue that since Weber applied the term "sacred" to tradition, and since "charisma" is Weber's term for sacredness, and since tradition-as-norms bears the charisma (ergo sanctity) transferred from the charismatic person of an earlier era, and since for Durkheim ritual was "practices relative to sacred things," therefore the association between charisma and (Durkheimian) ritual is intimate (p. 674). Parsons further ties up the connection by pointing out that Weber discusses action in a postcharismatic era as involving symbolic representations of "supernatural entities." What is the difference, Parsons asks, between "supernatural entities" (Weber) and "sacred things" (Durkheim)? Assuming none, he answers, "One could hardly ask for a closer correspondence" between Weber and Durkheim (p. 675). Notice that the constitutive role of Durkheimian ritual now becomes assigned to traditionalism. Accordingly, Parsons concludes that traditionalism is the stabilizing "element" in all forms of symbolic relationships: "The correspondence between the two [men] is complete" (p. 676). Again, finding traditionalism in all three types disrupts the internal integrity of ideal types.

But one would still hope for a closer correspondence. Parsons is aware of the importance of finding Durkheimian ritual in Weber's theory, even saying that not finding it would be a "serious blow" to the convergence theory (Parsons 1968b, p. 673). But as presented, this is at best an ad hoc correspondence, loosely strung together; Parsons himself calls it a "chain" (p. 674). Moreover, Parsons finds in the convergence a common emphasis on the "symbolic relation" (p. 675), without identifying the terms of the relation, i.e. what symbolizes and what gets symbolized. For Durkheim, one of these terms is invariably the society, the collectivity per se. While this is easiest to spot in the religious practices of mechanical solidarity, ritual and the sacred are essential to the maintenance and identity of society as such (see chapters 3 and 5). Parsons's concern with Durkheimian ritual, by contrast, is mostly tied to religion, where he identifies ritual as functionally similar to external social control. But for Durkheim the sacred and its ritual maintenance are not inherently "religious" except in a metaphoric or more general sense, one e.g. that would allow one to speak of moral individualism as "secular religion," hence Durkheim's quasi-religious (and purposely ironic) characterization of modern morality as "the cult of the individual." Societal maintenance is continued for organic solidarity in the ritual of deviance recruitment, for example. A Weberian rational-legal orientation therefore needs Durkheimian ritual to sustain it no less than charismatic and traditional orientations. A rational orientation (or any other) would be anomic without it. Parsons knew this, too, which in part explains why he needed charisma and tradition as "elements" of rationalism. It is still not clear how Parsons conceived the historical development of rationality as hinging on the weeding out of ritual while at the same time saw rationality as containing charisma and tradition. It would appear, in any case, that Weber used "ritual" in a more restricted sense than

Durkheim, more in keeping with its conventional association with certain kinds of religion. How else could Puritanism, or *any* social order, be hostile to ritual?

Finally, it should be noted that neither Weber nor Parsons claims that charisma itself is equivalent to the collectivity. This it would have to be, if it were the same as the Durkheimian sacred; there is no other way charisma could be an empirical phenomenon for science. At best what we have in Parsons's charisma is a feature of, or a symbol for, the invisible normative order he fashions as the cause of the empirical order. Neither is there, in Weber or Parsons, a categorical opposite of charisma analogous to the Durkheimian profane. But none of this means that Weber's sociology cannot be understood against the background of Durkheim. What it would take for Weberian ideas to display the Durkheimian sacred is that they be regularly and ritually sustained and re-created. This is true for all three ideal types of legitimacy, as well as for whatever ideas empirically prevail in a given place and time. Therefore no idea itself needs to be the source of the sacred in other ideas. See Pope, Cohen, and Hazelrigg (p. 425) for further criticism of Parsons's equation of Durkheim's sacred and Weber's charisma.

CHAPTER 8

1. To say that rationality is grounded in social practices is not to say that its groundedness is nonrational or irrational, but rather nonideational. While Sica may be correct in his Paretian objective of finding the "ultimate irrationality" (see Sica 1988, p. 38) in rationality, irrationality itself is an ideational concept conceived within a rational orientation, and as such "pure rationality" can contain it. Only rational actors could identify anything as irrational. Moreover, even if we use "irrationality" to refer to charismatic or traditional orientations (see pp. 213–14), this says nothing about the possibility of "pure rationality" methodologically conceived. Contrarily, to say that "pure rationality" is grounded in nonideational activity is to say that it is not contaminated by charismatic, traditional, or other "irrational" ideas, even though it may contain ideas about irrationality. Its purity is indicated by this lack of contamination, not by an ability to ground itself rationally. I would say on the basis of these considerations, therefore, that it is no less misleading to argue for the "irrational" foundations of rationality than it is to argue for the "sacrilegious" or unwholesome grounds of charismatic orientations. Notice that charismatic actors may find rationality itself tainted with the devil's work, just as rational actors find charisma irrational.

CHAPTER 9

1. Here I am departing from critics such as Pope, Cohen, and Hazelrigg (1975), who say that Parsons's distortions of Durkheim and Weber obscured differences between the two so fundamental that a convergence thesis is misguided on its face. These same critics, however, see the desirability of "synthetic theoretical constructions" that are "capable of subsuming two or more previous constructions that are

disparate in specific content and even in basic perspective" as long as they do not "read the later construction into its predecessors, as if to explicate their original meanings" (p. 426). I offer a "new convergence" as such a synthetic theoretical construction.

2. The compatibility between the Spector and Kitsuse approach and Durkheim's sociology does not mean that they are identical. For example, Durkheim produces an imagery of behaviors standing as candidate crimes according to their "distance" from the collective conscience. Ethnomethodologists would have trouble with this imagery because it implies a factual identity of behavior prior to its being labeled deviance or conformity. This is no less serious a problem than the more rigid assumption of factual conformity and objective deviance (see chapter 3). Neverthe-less, Durkheim's emphasis on ritual practices as opposed to stable categories of conformity and nonconformity dovetails with ethnomethodological notions of so-cial practices and artful repair, and this dovetailing advances insight into the character of functionalist reasoning. Here Merton's theorizing emerges as an em-pirical case of Durkheimian ritual claims-making activities.

CHAPTER 10

1. Other kinds of criticism allege that functionalism cannot handle history or social change (Turner and Maryanski 1979), that it is objectionably abstract and vague (Abrahamson 1978), and that it is illegitimately teleological and tautological (for an overview, see Ritzer 1988, pp. 222–25). Broadly, these criticisms fit within the two categories of criticism I am suggesting: conflict and analytic/empirical correctness. The tautology charge, for example, is intimately tied to my discussion of Merton's role theory in chapter 9, although in that context I viewed Merton's theory as an example of rational and "incarnate" order production as opposed to flawed scientific theory.

REFERENCES

Abrahamson, Mark. 1978. *Functionalism.* Englewood Cliffs, N.J.: Prentice-Hall.
———. 1981. *Sociological Theory: An Introduction to Concepts, Issues, and Research.* Englewood Cliffs, N.J.: Prentice-Hall.
Alexander, Jeffrey C. 1978. "Formal and Substantive Voluntarism in the Work of Talcott Parsons: A Theoretical and Ideological Reinterpretation." *American Sociological Review* 43:177–98.
———. 1982a. *Theoretical Logic in Sociology.* Vol. 1, *Positivism, Presuppositions, and Current Controversies.* Berkeley: University of California Press.
———. 1982b. *Theoretical Logic in Sociology.* Vol. 2, *The Antinomies of Classical Thought: Marx and Durkheim.* Berkeley: University of California Press.
———. 1983. *Theoretical Logic in Sociology.* Vol. 3, *The Classical Attempt at Theoretical Synthesis: Max Weber.* Berkeley: University of California Press.
———. 1984. *Theoretical Logic in Sociology.* Vol. 4, *The Modern Reconstruction of Classical Thought: Talcott Parsons.* Berkeley: University of California Press.
———. 1987a. "Action and Its Environments." In *The Micro-Macro Link*, edited by Jeffrey C. Alexander, Bernhard Giesen, Richard Münch, and Neil J. Smelser, pp. 289–318. Berkeley: University of California Press.
———. 1987b. "The Centrality of the Classics." In *Social Theory Today*, edited by Anthony Giddens and Jonathan H. Turner, pp. 11–57. Stanford: Stanford University Press.
———. 1988a. "Cultural and Political Crisis: 'Watergate' and Durkheimian Sociology." In *Durkheimian Sociology: Cultural Studies*, edited by Jeffrey C. Alexander, pp. 187–224. Cambridge: Cambridge University Press.
———, ed. 1988b. *Durkheimian Sociology: Cultural Studies.* Cambridge: Cambridge University Press.
Alexander, Jeffrey C., and Paul Colomy. 1990. "Neofunctionalism Today: Reconstructing a Theoretical Tradition." In *Frontiers of Social Theory*, edited by George Ritzer, pp. 33–67. New York: Columbia University Press.
Alexander, Jeffrey C., and Bernhard Giesen. 1987. "From Reduction to Linkage: The Long View of the Micro-Macro Link." In *The Micro-Macro Link*, edited by Jeffrey C. Alexander, Bernhard Giesen, Richard Münch, and Neil J. Smelser, pp. 1–42. Berkeley: University of California Press.
Andrews, Theodore. 1972. "Certification." In *Competency-Based Teacher Education: Progress, Problems, and Prospects*, edited by W. Robert Houston and Robert B. Howsam, pp. 143–70. Chicago: Science Research Associates.

Bakke, E. Wight. 1959. "Concept of the Social Organization." In *Modern Organization Theory*, edited by Mason Haire, pp. 16–75. New York: John Wiley and Sons.

Bales, Robert F. 1950. "A Set of Categories for the Analysis of Small Group Interaction." *American Sociological Review* 15:257–63.

Banton, Michael, and Jonathan Harwood. 1975. *The Race Concept*. New York: Praeger.

Barnard, Chester I. 1958. *The Functions of the Executive*. Cambridge: Harvard University Press.

Becker, Howard S. 1953. "Becoming a Marijuana User." *American Journal of Sociology* 59:235–42.

———. 1963. *Outsiders: Studies in the Sociology of Deviance*. New York: Free Press.

Bem, Daryl J. 1972. "Self-Perception Theory." In *Advances in Experimental Social Psychology*. Vol. 6, edited by L. Berkowitz. New York: Academic Press.

Bendix, Reinhard. 1962. *Max Weber: An Intellectual Portrait*. Garden City, N.Y.: Anchor.

———. 1968. "Bureaucracy." *International Encyclopedia of the Social Sciences*. New York: Macmillan and Free Press.

Berger, Peter, Brigitte Berger, and Hansfried Kellner. 1973. *The Homeless Mind*. New York: Random House.

Berger, Peter, and Thomas Luckmann. 1967. *The Social Construction of Reality: A Treatise in the Sociology of Knowledge*. Garden City, N.Y.: Anchor.

Bernard, Thomas. 1983. *The Consensus-Conflict Debate: Form and Content in Sociological Theories*. New York: Columbia University Press.

Bershady, Harold J. 1973. *Ideology and Social Knowledge*. New York: John Wiley and Sons.

Biggers, W. H. 1978. "Emotions and Pain." In *Chronic Pain: America's Hidden Epidemic*, edited by Steven F. Brena, pp. 74–81. New York: Atheneum.

Bittner, Egon. 1965. "The Concept of Organization." *Social Research* 32:239–55.

———. 1967. "The Police on Skid-Row: A Study in Peace Keeping." *American Sociological Review* 32:699–715.

Blau, Peter M. 1968. "Organization." *International Encyclopedia of the Social Sciences*. New York: Macmillan and Free Press.

———. 1970. "Weber's Theory of Bureaucracy." In *Max Weber*, edited by Dennis Wrong, pp. 141–45. Englewood Cliffs, N.J.: Prentice-Hall.

Bloor, David. 1976. *Knowledge and Social Imagery*. Boston: Routledge and Kegan Paul.

———. 1984. *Wittgenstein: A Social Theory of Knowledge*. New York: Columbia University Press.

Blumer, Herbert. 1969. *Symbolic Interactionism: Perspective and Method*. Englewood Cliffs, N.J.: Prentice-Hall.

Boden, Deirdre. 1983. "Talk International: An Examination of Turn-Taking and Related Phenomena in Eight Indo-European Languages." Presented at the meetings of the American Sociological Association, Detroit.

———. 1990. "The World As It Happens: Ethnomethodology and Conversation Analysis." In *Frontiers of Social Theory*, edited by George Ritzer, pp. 185–213. New York: Columbia University Press.

Bogen, David, and Michael Lynch. 1989. "Taking Account of the Hostile Native: Plausible Deniability and the Production of Conventional History in the Iran-Contra Hearings." *Social Problems* 36:197–224.

Boudon, Raymond. 1987. "The Individualistic Tradition in Sociology." In *The Micro-Macro Link*, edited by Jeffrey C. Alexander, Bernhard Giesen, Richard Münch, and Neil J. Smelser, pp. 45–72. Berkeley: University of California Press.

Bower, Joseph. 1968. "Descriptive Decision Theory from the 'Administrative' Viewpoint." In *The Study of Policy Formation*, edited by Raymond A. Bauer and Kenneth J. Gergen, pp. 105–48. New York: Free Press.

Brena, Steven F., ed. 1978. *Chronic Pain: America's Hidden Epidemic*. New York: Atheneum.

Brisset, Dennis, and Charles Edgley, eds. 1975. *Life as Theater: A Dramaturgical Sourcebook*. Chicago: Aldine.

Burke, J. Bruce. 1972. "Curriculum Design." In *Competency-Based Teacher Education: Progress, Problems, and Prospects*, edited by W. Robert Houston and Robert B. Howsam, pp. 34–55. Chicago: Science Research Associates.

Burns, Robert W. 1972. "The Central Notion: Explicit Objectives." In *Competency-Based Teacher Education: Progress, Problems, and Prospects*, edited by W. Robert Houston and Robert B. Howsam, pp. 17–33. Chicago: Science Research Associates.

Burns, Tom, and G. M. Stalker. 1961. *The Management of Innovation*. London: Tavistock.

Cavalli, Luciano. 1987. "Charisma and Twentieth-Century Politics." In *Max Weber, Rationality and Modernity*, edited by Scott Lash and Sam Whimster, pp. 317–33. Winchester, Mass.: Allen and Unwin.

Charon, Joel M. 1979. *Symbolic Interactionism: An Introduction, an Interpretation, an Integration*. Englewood Cliffs, N.J.: Prentice-Hall.

Chase, Donald J., William Harris, and Margaret F. Ishler. 1974. "Process to Product: A Competency-Based Teacher Education Program in Student Teaching." In *Competency-Based Teacher Education: A Potpourri of Perspectives*, edited by Richard E. Ishler, pp. 19–27. Washington, D.C.: Association of Teacher Educators.

Cicourel, Aaron V. 1964. *Method and Measurement in Sociology*. New York: Free Press.

———. 1968. *The Social Organization of Juvenile Justice*. New York: John Wiley and Sons.

———. 1973. *Cognitive Sociology: Language and Meaning in Social Interaction*. New York: Free Press.

Cicourel, Aaron V., et al. 1974. *Language Use and School Performance*. New

York: Academic Press.

Cicourel, Aaron, and John I. Kitsuse. 1963. *The Educational Decision Makers.* New York: Bobbs-Merrill.

Clinard, Marshall B. 1964. "The Theoretical Implications of Anomie and Deviant Behavior." In *Anomie and Deviant Behavior*, edited by Marshall B. Clinard, pp. 1–56. New York: Free Press.

Cohen, Albert. 1968. "Deviant Behavior." *International Encyclopedia of the Social Sciences.* New York: Macmillan and Free Press.

Cohen, Jere, Lawrence E. Hazelrigg, and Whitney Pope. 1975. "De-Parsonizing Weber: A Critique of Parsons' Interpretation of Weber's Sociology." *American Sociological Review* 40:229–41.

Collins, Randall. 1968. "A Comparative Approach to Political Sociology." In *State and Society: A Reader in Comparative Political Sociology*, edited by Reinhard Bendix, pp. 42–67. Boston: Little, Brown.

———. 1980. "Weber's Last Theory of Capitalism: A Systemization." *American Sociological Review* 45:925–42.

———. 1981a. "Micro-translation as a Theory-building Strategy." In *Advances in Social Theory and Methodology: Toward an Integration of Micro- and Macro-Sociologies*, edited by Karin Knorr-Cetina and Aaron V. Cicourel, pp. 81–108. Boston: Routledge and Kegan Paul.

———. 1981b. "On the Microfoundations of Macrosociology." *American Journal of Sociology* 86:984–1014.

———. 1985. *Three Sociological Traditions.* New York: Oxford University Press.

———. 1986. *Max Weber: A Skeleton Key.* Beverly Hills, Calif.: Sage.

———. 1987. "Interaction Ritual Chains, Power, and Property: The Micro-Macro Connection as an Empirically Based Theoretical Problem." In *The Micro-Macro Link*, edited by Jeffrey C. Alexander, Bernhard Giesen, Richard Münch, and Neil J. Smelser, pp. 193–206. Berkeley: University of California Press.

———. 1988. "The Durkheimian Tradition in Conflict Sociology." In *Durkheimian Sociology: Cultural Studies*, edited by Jeffrey C. Alexander, pp. 107–28. Cambridge: Cambridge University Press.

Colomy, Paul, and Gary Rhoades. 1988. "Specifying the Micro-Macro Link: An Application of General Theory to the Study of Structural Differentiation and Educational Change." Presented at the meetings of the American Sociological Association, Atlanta.

Cooley, Charles Horton. 1902. *Human Nature and the Social Order.* New York: Scribner.

Cooper, James M., and Wilford A. Weber. 1973. "A Competency Based Systems Approach to Teacher Education." In *Competency Based Teacher Education*, edited by James M. Cooper, M. Vere DeVault, et al., pp. 7–18. Berkeley, Calif.: McCutchan.

Coser, Lewis. 1971. *Masters of Sociological Thought.* New York: Free Press.

———. 1975. "Presidential Address: Two Methods in Search of a Substance."

American Sociological Review 40:691–99.

———. 1981. "The Uses of Classical Sociological Theory." In *The Future of Sociological Classics*, edited by Buford Rhea, pp. 170–82. London: George Allen and Unwin.

Coser, Rose Laub. 1990. "Reflections on Merton's Role-Set Theory." In *Robert K. Merton: Consensus and Controversy*, edited by Jon Clark, Sohan Modgil, and Celia Modgil, pp. 159–74. London: Falmer Press.

Coulter, Jeff. 1979. *The Social Construction of Mind: Studies in Ethnomethodology and Linguistic Philosophy*. New York: Rowman.

———. 1989. *Mind in Action*. Atlantic Highlands, N.J.: Humanities Press International.

Dalton, Melville. 1959. *Men Who Manage*. New York: John Wiley and Sons.

Davis, Kingsley. 1959. "The Myth of Functional Analysis as a Special Method in Sociology and Anthropology." *American Sociological Review* 24:757–72.

Dayan, Daniel, and Elihu Katz. 1988. "Articulating Consensus: The Ritual and Rhetoric of Media Events." In *Durkheimian Sociology: Cultural Studies*, edited by Jeffrey C. Alexander, pp. 161–86. Cambridge: Cambridge University Press.

DeMott, Benjamin. 1990. *The Imperial Middle: Why Americans Can't Think Straight about Class*. New York: William Morrow.

Denzin, Norman K. 1969. "Symbolic Interactionism and Ethnomethodology: A Proposed Synthesis." *American Sociological Review* 34:922–34.

———. 1970. "Symbolic Interactionism and Ethnomethodology." In *Understanding Everyday Life*, edited by Jack D. Douglas, pp. 259–84. Chicago: Aldine.

DiTomaso, Nancy. 1982. " 'Sociological Reductionism' from Parsons to Althusser: Linking Action and Structure in Social Theory." *American Sociological Review* 47:14–28.

Dodl, Norman R., et al. 1973. *The Florida Catalog of Teacher Competencies*. Tallahassee: Florida Department of Education.

Dodl, Norman R., and H. Del Schalock. 1973. "Competency Based Teacher Preparation." In *Competency Based Teacher Education*, edited by James M. Cooper, M. Vere DeVault, et al., pp. 45–52. Berkeley, Calif.: McCutchan.

Douglas, Jack D., and John M. Johnson, eds. 1977. *Existential Sociology*. New York: Cambridge University Press.

Dreyfus, Hubert. 1979. *What Computers Can't Do: The Limits of Artificial Intelligence*. New York: Harper Colophon.

Durkheim, Emile. 1933 [1893]. *The Division of Labor in Society*. Glencoe, Ill.: Free Press.

———. 1938 [1895]. *The Rules of Sociological Method*. New York: Free Press.

———. 1947 [1912]. *The Elementary Forms of the Religious Life*. Glencoe, Ill.: Free Press.

———. 1951 [1897]. *Suicide*. New York: Free Press.

———. 1953. *Sociology and Philosophy*. New York: Free Press.

Duster, Troy. 1981. "Intermediate Steps between Micro- and Macro- Integration:

The Case of Screening for Inherited Disorders." In *Advances in Social Theory and Methodology: Toward an Integration of Micro- and Macro- Sociologies*, edited by Karin Knorr-Cetina and Aaron V. Cicourel, pp. 109–35. Boston: Routledge and Kegan Paul.

Elam, Stanley. 1971. *Performance Based Teacher Education: What Is the State of the Art?* Washington, D.C.: American Association of Colleges for Teacher Education.

Evans-Pritchard, E. E. 1937. *Witchcraft, Oracles, and Magic among the Azande.* Oxford: Oxford University Press.

Fagerhaugh, Shizuko Y., and Anselm Strauss. 1977. *Politics of Pain Management: Staff-Patient Interaction.* Menlo Park, Calif.: Addison-Wesley.

Fine, Gary Alan. 1991. "On the Macrofoundations of Microsociology: Constraint and the Exterior Reality of Structure." *Sociological Quarterly* 32:161–77.

Fine, Gary Alan, and Sherryl Kleinman. 1986. "Interpreting the Sociological Classics: Can There Be a 'True' Meaning of Mead?" *Symbolic Interaction* 9:129–46.

Fishman, Mark. 1980. *Manufacturing the News.* Austin: University of Texas Press.

Freund, Julian. 1968. *The Sociology of Max Weber.* New York: Random House.

Garfinkel, Harold. 1952. "The Perception of the Other: A Study in Social Order." Ph.D. diss., Harvard University.

———. 1967. *Studies in Ethnomethodology.* Englewood Cliffs, N.J.: Prentice-Hall.

———. 1974. "The Origins of the Term 'Ethnomethodology.'" In *Ethnomethodology*, edited by Roy Turner, pp. 15–18. Baltimore: Penguin.

———. 1988. "Evidence for Locally Produced, Naturally Accountable Phenomena of Order*, Logic, Reason, Meaning, Method, Etc. In and As Of the Essential Quiddity of Immortal Ordinary Society (I of IV): An Announcement of Studies." *Sociological Theory* 6:103–9.

Garfinkel, Harold, Michael Lynch, and Eric Livingston. 1981. "The Work of a Discovering Science Construed with Materials from the Optically Discovered Pulsar." *Philosophy of the Social Sciences* 11:131–58.

Garfinkel, Harold, and Harvey Sacks. 1970. "On the Formal Structures of Practical Actions." In *Theoretical Sociology*, edited by J. C. McKinney and E. A. Tiryakian, pp. 338–66. New York: Appleton-Century-Crofts.

Gerth, H. H., and C. Wright Mills, eds. 1946. *From Max Weber: Essays in Sociology.* New York: Oxford University Press.

Giddens, Anthony. 1971. *Capitalism and Modern Social Theory: An Analysis of the Writings of Marx, Durkheim, and Max Weber.* New York: Cambridge University Press.

———. 1984. *The Constitution of Society: Outline of the Theory of Structuration.* Berkeley: University of California Press.

Gilbert, G. N., and M. Mulkay. 1984. *Opening Pandora's Box: An Analysis of Scientists' Discourse.* Cambridge: Cambridge University Press.

Goffman, Erving. 1959. *The Presentation of Self in Everyday Life.* Garden City, N.Y.: Doubleday.

———. 1961. *Encounters.* Indianapolis: Bobbs-Merrill.

———. 1967. *Interaction Ritual: Essays on Face-to-Face Behavior.* Garden City, N.Y.: Doubleday.

———. 1974. *Frame Analysis: An Essay on the Organization of Experience.* Cambridge: Harvard University Press.

———. 1981. *Forms of Talk.* Philadelphia: University of Pennsylvania Press.

Gouldner, Alvin. 1970. *The Coming Crisis of Western Sociology.* New York: Basic Books.

Grathoff, R. 1978. *The Theory of Social Action: The Correspondence of Alfred Schutz and Talcott Parsons.* Bloomington: Indiana University Press.

Gurwitsch, Aron. 1964. *The Field of Consciousness.* Pittsburgh: Duquesne University Press.

Halkowski, Timothy. 1990. " 'Role' as an Interactional Device." *Social Problems* 37:564–77.

Hall, Gene E., and Howard L. Jones. 1976. *Competency-Based Education: A Process for the Improvement of Education.* Englewood Cliffs, N.J.: Prentice-Hall.

Hazelrigg, Lawrence E. 1986. "Is There a Choice between 'Constructivism' and 'Objectivism'?" *Social Problems* 33:s1–s13.

Hekman, Susan J. 1983. *Weber, the Ideal Type, and Contemporary Social Theory.* Notre Dame, Ind.: University of Notre Dame Press.

Heritage, John. 1984. *Garfinkel and Ethnomethodology.* Cambridge: Polity.

Hewitt, John P. 1976. *Self and Society: A Symbolic Interactionist Social Psychology.* Boston: Allyn and Bacon.

Hewitt, John P., and Peter M. Hall. 1973. "Social Problems, Problematic Situations, and Quasi-theories." *American Sociological Review* 38:367–75.

Hilbert, Richard A. 1977. "Approaching Reason's Edge: 'Nonsense' as the Final Solution to the Problem of Meaning." *Sociological Inquiry* 47:25–31.

———. 1980. "Covert Participant Observation: On Its Nature and Practice." *Urban Life* 9:51–78.

———. 1981. "Toward an Improved Understanding of 'Role.' " *Theory and Society* 10:207–26.

———. 1982. "Competency Based Teacher Education versus the Real World: Some Natural Limitations to Bureaucratic Reform." *Urban Education* 16:379–98.

———. 1984. "The Acultural Dimensions of Chronic Pain: Flawed Reality Construction and the Problem of Meaning." *Social Problems* 31:365–78.

———. 1986. "Anomie and the Moral Regulation of Reality: The Durkheimian Tradition in Modern Relief." *Sociological Theory* 4:1–19.

———. 1987. "Bureaucracy as Belief, Rationalization as Repair: Max Weber in a Post-Functionalist Age." *Sociological Theory* 5:70–86.

———. 1989. "Durkheim and Merton on Anomie: An Unexplored Contrast and Its Derivatives." *Social Problems* 36:242–50.

————. 1990a. "Ethnomethodology and the Micro-Macro Order." *American Sociological Review* 55:794–808.

————. 1990b. "Merton's Theory of Role-sets and Status-sets." In *Robert K. Merton: Consensus and Controversy*, edited by Jon Clark, Sohan Modgil, and Celia Modgil, pp. 177–86. London: Falmer Press.

Horowitz, Irving L. 1962/67. "Consensus, Conflict, and Cooperation." In *System, Change, and Conflict*, edited by Nicholas Demerath and Richard Peterson, pp. 265–79. New York: Free Press.

Houston, W. Robert, and J. Bruce Burke. 1973. "Teacher Education as Interdisciplinary Study." In *Competency Based Teacher Education*, edited by James M. Cooper, M. Vere DeVault, et al., pp. 65–77. Berkeley, Calif.: McCutchan.

Howsam, Robert B., and W. Robert Houston. 1972. "Change and Challenge." In *Competency-Based Teacher Education: Progress, Problems, and Prospects*, edited by W. Robert Houston and Robert B. Howsam, pp. 1–16. Chicago: Science Research Associates.

Huaco, George. 1966. "The Functionalist Theory of Stratification: Two Decades of Controversy." *Inquiry* 9:215–40.

————. 1986. "Ideology and General Theory: The Case of Sociological Functionalism." *Comparative Studies in Society and History* 28:34–54.

Ishler, Richard E., and Joan D. Inglis. 1973. "The Development of a Comprehensive Competency-Based Teacher Education Program: A Model for Change." In *Competency Based Teacher Education*, edited by James M. Cooper, M. Vere DeVault, et al., pp. 7–18. Berkeley, Calif.: McCutchan.

Jefferson, Gail. 1984. "Caricature versus Detail: On Capturing the Particulars of Pronunciation in Transcripts of Conversational Data." *Tilburg Papers on Language and Literature No. 31.* University of Tilburg, Netherlands.

Jefferson, Gail, Harvey Sacks, and Emanuel A. Schegloff. 1987. "Notes on Laughter in the Pursuit of Intimacy." In *Talk and Social Organization*, edited by Graham Button and John R. E. Lee, pp. 152–205. Avon, U.K.: Multilingual Matters.

Jessor, Richard, et al. 1968. *Society, Personality, and Deviant Behavior.* New York: Holt, Rinehart and Winston.

Johnson, Barclay. 1965. "Durkheim's One Cause of Suicide." *American Sociological Review* 30:875–86.

Johnson, Charles E., and Gilbert F. Shearron. 1973. "Specifying Assumptions, Goals, and Objectives." In *Competency Based Teacher Education*, edited by James M. Cooper, M. Vere Devault, et al., pp. 43–56. Berkeley, Calif.: McCutchan.

Johnson, Doyle Paul. 1981. *Sociological Theory: Classical Founders and Contemporary Perspectives.* New York: John Wiley and Sons.

Johnson, Harry M. 1960. *Sociology: A Systematic Introduction.* New York: Harcourt Brace Jovanovich.

Jones, Howard. 1972. "Implementation of Programs." In *Competency-Based Teacher Education: Progress, Problems, and Prospects*, edited by W. Robert

Houston and Robert B. Howsam, pp. 102–42. Chicago: Science Research Associates.

Jones, Robert Alun. 1977. "On Understanding a Sociological Classic." *American Journal of Sociology* 83:279–319.

———. 1986. *Emile Durkheim: An Introduction to Four Major Works*. Beverly Hills, Calif.: Sage.

Joyce, Bruce. 1974. "Assessment in Teacher Education: Notes from the Competency Orientation." In *Exploring Competency Based Education*, edited by W. Robert Houston, pp. 191–208. Berkeley, Calif.: McCutchan.

Kean, John M., and Norman R. Dodl. 1973. "A Systems Approach to Curriculum Development." In *Competency Based Teacher Education*, edited by James M. Cooper, M. Vere DeVault, et al., pp. 33–41. Berkeley, Calif.: McCutchan.

Knorr-Cetina, Karin D. 1981. "Introduction: The Micro-sociological Challenge of Macro-sociology: Towards a Reconstruction of Social Theory and Methodology." In *Advances in Social Theory and Methodology: Toward an Integration of Micro- and Macro- Sociologies*, edited by Karin Knorr-Cetina and Aaron V. Cicourel, pp. 1–47. Boston: Routledge and Kegan Paul.

Kopel, Steven A., and Hal S. Arkowitz. 1974. "Role Playing as a Source of Self-Observation and Behavior Change." *Journal of Personality and Social Psychology* 29:677–86.

Kotarba, Joseph A. 1977. "The Chronic Pain Experience." In *Existential Sociology*, edited by Jack D. Douglas and John M. Johnson, pp. 257–72. New York: Cambridge University Press.

———. 1983a. *Chronic Pain: Its Social Dimensions*. Beverly Hills, Calif.: Sage.

———. 1983b. "Perceptions of Death, Belief Systems, and the Process of Coping with Chronic Pain." *Social Science and Medicine* 17:681–89

Lackey, Pat N. 1987. *Invitation to Talcott Parsons' Theory*. Houston: Cap and Gown Press.

Lash, Scott, and Sam Whimster, eds. 1987. *Max Weber, Rationality and Modernity*. Winchester, Mass.: Allen and Unwin.

Latour, Bruno. 1987. *Science in Action*. Milton Keynes, England: Open University Press.

Lidz, Victor. 1981. "Transformational Theory and the Internal Environment of Action Systems." In *Advances in Social Theory and Methodology: Toward an Integration of Micro- and Macro- Sociologies*, edited by Karin Knorr-Cetina and Aaron V. Cicourel, pp. 205–33. Boston: Routledge and Kegan Paul.

Linton, Ralph. 1936. *The Study of Man*. New York: Appleton-Century.

Livingston, Eric. 1986. *The Ethnomethodological Foundations of Mathematics*. London: Routledge and Kegan Paul.

Locke, John. 1959 [1690]. *An Essay concerning Human Understanding*. New York: Dover.

Loewith, Karl. 1970. "Weber's Interpretation of the Bourgeois-Capitalistic World in Terms of the Guiding Principle of 'Rationalization.'" In *Max Weber*, edited by Dennis Wrong, pp. 101–22. Englewood Cliffs, N.J.: Prentice-Hall.

Luhmann, Niklas. 1981. "Communication about Law in Interaction Systems." In *Advances in Social Theory and Methodology: Toward an Integration of Micro- and Macro- Sociologies*, edited by Karin Knorr-Cetina and Aaron V. Cicourel, pp. 234–56. Boston: Routledge and Kegan Paul.

Lukes, Steven. 1972. *Emile Durkheim: His Life and Work*. New York: Harper and Row.

Lyman, Stanford M., and Marvin B. Scott. 1970. *A Sociology of the Absurd*. New York: Appleton-Century-Crofts.

Lynch, Michael. 1982. "Technical Work and Critical Inquiry: Investigations in a Scientific Laboratory." *Social Studies of Science* 12:499–534.

———. 1985. *Art and Artifact in Laboratory Science: A Study of Shop Work and Shop Talk in a Research Laboratory*. London: Routledge and Kegan Paul.

———. 1991. "Pictures of Nothing? Visual Construals in Social Theory." *Sociological Theory* 9:1–21.

McDonald, Frederick J. 1974. "The Rationale for Competency Based Programs." In *Exploring Competency Based Education*, edited by W. Robert Houston, pp. 17–30. Berkeley, Calif.: McCutchan.

Manis, Jerome G., and Bernard N. Meltzer, eds. 1967. *Symbolic Interactionism: A Reader in Social Psychology*. Boston: Allyn and Bacon.

Mannheim, Karl. 1936. *Ideology and Utopia: An Introduction to the Sociology of Knowledge*. New York: Harcourt, Brace and World.

Maynard, Douglas W. 1980. "Placement of Topic Changes in Conversation." *Semiotica* 30:263–90.

———. 1984. *Inside Plea Bargaining: The Language of Negotiation*. New York: Plenum Press.

———. 1985a. "How Children Start Arguments." *Language in Society* 14:1–29.

———. 1985b. "On the Functions of Social Conflict among Children." *American Sociological Review* 50:207–23.

———. 1986. "Constituting the Child as a Clinical Object." Unpublished manuscript.

———. Forthcoming. "The Prospective Display Series in the Delivery and Receipt of Diagnostic News." In *Talk and Social Structure*, edited by Deirdre Boden and Don H. Zimmerman. Cambridge: Polity.

Maynard, Douglas W., and Steven B. Clayman. 1991. "The Diversity of Ethnomethodology." *Annual Review of Sociology* 17:385–418.

Maynard, Douglas W., and Thomas P. Wilson. 1980. "On the Reification of Social Structure." *Current Perspectives in Social Theory* 1:287–322.

Maynard, Douglas W., and Don H. Zimmerman. 1984. "Topical Talk, Ritual, and the Social Organization of Relationships." *Social Psychological Quarterly* 47:301–16.

Mead, George H. 1934. *Mind, Self, and Society*. Chicago: University of Chicago Press.

Mehan, Hugh, and Houston Wood. 1975. *The Reality of Ethnomethodology*. New York: John Wiley and Sons.

Menzies, Ken. 1977. *Talcott Parsons and the Social Image of Man*. London: Routledge and Kegan Paul.

Merskey, H., and F. G. Spear. 1967. *Pain: Psychological and Psychiatric Aspects*. London: Bailliere.

Merton, Robert K. 1957. "The Role-set: Problems in Sociological Theory." *British Journal of Sociology* 8:106–20.

———. 1968. *Social Theory and Social Structure*. New York: Free Press.

———. 1973. *The Sociology of Science*. Chicago: University of Chicago Press.

Merton, Robert K., and Robert Nisbet, eds. 1971. *Contemporary Social Problems*. New York: Harcourt Brace Jovanovich.

Miles, Robert. 1982. *Racism and Migrant Labor*. London: Routledge and Kegan Paul.

Mills, C. Wright. 1940. "Situated Actions and Vocabularies of Motive." *American Sociological Review* 5:904–13.

———. 1959. *The Sociological Imagination*. New York: Oxford University Press.

Molotch, Harvey, and Deirdre Boden. 1985. "Talking Social Structure: Discourse, Domination, and the Watergate Hearings." *American Sociological Review* 50:273–88.

Molotch, Harvey, and Marilyn Lester. 1974. "News as Purposive Behavior." *American Sociological Review* 39:101–12.

Mommsen, Wolfgang J. 1974. *The Age of Bureaucracy*. New York: Harper and Row.

———. 1987. "Personal Conduct and Societal Change: Towards a Reconstruction of Max Weber's Concept of History." In *Max Weber, Rationality and Modernity*, edited by Scott Lash and Sam Whimster, pp. 35–51. Winchester, Mass.: Allen and Unwin.

Münch, Richard, and Neil J. Smelser. 1987. "Relating the Micro and Macro." In *The Micro-Macro Link*, edited by Jeffrey C. Alexander, Bernhard Giesen, Richard Münch, and Neil J. Smelser, pp. 356–87. Berkeley: University of California Press.

Nisbet, Robert. 1966. *The Sociological Tradition*. New York: Basic Books.

———. 1974. *The Sociology of Emile Durkheim*. New York: Oxford University Press.

Pace, J. Blair. 1976. *Pain: A Personal Experience*. Chicago: Nelson-Hall.

Parkin, Frank. 1982. *Max Weber*. New York: Tavistock.

Parsons, Talcott. 1951. *The Social System*. New York: Free Press.

———. 1959. "Economy, Polity, Money, and Power." Unpublished manuscript, cited by Garfinkel (1967, p. 69).

———. 1968a. "Emile Durkheim." *International Encyclopedia of the Social Sciences*. New York: Macmillan and Free Press.

———. 1968b [1937]. *The Structure of Social Action*. New York: Free Press.

Parsons, Talcott, et al. 1951. *Toward a General Theory of Action*. New York: Harper and Row.

Parsons, Talcott, Robert F. Bales, and Edward A. Shils. 1953. *Working Papers in the Theory of Action*. New York: Free Press.

Peters, Thomas J., and Robert H. Waterman, Jr. 1982. *In Search of Excellence: Lessons from America's Best-Run Companies*. New York: Harper and Row.

Piven, Frances Fox, and Richard A. Cloward. 1971. *Regulating the Poor: The Functions of Public Welfare*. New York: Vintage.

Pollner, Melvin. 1974a. "Mundane Reasoning." *Philosophy of the Social Sciences* 4:35–54.

———. 1974b. "Sociological and Common-Sense Models of the Labelling Process." In *Ethnomethodology*, edited by Roy Turner, pp. 27–40. Baltimore: Penguin.

———. 1975. " 'The Very Coinage of Your Brain': The Anatomy of Reality Disjunctures." *Philosophy of the Social Sciences* 5:411–30.

———. 1987. *Mundane Reason: Reality in Everyday and Sociological Discourse*. New York: Cambridge University Press.

———. 1991. "Left of Ethnomethodology: The Rise and Decline of Radical Reflexivity." *American Sociological Review* 56:370–80.

Pope, Whitney. 1973. "Classic on Classic: Parsons' Interpretation of Durkheim." *American Sociological Review* 38:399–415.

Pope, Whitney, Jere Cohen, and Lawrence E. Hazelrigg. 1975. "On the Divergence of Weber and Durkheim: A Critique of Parsons' Convergence Theory." *American Sociological Review* 40:417–27.

Psathas, George, ed. 1973. *Phenomenological Sociology: Issues and Applications*. New York: John Wiley and Sons.

Ritzer, George. 1988. *Sociological Theory*. 2d ed. New York: Alfred A. Knopf.

———. 1990. "Metatheorizing in Sociology." *Sociological Forum* 5:3–15.

Roethlisberger, Fritz J., and William J. Dickson. 1939. *Management and the Worker*. Cambridge: Harvard University Press.

Rogers, Rolf E. 1969. *Max Weber's Ideal Type Theory*. New York: Philosophical Library.

Rose, Arnold M., ed. 1962. *Human Behavior and Social Processes: An Interactionist Approach*. Boston: Houghton Mifflin.

Roth, Guenther. 1978. "Introduction." In *Economy and Society*, by Max Weber, pp. xxxiii–cx. Berkeley: University of California Press.

———. 1987. "Rationalization in Max Weber's Developmental History." In *Max Weber, Rationality and Modernity*, edited by Scott Lash and Sam Whimster, pp. 75–91. Winchester, Mass.: Allen and Unwin.

Sacks, Harvey. 1984. "Methodological Remarks." In *Structures of Social Action: Studies in Conversation Analysis*, edited by J. Maxwell Atkinson and John Heritage, pp. 21–27. Cambridge: Cambridge University Press.

Sacks, Harvey, Emanuel A. Schegloff, and Gail Jefferson. 1974. "A Simplest Systematics for the Organization of Turn-taking for Conversation." *Language* 50:696–735.

Sauerbruch, Ferdinand, and Hans Wenke. 1963. *Pain: Its Meaning and Significance*. London: George Allen and Unwin.

Schacht, Richard. 1982. "Doubts about Anomie and Anomia." In *Alienation and Anomie Revisited*, edited by S. Giora Shoham and Anthony Grahame, pp. 71–91. Messina, Italy: Sheridan House and Ramot Educational Systems.

Schachter, Stanley, and J. Singer. 1962. "Cognitive, Social, and Physiological Determinants of Emotional States." *Psychological Review* 69:379–99.

Schalock, H. Del, and Jesse Garrison. 1973. "The Personalization of Teacher Education Programs." In *Competency Based Teacher Education*, edited by James M. Cooper, M. Vere DeVault, et al., pp. 33–43. Berkeley, Calif.: McCutchan.

Schegloff, Emanuel A. 1968. "Sequencing in Conversational Openings." *American Anthropologist* 70:1075–95.

———. 1972. "Notes on Conversational Practice: Formulating Place." In *Studies in Social Interaction*, edited by David Sudnow, pp. 75–119. New York: Free Press.

———. 1987. "Between Micro and Macro: Contexts and Other Connections." In *The Micro-Macro Link*, edited by Jeffrey C. Alexander, Bernhard Giesen, Richard Münch, and Neil J. Smelser, pp. 107–34. Berkeley: University of California Press.

Schegloff, Emanuel, and Harvey Sacks. 1973. "Opening Up Closings." *Semiotica* 7:289–327.

Schiller, Herbert I. 1989. *Culture, Inc.: The Corporate Takeover of Public Expression*. New York: Oxford University Press.

Schneider, Joseph W. 1985. "Social Problems Theory: The Constructionist View." *Annual Review of Sociology* 11:209–29.

Schutz, Alfred. 1962. *Collected Papers*. Vol. 1. The Hague: Martinus Nijhoff.

———. 1964. *Collected Papers*. Vol. 2. The Hague: Martinus Nijhoff.

———. 1966. *Collected Papers*. Vol. 3. The Hague: Martinus Nijhoff.

———. 1967 [1932]. *The Phenomenology of the Social World*. Evanston, Ill.: Northwestern University Press.

Seeman, Melvin. 1982. "A Prolegomenon on Empirical Research regarding Anomie." In *Alienation and Anomie Revisited*, edited by S. Giora Shoham and Anthony Grahame, pp. 121–38. Messina, Italy: Sheridan House and Ramot Educational Systems.

Seidman, Steven. 1984. "The Main Aims and Thematic Structures of Max Weber's Sociology." *Canadian Journal of Sociology* 9:381–404.

Selznick, Philip. 1948. "Foundations of the Theory of Organizations." *American Sociological Review* 13:25–35.

Shealy, C. Norman. 1976. *The Pain Game*. Millbrae, Calif.: Celestial Arts.

Shibutani, Tamotsu. 1961. *Society and Personality*. Englewood Cliffs, N.J.: Prentice-Hall.

Shils, Edward A. 1965. "Charisma, Order, and Status." *American Sociological Review* 30:199–213.

Shoham, S. Giora, and Anthony Grahame, eds. 1982. *Alienation and Anomie Revisited*. Messina, Italy: Sheridan House and Ramot Educational Systems.

Sica, Alan. 1988. *Weber, Irrationality, and Social Order.* Berkeley: University of California Press.

Smith, Dorothy E. 1974. "The Social Construction of Documentary Reality." *Sociological Inquiry* 44:257–68.

Spector, Malcolm, and John I. Kitsuse. 1977. *Constructing Social Problems.* Menlo Park, Calif.: Cummings.

Steffenson, James P. 1974. "Foreword." In *Exploring Competency Based Education,* edited by W. Robert Houston, pp. xiii–xvi. Berkeley, Calif.: McCutchan.

Stephan, Cookie White, and Walter G. Stephan. 1990. *Two Social Psychologies.* Belmont, Calif.: Wadsworth.

Sternbach, Richard A. 1968. *Pain: A Psychophysiologic Analysis.* New York: Academic Press.

Stinchcombe, Arthur L. 1975. "A Parsonian Theory of Traffic Accidents." *Sociological Inquiry* 45:27–30.

Stone, Gregory P., and Harvey A. Farberman. 1970. "On the Edge of Rapprochement: Was Durkheim Moving toward the Perspective of Symbolic Interaction?" In *Social Psychology through Symbolic Interaction,* edited by Gregory P. Stone and Harvey A. Farberman, pp. 100–112. Waltham, Mass.: Ginn-Blaisdell.

Suchman, Lucy A. 1987. *Plans and Situated Actions: The Problem of Human-Machine Communication.* Cambridge: Cambridge University Press.

Sudnow, David. 1965. "Normal Crimes: Sociological Features of the Penal Code in a Public Defender's Office." *Social Problems* 12:255–72.

———. 1967. *Passing On: The Social Organization of Dying.* Englewood Cliffs, N.J.: Prentice-Hall.

———. 1978. *The Way of Hands.* Cambridge: Harvard University Press.

Szasz, Thomas S. "The Psychology of Persistent Pain." In *Proceedings of the International Symposium on Pain* (Paris, April 11–13, 1967), edited by A. Soulairac, J. Cahn, and J. Charpentier, pp. 42–47. New York: Academic Press.

Takla, Tendzin, and Whitney Pope. 1985. "The Force Imagery in Durkheim." *Sociological Theory* 3:74–86.

Thomas, Adele K., and Patricia M. Kay. 1974. "Determining Priorities among Competencies: Judgments of Classroom Teachers and Supervisors." In *Exploring Competency Based Education,* edited by W. Robert Houston, pp. 155–71. Berkeley, Calif.: McCutchan.

Thompson, Kenneth. 1982. *Emile Durkheim.* New York: Tavistock and Ellis Horwood.

Tönnies, Ferdinand. 1963 [1887]. *Community and Society.* New York: Harper and Row.

Turner, Jonathan H., and Leonard Beeghley. 1981. *The Emergence of Sociological Theory.* Homewood, Ill.: Dorsey Press.

Turner, Jonathan, and Alexandra Maryanski. 1979. *Functionalism.* Menlo Park, Calif.: Benjamin/Cummings.

Turner, Ralph. 1962. "Role-Taking: Process versus Conformity." In *Human Be-*

havior and Social Processes, edited by Arnold M. Rose, pp. 20–40. Boston: Houghton Mifflin.

Unikel, J. P., and S. I. Chapman. 1968. "The Pain-prone Patient." In *Chronic Pain: America's Hidden Epidemic*, edited by Steven Brena, pp. 27–33. New York: Atheneum.

Vygotsky, L. S. 1962. *Thought and Language*. Edited by Eugenia Haufmann and Gertrude Vakar. Cambridge: MIT Press.

———. 1978. *Mind in Society: The Development of Higher Psychological Processes*. Cambridge: Harvard University Press.

Wallace, Ruth A., and Shirley F. Hartley. 1988. "Religious Elements in Friendship: Durkheimian Theory in an Empirical Context." In *Durkheimian Sociology: Cultural Studies*, edited by Jeffrey C. Alexander, pp. 93–108. Cambridge: Cambridge University Press.

Warner, R. Stephen. 1978. "Toward a Redefinition of Action Theory: Paying the Cognitive Element Its Due." *American Journal of Sociology* 83:1317–49.

Waterman, Floyd T. 1974. "Characteristics of Competency-Based Teacher Education Programs." In *Competency-Based Teacher Education: A Potpourri of Perspectives*, edited by Richard E. Ishler, pp. 1–6. Washington, D.C.: Association of Teacher Educators.

Weber, Max. 1949 [1903–17]. *The Methodology of the Social Sciences*. Translated and edited by Edward A. Shils and Henry A. Finch. Glencoe, Ill.: Free Press.

———. 1976 [1904–5]. *The Protestant Ethic and the Spirit of Capitalism*. Translated by Talcott Parsons. New York: Charles Scribner's Sons.

———. 1978 [1921]. *Economy and Society*. Translated by Ephraim Fischoff et al. Edited by Guenther Roth and Claus Wittich. Berkeley: University of California Press.

Weber, Wilford A., and Charles Rathbone. 1973. "Developing Instructional Strategies." In *Competency Based Teacher Education*, edited by James M. Cooper, M. Vere DeVault, et al., pp. 57–72. Berkeley, Calif.: McCutchan.

West, Candace. 1979. "Against Our Will: Male Interruptions of Females in Cross-sex Conversations." *Annals of the New York Academy of Sciences* 327:81–97.

West, Candace, and Don H. Zimmerman. 1977. "Women's Place in Everyday Talk: Reflections on Parent-Child Interaction." *Social Problems* 24:521–29.

———. 1983. "Small Insults: A Study of Interruptions in Cross-sex Conversations between Unacquainted Persons." In *Language, Gender, and Society*, edited by Barrie Thorne, Cheris Kramarae, and Nancy Henley, pp. 102–17. Rowley, Mass.: Newbury House.

Whalen, Jack, Don H. Zimmerman, and Marilyn L. Whalen. 1988. "When Words Fail: A Single Case Analysis." *Social Problems* 35:335–62.

Wieder, D. Lawrence. 1970. "On Meaning by Rule." In *Understanding Everyday Life*, edited by Jack D. Douglas, pp. 107–35. Chicago: Aldine.

———. 1974a. *Language and Social Reality: The Case of Telling the Convict Code*. The Hague: Mouton.

———. 1974b. "Telling the Code." In *Ethnomethodology*, edited by Roy Turner, pp. 21–26. Baltimore: Penguin.

Wiley, Norbert. 1988. "The Micro-Macro Problem in Social Theory." *Sociological Theory* 6:254–61.

Wilson, Thomas P. 1970. "Conceptions of Interaction and Forms of Sociological Explanation." *American Sociological Review* 35:697–710.

———. 1991. "Social Structure and the Sequential Organization of Interaction." In *Talk and Social Structure: Studies in Ethnomethodology and Conversation Analysis*, edited by Deirdre Boden and Don H. Zimmerman, pp. 22–43. Cambridge: Polity.

Wilson, Thomas P., and Don H. Zimmerman. 1979/80. "Ethnomethodology, Sociology, and Theory." *Humboldt Journal of Social Relations* 7:52–88.

Wippler, Reinhard, and Siegwart Lindenberg. 1987. "Collective Phenomena and Rational Choice." In *The Micro-Macro Link*, edited by Jeffrey C. Alexander, Bernhard Giesen, Richard Münch, and Neil J. Smelser, pp. 135–52. Berkeley: University of California Press.

Wittgenstein, Ludwig. 1953. *Philosophical Investigations.* New York: Macmillan.

———. 1956. *Remarks on the Foundations of Mathematics.* Oxford: Basil Blackwell.

———. 1958. *The Blue and Brown Books.* Oxford: Basil Blackwell.

Wolfe, Alan. 1991. "Mind, Self, Society, and Computer: Artificial Intelligence and the Sociology of Mind." *American Journal of Sociology* 96:1073–96.

Woolgar, Steve, and Dorothy Pawluch. 1985a. "How Shall We Move beyond Constructionism?" *Social Problems* 33:159–62.

———. 1985b. "Ontological Gerrymandering: The Anatomy of Social Problems Explanations." *Social Problems* 32:214–27.

Wrong, Dennis. 1961. "The Oversocialized Conception of Man." *American Sociological Review* 26:183–93.

———. 1970. *Max Weber.* Englewood Cliffs, N.J.: Prentice-Hall.

Zborowski, Mark. 1969. *People in Pain.* San Francisco: Jossey-Bass.

Zimmerman, Don H. 1970. "The Practicalities of Rule Use." In *Understanding Everyday Life*, edited by Jack D. Douglas, pp. 221–38. Chicago: Aldine.

———. 1974. "Fact as a Practical Accomplishment." In *Ethnomethodology*, edited by Roy Turner, pp. 128–43. Baltimore: Penguin.

———. 1976. "A Reply to Coser." *American Sociologist* 11:4–13.

———. 1988. "On Conversation: The Conversation Analytic Perspective." In *Communication Yearbook*, vol. 11, edited by J. A. Anderson, pp. 406–32. Beverly Hills, Calif.: Sage.

Zimmerman, Don H., and Melvin Pollner. 1970. "The Everyday World as a Phenomenon." In *Understanding Everyday Life*, edited by Jack D. Douglas, pp. 80–103. Chicago: Aldine.

Zimmerman, Don H., and Candace West. 1975. "Sex Roles, Interruptions, and Silences in Conversation." In *Language and Sex: Difference and Dominance,* edited by Barrie Thorne and Nancy Henley, pp. 105–29. Rowley, Mass.: New-bury House.

Zimmerman, Don H., and D. Lawrence Wieder. 1970. "Ethnomethodology and the Problem of Order: Comment on Denzin." In *Understanding Everyday Life*, edited by Jack D. Douglas, pp. 285–95. Chicago: Aldine.

INDEX

Abrahamson, Mark, 142
Alexander, Jeffrey C., 2, 3, 5, 16, 19, 26, 38, 68, 70, 123, 124, 189, 190, 194, 197, 198, 201, 212, 214; on "de-Parsonization," 121 (n. 3); on Durkheim and ritual, 226–27 (n. 1); neofunctionalism of, 190–91; on Parsons's empiricism, 223 (n. 7)
Alienation, 216
Andrews, Theodore, 157
Anomie: and clinical depression, 101–2; doubts about, 102; and Durkheim, 24, 30, 47, 48, 52, 53, 71, 153, 163–64, 165; Durkheim and Merton compared, 83–90, 183, 185, 186; and ethnomethodology, 58, 90–103, 171; in experimental settings, 92–93, 96–98; and Merton, 183–87; in natural settings, 98–101; and suicide, 84, 86–88, 102. *See also* Durkheim, Emile; Merton, Robert K.
Arkowitz, Hal S., 73, 101
Artificial intelligence, 42–43
Azande, practices of, 75, 135–37, 138, 185

Bakke, E. Wight, 142
Bales, Robert F., 3, 19, 172, 181, 200
Banton, Michael, 82
Barnard, Chester I., 142, 168
Becker, Howard S., 73, 101

Beeghley, Leonard, 142
Bem, Daryl J., 73
Bendix, Reinhard, 142, 148
Berger, Brigitte, 68
Berger, Peter, 68, 73, 94, 98–99
Bernard, Thomas, 211
Bershady, Harold J., 14, 15, 16, 38, 131
Biggers, W. H., 101
Bittner, Egon, 8, 62, 82, 95, 142, 186, 195; on bureaucracy, 149–50, 186; study of police, 39–42, 44, 50, 90
Blau, Peter M., 142, 143
Bloor, David, 35, 69, 70, 226 (n. 5)
Blumer, Herbert, 73
Boden, Deirdre, 197, 198, 212, 215, 219
Bogen, David, 212
Boudon, Raymond, 190
Bower, Joseph, 142
Brena, Steven F., 101
Brisset, Dennis, 73
Bureaucracy: and Durkheimian "sacred," 165; and ethnomethodology, 141, 149–51, 155–56, 196, 227 (n. 1); functionalist version of society as, 166; and teacher education, 157, 159–60; and Weber, 24, 62, 111, 119, 121, 132, 141–49, 151, 155–56. *See also* Rationalization
Burke, J. Bruce, 157
Burns, Robert, 157, 158
Burns, Tom, 142

Cavalli, Luciano, 151
Chapman, S. I., 101
Charon, Joel M., 72–73
Chase, Donald J., 157, 158, 160
Cicourel, Aaron V., 82, 150, 195, 206
Claims-making activities, 185–86, 232
    (n. 2)
Clayman, Steven, 8, 12, 197, 219
Clinard, Marshall B., 82, 102, 184
Cloward, Richard A., 215
Cognition, 10, 195. *See also* Experi-
    ence; Ideas, role of; Subjectivity
Cohen, Albert, 85
Cohen, Jere, 5, 23, 28, 67, 106, 124,
    133, 231–32 (n. 1, chap. 9)
Collins, Randall, 32, 67, 82, 106, 115,
    118, 124, 151, 190, 194, 212, 217;
    "interaction ritual chains," 189,
    205–7, 209–11, 214, 216
Colomy, Paul, 190
Comte, Auguste, 29
Conversation analysis, 9, 25, 188–89,
    197–203, 218, 219; empirical
    method of, 198–200, 201, 202
Cooley, Charles Horton, 72
Cooper, James M., 157
Coser, Lewis, 28, 47, 68, 84, 85, 107,
    130, 142, 143, 151, 194, 210
Coser, Rose Laub, 177
Coulter, Jeff, 35, 195

Dalton, Melville, 142, 168
Darwinism, 18
Davis, Kingsley, 2
Dayan, Daniel, 213, 214
DeMott, Benjamin, 215
Denzin, Norman K., 12, 194
Dickson, William J., 142, 168
DiTomaso, Nancy, 34, 64
Dodl, Norman R., 157, 158–59
Douglas, Jack D., 73
Dreyfus, Hubert, 43
Durkheim, Emile, 1–2, 3, 5, 6, 9, 12,
    13, 14, 18, 26, 64, 65, 79–82, 104,

132, 133, 134, 141, 161, 167, 169,
    183, 185, 189, 194, 212, 217, 221
    (nn. 3, 4), 226 (nn. 5, 6), 229–31
    (n. 7); anomie, 24, 47, 48, 52, 53,
    71, 83–90, 101–3, 153, 163–64,
    165, 182, 183, 185; collective con-
    science, 7, 23, 27, 31, 47–48, 52–
    53, 69, 71, 75, 84, 85, 87, 89, 92,
    153, 169, 182, 187, 232 (n. 2);
    "constraint," 28, 29, 42, 44, 45, 46,
    50, 52, 54, 69, 78, 87, 89, 139,
    163; crime, 47–48, 52, 85–89, 182,
    183, 231–32 (n. 1); "dynamic den-
    sity," 222 (n. 1), 225 (n. 3); empiri-
    cal method of, 27, 29, 38–39, 52,
    54, 70, 163, 189; "exteriority," 8,
    28, 29, 42, 44, 45, 46, 69, 87, 139,
    163, 195; functionalism, 26; ideal-
    ism alleged in, 18, 66, 72, 78, 80,
    82, 224 (n. 2, chap. 3), 225–26
    (n. 4); mechanical and organic soli-
    darity, 29, 30, 31–32, 37, 68–69,
    70, 71, 74, 79, 88, 103, 222–23
    (nn. 1, 3), 229 (n. 6), 229–30
    (n. 7); morality, 24, 27, 29–32, 34–
    35, 37–38, 46, 47–48, 52, 53, 54,
    55, 57, 68, 69, 70, 74, 84, 85–86,
    87–88, 89, 90, 103, 162, 189, 222
    (n. 1), 222–23 (n. 3), 224 (n. 2),
    225 (n. 3); organicism, 26, 27–29,
    54–55, 84, 189; ritual, 7, 37, 47–
    48, 71, 85–86, 87, 88, 90, 92, 93,
    139, 152, 153, 154, 164, 165, 171,
    182, 186, 189, 207, 222 (n. 2),
    222–23 (n. 3), 226–27 (n. 1), 229–
    31 (n. 7), 232 (n. 2); society/
    morality equivalence, 24, 29–30,
    32, 46, 54, 55, 58, 65, 84, 104,
    111–12, 162, 170, 174, 222
    (nn. 1, 3), 224 (n. 2); society/reality
    equivalence, 24, 66, 67–70, 71, 72,
    76, 78, 82, 129, 163, 181, 204, 224
    (n. 2), 224–25 (n. 2); subjectivity,
    28, 67–69, 89–90, 139, 162; sui-

cide, 30, 84, 85, 86–88. *See also* Durkheim-Weber convergence; Ethnomethodology; Parsons, Talcott

Durkheim-Weber convergence: and ethnomethodology, 24, 162–65, 171, 188, 189, 231–32 (n. 1); and Parsons, 3, 5, 15, 18–19, 23, 104, 132–34, 161–62, 223–24 (n. 7), 227–31 passim

Duster, Troy, 190

Edgley, Charles, 73

Elam, Stanley, 157

Ethnomethodological theory, 7, 8, 24, 162, 170, 176–77, 188, 189, 205, 207, 210. *See also* Ethnomethodology

Ethnomethodology: and anomie, 58, 90–103, 171; anti-reification methodology of, 108–9, 111, 163, 192–93, 195; artful practices, 4, 41–42, 43–45, 46, 51–52, 66, 75–76, 77, 80, 83, 90, 92, 95, 109, 112, 129, 139, 140, 165, 192, 193, 195; compellingness of ideas for actors, 24, 130, 139–40, 141, 164, 194; and conflict theory, 211–17; constraint, 42, 44–45, 46, 50–52, 58, 61–62, 74, 75, 76, 78, 90, 91, 92, 95, 96, 99, 100, 101, 102, 163, 191–92, 194, 202, 204; defined, 3–4; empirical method of, 3–4, 5, 6, 7, 9, 23, 24, 39, 48, 51, 83, 90, 102, 105, 109, 110, 122, 126, 141, 161, 162, 163, 196–97, 198, 199–200, 201, 204, 211, 218; historical context of, 3–5; indifference to actors' ideas, 81, 111, 114–16, 117, 150, 164; indifference to structure, 25, 108–15, 164, 192–93, 194–96, 200, 202, 203, 215; and interaction ritual chains, 207; and Marx, 212–13, 215, 216; and micro-macro so-

ciology, 25, 188, 189–203, 210–11, 217; and neofunctionalism, 190–92; origins in Parsonian functionalism, 10–13, 22–23, 25, 27; and phenomenology, 5, 10–11, 22, 126–27, 210; and "radical reflexivity," 218–19; recovery of Durkheim, 24, 27, 34–35, 37–38, 42, 44, 45, 46, 48, 52–53, 55, 57–58, 63–65, 66, 78, 80–81, 84, 93, 95–96, 111, 162–65, 188; recovery of Weber, 24, 105, 108, 111, 117–18, 126, 134–35, 149, 162–65, 188; roots in classical theory, 1–2, 5–6, 9–10, 24–25, 161, 212, 217, 221–22 (n. 4); and sociological theory, 7–10. *See also* Conversation analysis; Ethnomethodological theory; Garfinkel, Harold

Evans-Pritchard, E. E., 135–36

Exchange theory, 193

Experience, 42, 50–51, 223 (n. 5); and anomie, 83, 85, 86, 89, 90, 98–99, 102–3, 164; and Durkheim, 24, 28, 53, 66, 67–71, 72, 74, 79, 80, 141, 181–82; and ethnomethodology, 72, 78, 80, 110, 139, 204–5; "experience structures" in Weber, 10, 123; and Garfinkel, 10, 97, 123; of "nonsense," 94; of pain, 73, 98–101; and Parsons, 225 (n. 3); and social construction theory, 72–73. *See also* Ideas, role of; Subjectivity

Factual order, 2, 19–21, 24, 25, 30, 32, 38, 54, 59, 89, 117, 178, 209, 225 (n. 3), 227–28 (n. 4); defined, 19–20; equivalence to normative order, 55, 57–58, 64–65, 104, 111, 112; ethnomethodology's rejection of, 57, 104–5, 108, 111, 112; and Weber, 105, 108, 125

Fagerhaugh, Shizuko Y., 100

Farberman, Harvey A., 221 (n. 4)

Fine, Gary Alan, 190, 221 (n. 4)

Fishman, Mark, 213

Freund, Julian, 142

Functionalism. *See* Functionalist sociology

Functionalist sociology, 1–3, 4, 5, 6, 11, 21, 22, 25–26, 27, 37, 38, 42–43, 44, 45, 48, 55, 58, 61, 65, 83, 84, 86, 89, 90, 107, 108, 113, 121, 122, 130, 142, 143, 144, 145, 146, 169, 188, 189, 196, 208, 211, 214, 217, 221 (n. 3), 224 (n. 1), 229–31 (n. 7), 232 (nn. 1, 2); as bureaucratic, 7, 25, 166–68, 169, 181; complexity of, 19, 173; conflict theorists' criticism of, 211; derivation from Durkheim and Weber, 1–3, 5, 13, 15, 18–19, 23–24, 30, 212; as folk science native to Western culture, 2, 6–7, 25, 59–60, 81–82, 114, 115, 117, 162, 165–69; as "normative paradigm," 32–33; Parsons's theoretical bedrock of, 13–15, 84, 115; as rationalization, 7, 170–81, 182, 187; readings of Weber, 142–43, 149, 150; as ritual repair, 7, 170–71, 173, 174, 175, 177, 180, 182–87; and voluntarism, 221 (n. 1); Wrong's criticism of, 34. *See also* Merton, Robert K.; Parsons, Talcott

Garfinkel, Harold, 1–2, 3–4, 5, 6, 8, 11, 12, 13, 21, 24, 25, 36, 38, 39, 42, 45, 46, 58, 82, 105, 111, 123, 126, 139, 153, 160, 163, 167, 169, 182, 193, 195, 196, 197, 198, 201, 203, 206, 207, 211, 212, 218, 221 (n. 4); "breaching" experiments, 83, 92–93, 96; "counseling" experiment, 127–28; documentary method of interpretation, 51, 170, 191, 195; indexical expressions, 46, 48–50, 55–56; reflexivity, 46, 56–

57, 104, 129, 162, 174; thematic connection to Parsons, 1–2, 3–4, 10–12, 22–23; premedical student experiment, 96–98; studies of institutionalized rules, 43–44; studies of rational grounds of "shared understanding," 127–29, 155, 158, 171; study of "Agnes," 113–14; study of coding practices, 62–63; study of pulsar discovery, 76–78, 81, 204; study of suicide investigation, 73–74, 81. *See also* Ethnomethodology

Garrison, Jesse, 157

Gerth, H. H., 145

Giddens, Anthony, 28, 29, 32, 54, 68, 70, 71, 79, 82, 87, 88, 89, 106, 107, 115, 116, 117, 118, 119, 123, 124, 130, 131, 142, 148, 151, 190, 192, 212; criticism of ethnomethodology, 210

Giesen, Bernhard, 189, 190, 194, 197, 201

Gilbert, G. N., 78

Goffman, Erving, 12, 62, 73, 101

Gouldner, Alvin, 211

Grathoff, R., 22

Gurwitsch, Aron, 10, 50, 205

Halkowski, Timothy, 195

Hall, Gene E., 157, 158

Hall, Peter M., 186

Harris, William, 157, 158, 160

Hartley, Shirley F., 207

Harwood, Jonathan, 82

Hazelrigg, Lawrence E., 5, 23, 28, 67, 106, 124, 133, 186, 231–32 (n. 1, chap. 9)

Hekman, Susan J., 107, 111, 132, 143, 162

Heritage, John, 3, 4, 7, 13, 18, 19, 36, 125, 126, 165, 167, 168, 197, 198, 199, 201; on Garfinkel and Parsons, 10–12, 21–23, 122–23

Hewitt, John P., 186
Hilbert, Richard A., 4, 34, 62, 65, 74, 82, 83, 86, 102, 174, 182, 189, 192, 195, 206, 211, 219; study of chronic pain, 98–101; study of "nonsense," 93–95, 183, 186; study of teacher education, 156–60, 171–73
Hobbes, Thomas, 13, 16–17, 20, 54, 89, 108, 222 (n. 6), 224 (n. 1, chap. 4)
Hobbesian problem of order, 10, 13, 16, 17–18, 55, 191, 222 (n. 6)
Horowitz, Irving L., 211
Houston, W. Robert, 157
Howsam, Robert B., 157
Huaco, George, 211

Idealism: alleged in Durkheim, 18, 66, 72, 78, 80, 82, 224 (n. 2, chap. 3), 225–26 (n. 4); and Weber, 18, 105, 123, 124
Ideas, role of: Durkheim, 78–80, 89, 225–26 (n. 4); Weber, 24, 117–18, 123–24, 125, 133, 143–45, 147, 151, 152, 171. See also Experience; Subjectivity
Ideology, 118, 211, 213
Impression management, 62, 213, 214
Indexicality, 46, 48–50, 51, 55–56, 58, 90, 91, 94, 104, 195, 208; defined, 48
Inglis, Joan D., 157, 158
Interaction ritual chains, 189, 205–11, 214, 216; empirical nature of, 206, 207, 208–9
Intersubjectivity, 12, 20, 122, 125–29, 161, 164, 195. See also Shared understanding; Subjectivity
Ishler, Margaret F., 157, 158, 160

Jefferson, Gail, 9, 195, 197, 199
Jessor, Richard, 102
Johnson, Barclay, 88

Johnson, Charles E., 158
Johnson, Doyle Paul, 142
Johnson, Harry M., 102
Johnson, John M., 73
Jones, Howard L., 156, 157, 158
Jones, Robert Alun, 70, 221 (n. 4)
Joyce, Bruce, 157

Katz, Elihu, 213, 214
Kay, Patricia M., 157
Kean, John M., 157
Kellner, Hansfried, 68
Kitsuse, John I., 82, 95, 150, 185–86, 195, 212, 232 (n. 2)
Kleinman, Sherryl, 221 (n. 4)
Knorr-Cetina, Karin D., 190, 194
Kopel, Steven A., 73, 101
Kotarba, Joseph A., 73, 99, 100, 102

Labeling theory, 12, 73
Lackey, Pat N., 19, 38, 173, 181
Lash, Scott, 133
Lester, Marilyn, 212
Lidz, Victor, 190
Lindenberg, Siegwart, 193
Linton, Ralph, 174, 175
Livingston, Eric, 76–78, 196, 204
Locke, John, 16, 17–18, 36, 108
Loewith, Karl, 151
Luckmann, Thomas, 73, 94, 98–99
Luhmann, Niklas, 190
Lukes, Steven, 28, 29, 30, 68, 69, 70; on Durkheim and morality, 222–23 (n. 3)
Lyman, Stanford M., 12, 73, 194
Lynch, Michael, 19, 76–78, 195, 196, 204, 212

McDonald, Frederick J., 157, 158
Malthusian doctrine, 18
Manis, Jerome G., 73
Mannheim, Karl, 69, 120
Marshall, Alfred, 13, 221 (n. 1)

Marx, Karl, 9, 25, 123, 124, 189, 211, 212, 213, 215, 216, 217
Maynard, Douglas W., 8, 12, 108, 195, 197, 199, 205, 212, 215, 219
Mead, George H., 72
Mehan, Hugh, 5, 8, 73, 78, 212
Meltzer, Bernard N., 73
Menzies, Ken, 26
Merskey, H., 101
Merton, Robert K., 3, 19, 149; adoption of rational orientation, 179, 185; anomie theory, 83–86, 88–89, 183–87; compared with Durkheim, 85–86, 88–89, 183, 185, 186; interpretation of Durkheim, 84; role theory, 174–80, 232; self-fulfilling prophesy, 178
Micro-macro debate, 188, 189, 192, 193; terms of, 190
Miles, Robert, 82
Mills, C. Wright, 37, 145, 186, 211
Molotch, Harvey, 212, 215
Mommsen, Wolfgang J., 151
Mulkay, M., 78
Münch, Richard, 197, 201

Neofunctionalism, 190–92
Nisbet, Robert, 85, 86
Normative order, 2, 19–21, 22, 23, 25, 30, 32, 36, 38, 54, 105, 123, 132, 183, 223 (nn. 4, 6), 225–26 (nn. 3, 4), 227–28 (n. 4), 229–31 (n. 7); defined, 20; and Durkheim, 30, 224 (n. 2, chap. 3); equivalence to factual order, 55, 57–58, 64–65, 104, 111, 112; ethnomethodological rejection of, 44, 53, 104, 111, 112; as source of intersubjectivity, 20, 125; and Weber, 125

"Occasioned corpus," 109–11, 112–13

Pace, J. Blair, 100, 101
Pain, experience of, 73, 96, 98–102

Pareto, Vilfredo, 13, 221 (n. 1)
Parkin, Frank, 119, 149
Parsons, Talcott, 1–3, 4, 5, 6, 7, 10, 11, 12, 25, 31, 32, 37, 38, 43, 46–47, 61, 83, 84, 89, 107, 110, 115, 154, 162, 164, 172–73, 174, 176, 189, 209, 212, 217, 227 (nn. 2, 3); adoption of rational orientation, 22, 115–16, 117, 130, 142, 165–67; assessment of utilitarianism, 12, 15, 16–18; compared with Durkheim, 47, 48, 67; compared with Weber, 108, 124–25, 126; disruption of Weber's ideal types, 129–30, 131–32, 133, 164, 229–30 (n. 7); and empiricism, 3, 4, 38–39, 42, 54, 123, 223 (n. 7); interpretation of Durkheim, 30, 46, 47–48, 53–54, 55, 67, 70, 71–72, 78–82, 167, 169, 223 (n. 4), 224 (n. 2, chap. 3), 225 (n. 3), 225–26 (n. 4), 227 (n. 4), 231 (n. 1, chap. 9); interpretation of Weber, 104, 105, 125, 130, 132–34, 149, 153, 227–31 passim; and positivism, 12–13, 15–16, 18, 20, 21, 22, 67, 224 (n. 2, chap. 3), 225–26 (nn. 3, 4); rejection of Durkheim, 30, 46, 55, 66, 71–72, 78, 82, 222 (n. 1), 224 (n. 2, chap. 3), 225–26 (n. 4); rejection of Weber, 131, 152; and subjectivity, 20, 21–22, 47, 67, 70, 71, 105, 108, 117, 122–23, 126, 132, 223 (nn. 4, 5), 224 (n. 2, chap. 3), 225 (nn. 3, 4), 227 (n. 4); suppression of classical ideas, 1, 5–6, 12, 23–24, 105, 161, 212, 221 (n. 4); thematic connections to Garfinkel, 1–2, 3–4, 10–12, 22–23; and the "unit act," 14, 21; voluntarism, 2, 12, 15, 18, 19–21, 24, 25–26, 104, 118, 188, 221 (n. 1), 222 (n. 5). See also Functionalist sociology

Pawluch, Dorothy, 186
Peters, Thomas, 142
Phenomenology, 5, 10, 11, 22, 50, 73, 126, 205, 210
Piven, Frances Fox, 215
Police, practices of, 39–42, 43, 50, 59, 75, 90, 109
Pollner, Melvin, 2, 8, 57, 60, 80, 81, 82, 95, 120, 154, 170, 179, 185, 192, 195; comparison of rational and religious reasoning, 135, 138–39; "occasioned corpus," 109–11, 112–13; and "radical reflexivity," 218–19; reanalysis of Evans-Pritchard's Azande study, 75, 135–37, 185; study of traffic court, 74–76, 137–38
Pope, Whitney, 5, 23, 28, 32, 67, 82, 88, 106, 124, 133, 231–32 (n. 1, chap. 9)
Positivism, radical, 12–13, 15–16, 18, 20, 67, 225 (n. 3)
Psathas, George, 73
Psychology, 28, 30, 54, 64, 79, 98, 102, 106, 139, 193

Rathbone, Charles, 157
Rational choice theorists, 193
Rational orientation. *See* Rationality
Rationalism. *See* Rationality
Rationality: and Durkheim, 29, 30, 35, 37, 68, 70, 74, 103, 222–23 (n. 3), 224 (n. 1, chap. 4); as Durkheimian "sacred," 165; and ethnomethodology, 122, 135, 137–38, 139, 150, 154–55, 156, 164, 165, 171; as a feature of Parsonian functionalism, 2, 115, 117, 142, 149, 162, 165–70, 174, 177, 179–80, 183, 185, 186; and Garfinkel, 129, 161, 171; and Hobbes, 17; and Locke, 17; nonideational foundations of, 135, 139, 142, 152, 153–55, 231 (n. 1, chap. 8); and

Parsons, 21, 22, 24, 133–34, 152, 153, 164, 228 (n. 5); "pure rationality," 24, 119, 130, 142, 152, 153, 154, 165, 171; and radical positivism, 15, 16; and utilitarianism, 15; and Weber, 7, 115, 116, 117, 118, 119–20, 121, 124, 134, 141, 144, 147, 148, 149, 151–52, 164, 229 (n. 6). *See also* Rationalization
Rationalization, 7, 182; of the collective conscience, 169–81; and ethnomethodology, 152–56, 160; of teacher education, 156–60; and Weber, 24, 130, 133, 141–42, 151–52, 171. *See also* Functionalist sociology; Rationality; Weber, Max
Reflexivity, 46, 56–57, 58, 60–61, 62, 72, 78, 90, 104, 111, 129, 162, 174, 180, 218–19; defined, 56; radical, 218–19. *See also* Garfinkel, Harold
Religion, 52, 69, 70, 71, 79, 80, 102, 118, 124, 133, 134, 135, 139, 146, 154, 165, 226–27 (n. 1), 229 (n. 6), 229–31 (n. 7)
Religious experience and practices. *See* Religion
Rhoades, Gary, 190
Ritual repair, 7, 71, 92–93, 96, 163–64, 165, 170–71, 177, 180, 182, 185, 186, 226–27 (n. 1)
Ritzer, George, 2, 190
Roethlisberger, Fritz J., 142, 168
Rogers, Rolf E., 142
Roles: "role making," 33; role-sets, 174–76, 179, 180
Rose, Arnold M., 73
Roth, Guenther, 146–47, 151–52
Rules, 20, 24, 27, 30, 32, 46, 47, 48, 53–54, 57, 58, 64, 67, 71, 81, 92, 113, 114, 110, 121, 127, 144, 147–49, 154, 157, 167, 168, 169, 170, 172, 173, 174, 177–78, 179, 180, 186, 187, 189, 222 (n. 3), 224

(n. 2, chap. 3); analytic insufficiency of, 30–38, 59; descriptive use of, 61; and Durkheim, 30–32, 47, 222–23 (n. 3); ethnomethodological interest in, 58–60, 112, 150; lack of empirical evidence for, 39–44; prescriptive use of, 62–64, 121

Sacks, Harvey, 9, 195, 197, 198, 199
Sauerbruch, Ferdinand, 101
Schachter, Stanley, 73, 101
Schalock, H. Del, 157
Schegloff, Emanuel A., 9, 193, 195, 197, 199, 200, 201, 202–3
Schiller, Herbert I., 213, 216
Schneider, Joseph W., 186
Schutz, Alfred, 10, 22, 123, 126–27, 198
Scott, Marvin B., 12, 73, 194
Seeman, Melvin, 102
Seidman, Steven, 142
Selznick, Philip, 142, 168
Shared understanding, 3, 20, 22, 101, 122, 125, 164; and Garfinkel, 128–29. See also Intersubjectivity
Shealy, C. Norman, 101
Shearron, Gilbert F., 158
Shibutani, Tamotsu, 73
Shils, Edward A., 3, 19, 172
Sica, Alan: on Weber and irrationality, 231 (n. 1, chap. 8)
Singer, J., 73, 101
Smelser, Neil J., 197, 201
Smith, Dorothy, 82, 160, 216
Social construction of reality, 72–73, 81–82
Social structure, 3, 10, 85, 108, 109, 110, 111, 113, 115, 125, 129, 154, 161, 163, 164, 166, 167, 169, 192, 194, 200, 201–2, 204, 205, 211. See also Factual order
Spear, F. G., 101
Spector, Malcolm, 95, 185–86, 212, 232 (n. 2)

Stalker, G. M., 142
Steffenson, James P., 157
Stephan, Cookie White, 12
Stephan, Walter G., 12
Sternbach, Richard A., 100, 101
Stinchcombe, Arthur L., 181
Stone, Gregory P., 221 (n. 4)
Strauss, Anselm, 100
Subjectivity, 79, 136, 138, 141, 153, 157, 164, 167, 224 (n. 2, chap. 4), 227 (n. 1); and anomie, 99, 103; and Durkheim, 28, 47, 67–69, 89–90, 139, 162; and ethnomethodology, 83, 122, 139, 193, 194, 210; and functionalism, 167, 168; and Garfinkel, 22–23, 55, 142; and Parsons, 14, 20, 21–22, 47, 67, 70, 71, 105, 108, 117, 122–23, 124–25, 126, 132, 223 (nn. 4, 5) 224 (n. 2, chap. 3), 225 (nn. 3, 4), 227 (n. 4); and radical positivism, 16; and Schutz, 123, 126, 129; and social construction theory, 72; and Weber, 106–7, 109, 111, 114, 115–20, 122, 123–25, 132, 134, 139, 141, 143–48, 149, 162, 165, 189, 195, 202, 227 (n. 2), 229 (n. 6); Weber and Parsons compared, 124–25, 126. See also Experience; Ideas, role of; Intersubjectivity
Suchman, Lucy A., 43
Sudnow, David, 8, 45, 64, 195–96
Suicide, 30, 73–74, 84, 85, 86–88, 102
Symbolic interactionism, 12, 33–34, 73, 193, 221 (n. 4)
Szasz, Thomas S., 101

Takla, Tendzin, 32
Teacher education, 156–60, 171–73, 181
Thomas, Adele K., 157
Thomas, W. I., 72
Thompson, Kenneth, 85

Tönnies, Ferdinand, 29, 35, 37
"Traditional sociology," eth-
nomethodology's criticism of, 2, 5,
6–7, 8, 58, 80, 109, 162, 168–69
Troxell, Eugene, 224 (n. 1, chap. 3)
Turner, Jonathan H., 142
Turner, Ralph, 33–34

Unikel, I. P., 101
Utilitarianism, 12, 13, 14, 15–18, 20,
22, 34, 54, 89–90, 167, 222 (n. 5)

Vygotsky, L. S., 72

Wallace, Ruth A., 207
Warner, R. Stephen, 5, 14, 33, 82; on
Parsons and Hobbes, 222 (n. 6); on
Parsons and subjectivity, 224–25
(n. 2, chap. 4)
Waterman, Floyd T., 158
Waterman, Robert H., 142
Weber, Max, 1–2, 3, 5, 6, 8, 9, 10, 12,
13, 14, 18, 23, 32, 62, 104, 111,
112, 140, 161, 167, 189, 212, 217,
221 (n. 3); bureaucracy, 24, 62,
111, 119, 121, 132, 141–49, 151,
155–56; Calvinism, 145; capitalism, 105, 123–24, 146, 151, 152;
compared with Parsons, 124–25,
126; compellingness of ideas for
actors, 24, 122, 133, 134–35, 163;
distancing from substance of actors'
ideas, 117–20, 122, 147–48, 164;
empirical method of, 122–24, 130,
189; ideal types, 24, 129–32, 133,
143, 162, 164, 165, 227 (nn. 1, 2),
229 (n. 6); idealism, 18, 105, 123,
124; rationality, 7, 115, 116, 117,
118, 119–20, 121, 124, 133, 134,
141, 144, 146, 147, 148, 149, 151,
152, 164, 229 (n. 6); rationalization, 24, 130, 133, 141–42, 151–

52, 171, 187; reification, 24, 105–
8, 112, 114, 115, 120, 143, 145,
163, 189; social organization, 106–
8, 111, 114, 129, 132, 147; social
relationships as probability, 107–8;
sociology of law, 119, 147; subjectivity, 106–7, 109, 111, 114, 115–
20, 122, 123–25, 126, 132, 134,
139, 141, 143–48, 149, 162, 165,
189, 195, 202, 227 (n. 2), 229
(n. 6); types of subjective orientation to action, 115–16, 132; types
of subjective orientation to legitimacy and authority, 116–17; universal "psychological roots" of
ideas, 24, 118, 122, 134, 139–40.
See also Durkheim-Weber convergence; Ethnomethodology; Parsons, Talcott
Weber, Wilford A., 157
Wenke, Hans, 101
West, Candace, 195, 199, 200
Whalen, Jack, 199
Whalen, Marilyn L., 199
Whimster, Sam, 133
Wieder, D. Lawrence, 2, 3, 8, 12, 19,
21, 25, 58, 60, 62, 80, 169, 174,
185, 194, 196, 207; on ethnomethodology, 112; study of convict code, 60–62
Wiley, Norbert, 190
Wilson, Thomas P., 7, 108, 199; on
ethnomethodology and theory, 8–9;
on conversation and social struc-
ture, 201–2, 209–10; "normative
paradigm," 32
Wippler, Reinhard, 193
Wittgenstein, Ludwig, 35–37, 50,
180–81
Wolfe, Alan, 43
Wood, Houston, 5, 8, 73, 78, 212
Woolgar, Steve, 186
Wrong, Dennis, 34, 107, 142, 143,
149, 151, 156

Zborowski, Mark, 73
Zimmerman, Don H., 2, 3, 7, 8, 12,
19, 21, 25, 57, 58, 60, 80, 82, 120,
154, 169, 170, 179, 185, 192, 194,
195, 196, 197, 198, 199, 200; on

ethnomethodology and theory, 8–9;
"occasioned corpus," 109–11, 112–
13; study of welfare establishment,
63–64, 149